NEVER TOO LATE

*A Prosecutor's Story
of Justice in the Medgar Evers Case*

BOBBY DELAUGHTER

A LISA DREW BOOK
SCRIBNER
NEW YORK LONDON TORONTO SYDNEY SINGAPORE

SCRIBNER
1230 Avenue of the Americas
New York, NY 10020

SCRIBNER and design are trademarks of
Macmillan Library Reference USA, Inc., used under license
by Simon & Schuster, the publisher of this work.

Designed by Colin Joh
Set in Aldine

Manufactured in the United States of America

1 3 5 7 9 10 8 6 4 2

Library of Congress Cataloging-in-Publication Data
DeLaughter, Bobby.
Never too late: a prosecutor's story of justice in
the Medgar Evers case/Bobby DeLaughter.
1. Beckwith, Byron de la—Trials, litigation, etc.
2. Trials (Murder)—Mississippi—Jackson.
I. Title.

KF224.B34 D45 2001
345.73'02523—dc21
00-030106

ISBN 0-684-86503-3

For Peggy and the kids:
Burt, Claire, Drew, JJ, Joel, and Jared
Also, for my mother and father,
With all my love

Acknowledgments

Much appreciation to Lisa Drew, my editor and publisher at Scribner, and to my agents, Maureen and Eric Lasher, for their extraordinarily patient tutelage and guidance throughout my inaugural sojourn into the labyrinth of the publishing landscape.

Many thanks to Anne Stascavage, who also provided editing assistance. She proved exceptionally helpful, particularly on initial questions of tone.

Although their names are mentioned in the book, I wish to here express my gratitude to court reporter Kaye Kerr and Hinds County circuit clerk Barbara Dunn for going beyond the call of duty. Kaye not only provided court transcripts, but transcribed all witness interviews and grand jury testimony for me during the investigation. Barbara has always been of invaluable assistance in furnishing access to court documents and evidence.

Last, but not least, I thank my family for their continued love, support, and forbearance.

CONTENTS

AUTHOR'S NOTE
AND INTRODUCTION

This is the true and complete story of the most important and fascinating case I have tried during my twenty-plus years in the courtroom. I realized its special nature early in the investigation and began keeping a journal. Soon after the conclusion of the case, I decided to write a memoir drawing upon my journal, letters, newspaper articles, reports of the Jackson Police Department and FBI, court transcripts, taped interviews gathered during the investigation and trial, and my memory.

I initially intended to write a private memoir for my children so, after attaining the necessary maturity, they would know and fully understand everything that happened as well as my feelings and motivations along the way.

Through the friendship and encouragement of writer Willie Morris, I became convinced that I should share my story on a much larger scale. Although the thought of writing a book for publication was rather intimidating to me, Willie was relentless. "You not only *can* do it," he urged, "you *must* do it." Indeed, as noted by Edmund Bergler, "the real writer is haunted by a plot which he must write out of inner necessity."

After three years of writing, I finished the final chapter during the last week of July 1999 and spoke to Willie by phone that evening. He shared my excitement, volunteered to write the introduction, and invited my wife, Peggy, and me to come over one night the following week to join him and his wife, JoAnne, to eat pizza and watch *Judgment at Nuremberg* on video. We would talk more about the introduction then, he said. It never happened. On Monday, August 2, 1999, Willie's kind and generous heart stopped beating.

I would never presume to write that which Willie, another Faulkner, was to pen, nor could I bring myself to ask a substitute to fill the void. I know firsthand Willie's feelings about this story. We discussed it many an evening over an equal number of bottles of Willie's favorite merlot. An understanding was reached. Willie would write of the making of *Ghosts of Mississippi,* the Rob Reiner movie about the reinvestigation and reprosecution of white supremacist Byron De La Beckwith for the 1963 assassination of civil rights leader Medgar Evers, and indeed Willie did so in *The Ghosts of Medgar Evers* (Random House, 1998). I, on the other hand, would write the definitive and detailed account of the case itself.

Good friend and consummate writer that he was, Willie couldn't resist revealing his feelings about the case and me in his book. While unusual, it is only fitting that his words serve as a prelude to the journey to justice chronicled in the pages that follow:

In 1994 I was drawn to an extraordinary story. That year in Jackson, Mississippi, I covered for a national magazine the third and final trial of the radical white supremacist Byron De La Beckwith for the June 12, 1963, assassination of the thirty-seven-year-old Mississippi civil rights leader Medgar Evers, shot in the back in the driveway of his house.

"The case against Byron De La Beckwith," one journalist wrote, "was brought back not because of any one event, but by a confluence of many events in a slow tide of change." A younger generation of whites accepted integration, in part out of repulsion toward everything the Beckwiths had once stood for.

One of these younger whites was an assistant district attorney named Bobby DeLaughter, who would handle the new investigation against staggering odds and eventually at great personal and professional cost.

He is an introverted, complicated man and, as with Myrlie Evers, only reveals himself to people he really trusts. He is modestly self-confident and brave. He is deeply religious but does not advertise it. He is the long-distance runner. Yet beneath the often stoic facade there are intensely strong emotions, and also a strain of irrepressible humor, buttressed by a gift for telling stories.

Without Bobby DeLaughter, Beckwith would never have been convicted and in the years to come the country will need all the heroes and heroines it can get, no matter what their color.

The 1994 trial and the investigative work that led to it culminated one of the most unusual episodes of criminal prosecution in American history. "It tells a story that stays with you—a story about conscience. Bobby DeLaughter and Myrlie Evers: two who grew in conscience, courage, and trust." As a book lives or dies on its inherent life-giving truth and passion, this story, I believe, will endure.

If My people who are called by My name humble themselves, pray, seek My face, and turn from their wicked ways, then I will hear from Heaven, and will forgive their sin, . . . heal their land, [and] let justice roll down like waters, and righteousness like an ever-flowing stream, [for] the Lord of Hosts is exalted by justice.
—2 Chronicles 7:14, Amos 5:24, and Isaiah 5:16 (NRSV)

NEVER TOO LATE

PROLOGUE

The murderer will be free? Could I have heard correctly? His conviction vacated, the jury's unanimous guilty verdict held for naught? Nationwide celebrations for justice will turn to cries of outrage. Salutes to a state that had long suffered a poor reputation for affording basic civil rights and humanity will evolve into "I told you so; nothing has really changed in Mississippi in thirty years." I recall my Faulkner: "The past is not dead; it's not even past." My antagonists will relish running me out of town, and my dream of one day becoming a judge will probably remain just that: a dream.

It's Monday, December 22, 1997. I have just received word from a source that enough judges of the Mississippi Supreme Court have voted to overturn the conviction of Byron De La Beckwith. The decision will be made public in a matter of hours.

I can't bring myself to stay in the office today. It's almost Christmas and I have bought no presents—zilch. Merry damn Christmas. To hell with it. I did the right thing and that's all that matters. I'll just take the day off, go to the mall, and concentrate on Christmas and my family. I won't even think about Beckwith or Medgar Evers. Yet, as I inch my Jeep along in the bumper-to-bumper traffic, the words of Louis L'Amour, in *The Daybreakers,* ring in my head instead of Christmas carols: "The words a man speaks today live on in his thoughts or the memories of others, and the shot fired, the blow struck, the thing done today is like a stone tossed into a pool and the ripples keep widening out until they touch lives far removed from ours."

My God, how I've come to realize how true those words are. A single blast from a 1917 Enfield .30-06 rifle, fired shortly after midnight in the early-morning hours of June 12, 1963, from a thicket of sweet gum and honeysuckle in Jackson, Mississippi, had, and is still having, such an effect. It ended the life of Medgar Evers, field secretary of the NAACP in Mississippi, and it followed his white assassin, Byron De La Beckwith VI, who was tried unsuccessfully twice in 1964 by all-white juries for murdering the man he later described as "Mississippi's mightiest nigger."

A quarter century later, the ripples emanating from that shot tore through the heart and soul of a third person—an unsuspecting and rather unlikely one—a white prosecuting attorney who tried to free himself of the shackles of his past and assumed the challenge of rebuilding the case against Beckwith. On February 5, 1994, thirty-one years later, he played an instrumental role in securing for the Evers family those long-elusive words, "We, the jury, find the defendant guilty, as charged." For the Everses, those words brought some degree of closure. For Mississippi, it was an exorcism of sorts. With the world watching, the state cast out many demons of racism that had possessed it for so many years.

Those words of the jury, "guilty, as charged," were also a crucial step in the catharsis experienced by that young assistant district attorney who spearheaded the state's successful prosecution. His name is Bobby DeLaughter, and I know him better than anyone—his thoughts, his exuberance, his pain, his motivation, the secret feelings that he protects so surely that even those people closest to him describe him as taciturn. I know the effect that bullet in 1963 had on him and his family. I *am* Bobby DeLaughter. To the tune of Bing Crosby's "White Christmas" on the radio, I find myself reflecting on it all. When, how, and why did I get mixed up in this whirlwind? Ah, yes, I read my newspaper.

CHAPTER ONE

A CURIOSITY

It was Sunday, October 1, 1989, and the morning paper had just arrived. Clad in my robe and slippers, my first cup of coffee in hand, I groggily made my way out the front door, across the sidewalk, and down the driveway. I stooped to pick up the paper.

Back inside, I poured another cup of Maxwell House and flipped through the headlines of the various sections of the *Clarion-Ledger* to see what I wanted to read first. Zsa Zsa Gabor had been convicted of slapping a cop in Los Angeles. Mississippi author Willie Morris had come out with another book, *Good Old Boy and the Witch of Yazoo,* and a storm was brewing over the federal response to Hurricane Hugo.

No storm brewing here in Jackson, Mississippi, though. Forecast for the day: mostly sunny with only a slight chance of rain and an expected high of seventy-seven degrees. The prediction appeared to be on the mark as I glanced out of the kitchen window. There wasn't a cloud in the sky and bright sunshine was gradually shooting over the eastern horizon. No storm brewing here.

I settled down on the couch and began my reading in earnest. "State Checked Possible Jurors in Evers Slaying," read the front-page headline. Jerry Mitchell, whose assignment included the courthouse beat, had written the article. His bright orange hair and matching necktie against a customary lime green shirt made him a somewhat conspicuous presence in the courtroom. My dealings with Jerry had been positive, and I had never minded discussing with him what I ethically could about any of my cases.

Although Jerry's normal beat included the trials and general goings-on around the courthouse, lately he had been following a tangent involving the 1960s racial strife in Mississippi. Since the movie *Mississippi Burning* had come out, everything penned by Jerry had racial overtones. Initially, his articles had dealt with, as had *Mississippi Burning,* the murders of three civil rights workers in Philadelphia, Mississippi.

Next, a series of articles appeared on a defunct state agency called the Mississippi Sovereignty Commission, established in the 1950s. Its initial purpose was to perpetuate segregation in the state, and it evolved into a state-operated spy corps. When the commission shut down in the early 1970s, the Mississippi legislature ordered all of its records sealed until well into the next century. The ACLU and several individual plaintiffs, trying to have the records opened to the public, had taken their cause to federal court.

Jerry had apparently obtained some access to a portion of these records. His October 1, 1989, article claimed that agency documents revealed that the Sovereignty Commission had investigated prospective jurors in the second 1964 trial of Byron De La Beckwith for the 1963 murder of NAACP leader Medgar Evers.

Both trials resulted in hung juries, and Beckwith was released following the second. The article I was reading implied that an investigator with the Sovereignty Commission had tampered with the jury, and even quoted one of my law school professors, Aaron Condon, as saying that jury tampering was possible.

As I read, questions went through my mind. According to the article, Andy Hopkins, the investigator involved, was dead, so even if his actions constituted jury tampering and the statute of limitations had not run, the culprit was certainly beyond the long arm of the law. Nevertheless, a seed of curiosity had been planted, and it caused me to reflect on the 1960s. I was not, however, thinking about the Beatles, bell-bottom pants, or Joe Namath. I was conjuring up other memories that had long since been shoved to the dark recesses of my brain. What did I remember about the racial strife in 1960s Mississippi, and in particular, what did I recall about Byron De La Beckwith's 1964 trials?

I thought back to my first visit to the University of Mississippi campus nestled in the small hamlet of Oxford. It was 1962 in the wake of James Meredith's forced admission to the Ole Miss Law School, and my mother had a cousin living on campus. Riots had broken out, the Kennedys had sent in federal troops to restore and maintain order, and we (my mother, little brother, and I) went along with my aunt to check on our cousin and her husband, who was also in law school. He is now a federal judge; James Meredith is a former aide to ultraconservative U.S. senator Jesse Helms; and the Ole Miss Law School, only a few years ago, mourned the death of its African-American dean, who suffered a fatal heart attack while visiting New Orleans. Things have, indeed, changed.

I was eight then, and my brother, Mike, was half that age. The campus didn't look like any school I had ever seen, not that I had seen many, if any, colleges. That place, however, looked more like the army-occupied towns that I had seen in television episodes of *Combat* than any school. It was a place of wonder for little boys. Pup tents stretched as far as the eye could see across the intramural fields (where the athletic dorm now stands), and a soldier stood at every door.

Lt. Gov. Paul Johnson would be elected Mississippi's next governor by a landslide for taking a stand at the campus's main entrance, refusing to allow Meredith and his federal entourage to enter. I went to a political rally with my parents at Poindexter Park during that gubernatorial campaign, sporting a button with Johnson's slogan: Stand Tall with Paul!

Also standing tall at Ole Miss was a great-uncle of mine, Buddie Newman, who was then a state legislator and would eventually become the Speaker of the Mississippi House of Representatives, arguably the most powerful position in state government at the time.

Still, in later years, I discovered that a local judge actively involved with the state power structure was also at that campus entrance. Judge Russel Moore was of the "old school" in Mississippi politics. A staunch segregationist in the 1960s, as most white Mississippians then were, he, like my uncle Buddie, served as one of Gov. Ross Barnett's top advisers and supporters. Also like my uncle and many others, however, Russel later experienced a change of heart. I married his stepdaughter Dixie, named after the Ole Miss fight song.

I met Dixie during the summer of 1973. I had known since I was in the ninth grade that I wanted to be a lawyer and had planned my education since then around that ambition. When we met, Dixie and I were nineteen years old, an age when most of my friends had not yet decided what to do with their lives. As Dixie and I began dating, I soon realized that I had found someone who understood my goals. The man she called Dad was a circuit judge. She had heard the law discussed and had been around it most of her life.

To the dismay of both families, we married in November 1973. We were determined to make our own way in the world, and once that became apparent to Judge Moore and he realized that I was not looking for any handouts, our relationship softened and warmed.

Judge Moore and I practiced law together for a few years after he retired from the bench. He was a friend as well as a father-in-law. We often discussed politics and dissected points of law. Novel legal questions and arguments intrigued both of us.

As I read my newspaper that Sunday morning in October 1989, I had clear recollections of my early boyhood of 1962. One thing, though, of which I had little or no memory was the assassination of Medgar Evers the following year and the ensuing trials of Byron De La Beckwith.

I vaguely recalled friends of my parents' visiting in our home, or vice versa, and the subject of the trials being brought up. The jury was still out, and someone made the statement that, while Beckwith was guilty, the state couldn't prove it. He would probably not be convicted, and surely they (the jury) would not impose the death penalty even if he were by chance found guilty. That's all that I could remember.

Dixie wasn't at home. She was gone a lot since going to work for the *Clarion-Ledger* circulation department. Most mornings, it was up to me to rouse our three kids: Burt, ten, Claire, six, and Drew, four. I couldn't linger too long reading the paper. It was time to get them ready for church.

Hinds County is one of the few in Mississippi that has two county seats: Jackson and Raymond. Jackson, the capital and largest city in the state, is where our offices are housed and where we try the majority of our cases. Raymond, a small Civil War–era town, is situated in the rural area of the county.

Most crimes committed outside the Jackson metropolitan area are tried in the Raymond courthouse. It's a two-story structure, with massive white columns, built by slave labor and used as a hospital in the Civil War. That's where I was heading the next morning to help my boss, District Attorney Ed Peters, try the Trussell case.

A teacher at the local community college had been attacked in a school bathroom. She wasn't raped, but she had the ever-living hell beat out of her, and before the assailant was caught, he phoned her repeatedly and told her all that he would have liked to have done to her. By tracing these calls, the police had found him.

I played out our case in my mind as I drove. Ed would pick the jury, I would deliver the opening statement and put on our case, and then Ed would cross-examine the defense witnesses. We would split the closing argument. Such was the way we normally divided the labor in the cases that Ed and I tried together, and frankly, I thought we made a helluva team.

Ed had been district attorney for seventeen years. He is quick on his feet and shoots from the hip—but with deadly accuracy. Tall and lanky, he is a formidable presence in the courtroom. His slow Southern drawl and pleasant manner have lured many defendants into his trap during cross-examination, only to realize their mistake too late. Ed's demeanor then becomes that of a predator—lithe, quick, and lethal. This persona, combined with his prematurely gray hair, has earned him the nickname the Silver Fox.

It's hard to imagine Hinds County without Ed Peters as its DA. He has become a fixture on which everybody depends, but takes for granted.

Shortly after the courthouse renovation was completed and we moved in, someone called the office and inquired as to the identity of the two large statues atop the building. The secretary, without hesitation, correctly identified for the caller the one facing north as Moses, but instead of relating that the other one was Socrates, she said, "And we think the other one is Mr. Peters."

Conversely, I am more organized, methodical, and research-wise. Plus, with ten years of private practice under my belt as a defense attorney, I was able to predict many strategic moves of my adversaries. We complemented each other quite well and with good results. I had not lost a case in the two years I had been at the DA's office.

I neared the courthouse square, found a place to park, grabbed my file, and hustled inside. Jurors were making their way up the more-than-century-old stairs, which creaked with each step. I stuck my head in the court clerk's office first, where all of the court personnel gathered for coffee and gossip. Barbara Dunn, the clerk, was there, along with her deputy clerks, Patsy and Martha. Fortunately, Ed, Judge L. Breland Hilburn, the court reporter Kaye K. Kerr, and the two bailiffs, Steve Libenschek and Jeff Murray, were there, as well. Nobody had gone up to the courtroom yet. Nothing is more embarrassing than walking into a courtroom with the judge on the bench and jurors waiting.

While I don't remember all that we talked about as we waited for all of the jurors to report in, I know it was not the Beckwith case or Jerry Mitchell's article of the day before. We had a case to try and the day was spent on jury selection.

Tuesday morning, though, when I unfurled the morning paper, I noticed that Jerry had written another article about the Beckwith case. This time, it wasn't about a tangential issue like jury tampering. This one said that Myrlie Evers, widow of the slain civil rights leader, wanted the case reopened if the evidence was available.

During one of our breaks, I noticed the day's *Clarion-Ledger* folded on a table in Barbara's office. The article about Myrlie Evers was visible. I asked Ed what he thought about it, what our response was going to be, if we had one. He said that a request to reopen the case came up every so often and his response was always that there was no constitutional way, and any first-year law student knows it.

Ed's plan was simply to ignore it; once again, it would just go away. That made sense to me. After all, it had been twenty-six years, and our state supreme court had reversed cases for delays of only a few years. There was no reason to give a second thought to any attempt to launch a case in which we would immediately get shot out of the water on speedy-trial grounds. We finished Trussell's trial the next day—with a conviction.

"It will just go away." Go away? What in life ever just goes away forever? Sooner or later, in the great circle of life, all things, good and evil, pleasures and irritants, resurface, like the proverbial bad penny, and leave their mark on those whom fate puts in the path. We may temporarily ignore the elements and forces in our world, to be sure, but ignore, for instance, a deep wound, and it will only fester.

In October 1989, I wasn't sure whether the Beckwith case was a bad penny or a festering wound, but it became evident to me that it was not just going to quietly evaporate.

Public reaction to Mitchell's articles was immediate and divisive. Monday, October 9, at the Hinds County Board of Supervisors' meeting, Supervisor Bennie Thompson (now a U.S. congressman) moved for the board to pass a resolution asking Mississippi attorney general Mike Moore and Ed Peters to reopen the Beckwith case. It failed when nobody seconded the motion.

George Smith, then the county's only other black supervisor in addition to Thompson, said the request, if it came, should come from Myrlie Evers. There was, of course, an article in the paper the next day detailing the motion and the vote, and in Wednesday's edition an editorial asked why the supervisors remained quiet when they should have gone on record for justice.

But, if there was no evidence, where would the justice be in reopening the case? If the law was clear that it could not be done, would there be justice in ignoring the law and reprosecuting the case anyway? It seemed to me that the *Clarion-Ledger* was saying, "Damn the Constitution, damn the law, damn the evidence or the lack thereof; we want this case reprosecuted and don't confuse us with the law and the evidence." For our reluctance to rush out and indict someone before getting any evidence, Ed and I were labeled by some as racists.

Conversely, I also received calls and letters from people on the opposite end of the spectrum, who hoped we were not considering reopening the case, no matter what the law was or what evidence we ever amassed. The decision to prosecute any case should be based upon the law and the evidence, but to this group, Beckwith's guilt was not the issue. I was repeatedly told, "We know he's guilty, everybody knows that; but that's not the point." As incredible as I found such statements, I decided to listen and learn. As misguided as it was, the feeling was there, and if I didn't find a way to deal with it, there was no hope of ever winning over a jury drawn from people with this attitude.

So, I would ask, "What *is* the point?" Without exception, I got one of four responses: "He's too old"; "The case is too old"; "It will cost the taxpayers too much money"; "It will open up an old wound."

I respect anyone's right to disagree with my position, but these people were downright nasty about it. Where was such virulence coming from? Our society had become a fully integrated one over the past twenty-five years. An observation of Tony Horwitz, in his *Confederates in the Attic,* equally applied to the paradox I was witnessing: "Blacks and whites mingled freely at schools, restaurants, and other public places. Yet for reasons no one fully understood, this intimacy had spawned a subterranean rage" within some.

The easy way out would have been to immediately convene a grand jury (just as some vocal blacks wanted) and honestly tell the panel, "We have nothing," whereupon a "no bill" would have been returned. That would've been the end of it (just as some vocal whites desired).

But I felt that Mississippi and I were being put to the test. We say that no man is above the law; but what if he is seventy years old? We claim that we value all human life; but what if the life is that of a civil rights activist in 1963 Mississippi? There is no statute of limitations for murder; but what if it's been a quarter century? In pursuing justice and maintaining freedom, how much taxpayer money is too much? Finally, if justice has never been finalized in such a despicable and immoral atrocity and pursuing it will open an old wound, is it not then a wound that needs to be reopened and cleansed, instead of continuing to fester over the years, spreading its poison to future generations?

The interest generated by the mere mention of reopening this case, and the intensity of that interest, pro or con, made it that much more interesting to me. What the hell did we have here? I had not seen nor heard of any other case that could so arouse people's passions, and with so little real information at their fingertips.

The only way for this to go anywhere, whether it be a file cabinet or a courtroom, was to take a genuine look at it, make a credible investigation, and report our findings to a grand jury for its decision.

The law and the evidence were immaterial to the extremists on both ends. But by reopening the case, just to the extent of seeing if it could be reprosecuted, and then letting that decision be made by a grand jury, even if there was no prosecution, we would have done our job and life would go on.

Over the next several weeks, I brought the subject up with Ed, and on Halloween, 1989, Jerry Mitchell had another article under his belt. This one announced that the DA had joined in the reopening of the case; but it was, at that time, only to see if any jury tampering had occurred. This is what I had asked for, so I was the assistant given the assignment. Be careful what you ask for because you may get it.

The negative calls before were nothing compared to those we received after that article came out.

What I couldn't understand then and cannot understand to this day is how anyone could say that Ed and I were doing this for political gain. Having anything to do with this case was the most politically hot, politically divisive thing anyone in our position could possibly do. It was a lose-lose situation from the very beginning politically; and we knew it.

"Bobby DeLaughter, have you lost your ever-loving mind?" Barbara Dunn asked in one of those sawmill whispers as I sat in her office and told her what I needed. As circuit clerk, Barbara maintains custody of all court minutes, files, and exhibits that are introduced into evidence in all of the trials.

I was investigating possible jury tampering in a trial twenty-five years earlier in a case I knew little or nothing about. I did not have the luxury of going in the file room of the DA's office and pulling out a neat, organized file bearing Beckwith's name. I would have settled for any file—even one that was a jumbled mess. We had zilch.

Our files went back only as early as 1972, when Ed first took office as district attorney. I had telephoned Bill Waller to see if he had kept any of his files. Waller was the district attorney who prosecuted Beckwith in 1964. He was later elected governor of Mississippi and, in fact, as governor dissolved the state Sovereignty Commission. By 1989, he had reestablished his private practice of law in Jackson, with an office near the courthouse.

When I asked Waller about the file, he said that he felt certain that he had left all of his district attorney files to his successor in office, Jack Travis. Waller promised, though, that he would double-check with John Fox, Waller's assistant in 1964.

So, I had stopped in Barbara's office, which is located in the courthouse basement, on my way in to work that morning to see what minutes, files, and evidence her predecessors might have maintained.

Barbara agreed to help, but she wasn't sure that a predecessor in office hadn't destroyed the materials. State law, she explained, would have permitted it after ten years.

It was close to nine-thirty by the time I stepped into the lobby of the DA's office.

The courthouse had recently undergone a complete renovation. The fifth (and top) floor, where the DA's office is located, was once the old jail. In the years to come I would often wonder where Beckwith's cell was located when he was jailed here in 1963 awaiting trial.

Back in my office, I opened an envelope that Ed had left for me in my box. Attached to a typed letter, a note in Ed's handwriting said, "You may find this interesting. I received it a couple of years ago and just ignored it. Use it as you see fit."

The attached letter was dated October 7, 1987, and was on the printed letterhead of Byron De La Beckwith, complete with his phone number and address in Signal Mountain, Tennessee.

Beckwith had sent it to Ed two years earlier, expressing his gratitude for Ed's not reopening his case. Beckwith predicted the outcome of a third trial:

Surely a 3rd trial of me would turn Jackson, and indeed much of Hines [*sic*] County, into a huge "Roman Circus fiesta" filling the air and streets with the bitterness and blackness of beasts, topped off and stirred with a vast multitude of trash of the white variety, and every afore named [*sic*] participant among the multitudes of legal Leaders//??!! dragging their empty purses behind them like a passell [*sic*] of "pickers" going to 'de cotton patch to empty a vast veritable fortune of funds (4 'dey services) out of the pockets of the responsible, white, Christian tax paying public—of them who like thee and me and our people for generations WHO BUILT THIS REPUBLIC.

Attempting, I guess, to find a silver lining in the otherwise dark cloud that another trial would create, Beckwith continued:

One good thing that could come of such a trial would be it could probably, like the flood of 1927 which we lived through in the Delta, unleash a delluge [*sic*] of white damnation that, in its pent up fury, is NOW of such strength that it would flood, drownd [*sic*] out and burry [*sic*] in the muck all but a remnant of the evil ones assaulting us—and as before in all floods—the white Christian remnant would then, as Omar Khyyam [*sic*] said—"SHATTER

THIS SORRY SCHEME OF THINGS ENTIRE THEN SHAPE IT NEARER TO (OUR) THE HEARTS DESIRE." As in WW-II., I, as many others of us said—"if we must have war—then let it be in our life time [*sic*] that we be participants in the victory". and I'll add GOD'S WILL BE DONE. Amen.

This guy, I thought, *is crazier than a shit-house rat.* I was repulsed at his attempt at levity:

To ad [*sic*] a humurous [*sic*] note to all of this, may I observe, me being a Native Son of California—then at the death of my father in 1925, mother and I moving back to Miss where I was raised on her/the family cotton plantation—California got rid of a dear little white child, and lo—in 1965 California fell "heir" to a drove of darkies from Mississippi as the Evers' ooozzzed into the Los Angeles area!!! WITH AN AVALANCHE OF DIXIE DARKIES AND ALL THE OTHER "STUFF" UNLOADING IN LOS ANGELES—'TIS NO WOUNDER [*sic*] THAT THE EARTH SHIVERS AND SHAKES AT THE REVULTION [*sic*] OF THE INFLUX! God's will be done. Amen.

Although this letter was no evidence that its author murdered anyone, it didn't exactly endear him to me. Nor did it strike me as being penned by some harmless old man, once a racist along with most other Southerners in the 1960s but mellowed over the years. I came from a segregationist background, but I had never heard nor read anything like this letter in my life. The person who wrote this letter was certainly perverse and brazen enough to try to tamper with a jury or have some of his friends do it.

I picked up the phone and called Chief of Detectives Don Bartlett. Maybe he could put his hands on the investigative report of the Evers assassination. Waller's file would be more beneficial, if it could be found. The police file, if it still existed, would start from the time the first officer arrived on the scene and progress through the entire investigation. Every tip called in, any lead that was followed (even the dead ends), would be included. Thus, the wheat would be lost among the chaff. Waller's file, on the other hand, would focus on the wheat, since he would have winnowed the valuable details from the worthless tittle-tattle.

As I hung up the phone, Clara Mayfield, our office manager, came in my office and sat down. She said that the county stored a lot of old files in a large warehouse that it leased from Hood Industries, a local furniture manufacturer. While looking for some other old files several years earlier, Clara had seen some boxes with Jack Travis's name on them. The DA file on Beckwith might be there, she explained, and volunteered to assist me in the search. But, we needed to get a key from Barbara Dunn.

Although she gives me a hard time, Clara is competent, intelligent, and, like Barbara, has a heart of gold. Both ladies always pull through in a clutch. As Clara was leaving my office, Barbara walked in and handed some papers to me.

The documents were copies from the minute books of the court, containing the names of the jurors in both 1964 trials. No addresses were listed. This was the first step in locating and interviewing the jurors to determine what, if any, contact was made with them by the Sovereignty Commission or other persons that would constitute jury tampering.

"Thanks, Barbara; I didn't expect anything this quickly."

"That, as you can see, came from the minutes. We still have the minute books in our office. It may take me a while, though, to find the court file itself," she said. "But if it can be found, I'll get it."

I thanked her again and then asked her about going to the Hood Industries warehouse. She agreed and volunteered to send one of her deputy clerks, Henry Brinston, with us to lend a hand. She could not, however, spare Henry until Friday. It was Wednesday and I would just have to wait.

It was close to noon and I was famished. "Cynthia!" I hollered.

"Yes, I am starving!" Cynthia Hewes, in the office next door, knew exactly why I was calling her name. We had been acquaintances in law school, old courtroom foes when I was in private practice, and now we split prosecuting the crimes of violence.

Cynthia was also my best friend in the office. Smart, quick on her feet, and relentless once she sets her sights, she will tear your throat out in the courtroom. I should know. I ran up against that buzz saw too many times when I was on the opposite side of the fence. It was a lot more enjoyable sitting at the same counsel table and watching her lay into some other poor dolt.

Four or five of us in the office usually went to lunch together. R. D. "Doc" Thaggard, the investigator assigned to Cynthia and me, was one of them. He is the quietest, least hurried, yet most efficient person that I know. A man of few words, Doc speaks infrequently and without much emotion, but when he talks, he *says* something. Even though he has an exasperating job keeping up with witnesses, many of whom are transients, and he works under the hectic pressure of the cases flooding our office, I have only seen Doc lose his cool once or twice.

Nobody can find witnesses like Doc. It's uncanny. Cynthia always said the only reason the authorities never found Jimmy Hoffa was that they never asked Doc to look for him.

Appearing at my door, Cynthia said, "How does CS's sound? Doc is going to meet us downstairs. He had to check on some subpoenas in the clerk's office."

"Sounds great. Let's go. Is Tommy going?" I was referring to Tommy Mayfield, Clara's husband.

Then I heard him in the lobby: "Y'all come on now. I ain't holding this elevator all day."

During the drive over to CS's, I pulled Beckwith's letter out of my coat pocket, and I let Tommy read it to everyone.

The Good Lord surely threw the mold away after creating "the little Mayfield boy," as former governor Ross Barnett called him. Short, bearded, feisty, and usually dressed in jeans, he looks more like Gabby Hayes than he does a lawyer, and he would consider that a compliment. He is a walking encyclopedia of law, capable of reciting obscure cases by book and page number, and the year they were decided, as well as by name.

After placing our orders and getting our glasses of iced tea, Doc looked at me and asked for the Beckwith jury list. "I figure you are going to ask me to find them and talk to them. Am I right?"

"You always are."

"Make me a copy when we get back to the office and I will get on it as I can. When do you need their statements?"

"The next grand jury meets next month. I would like to present them with something and get this behind us one way or the other. Start off with the jurors in the second trial. That's the trial Mitchell mentioned in his article about this tampering issue."

I could see Doc's face tighten up a little at the mere mention of Jerry Mitchell's name. Doc had nothing for reporters.

"And, Doc," I pressed on, "in addition to asking them about any contact by anyone, ask them about their feelings or opinions on the case back then, and what it would take to convict him today."

Cynthia leaned over the table and said, in a hushed tone but loud enough to be heard over nearby pinball machines, "It sounds to me like you are planning on going beyond jury tampering. Are you seriously thinking about reprosecuting the murder case, Bobby?"

"Just curious and thinking what-if."

"Shit fire, Bobby Joe [Tommy's nickname for me], if you ask me— and I know you didn't, but I'm going to tell you anyway—the old son of a bitch ought to be indicted for being so damn spiteful. Which reminds me, here's your letter back. You do know that son of a bitch is crazy, don't you? You do realize that?"

Tommy then gave us the whole scoop on how Bill Waller tried to get Beckwith examined involuntarily at the state hospital for the insane following his arrest in 1963. If Waller had been successful and Beckwith had been found incompetent to stand trial, Beckwith's commitment would have been indefinite and Waller would not have had to bother with a trial. Beckwith's lawyers resisted and the issue was decided in his favor by the Mississippi Supreme Court. Waller thus had his back against the wall and was forced to trial.

When we got back to the office, I made a copy of the jury lists for Doc and stuck my copy in a manila file folder. With that, the first file of the reprosecution of Byron De La Beckwith was opened.

Around two-fifteen Barbara walked in and laid a court file on my desk. I picked it up and read the cover: "*State of Mississippi v. Byron De La Beckwith*, No. 17,824."

"Barbara, this is great. I didn't expect you to find it this soon, if it could be found at all."

"I know how after—what is it, twenty-five years?—you are in such a hurry." The sarcasm was biting.

"Barbara, I'm just doing my job. If we just go through the motions on this thing and announce that there is nothing to it, it will be worse than if we did nothing. I'm going to do my job, conduct as genuine and as thorough an investigation as I can, present it to a grand jury, and let the chips fall where they may. I want this behind us as much as anybody."

"And anything that I can do to speed up the process, you let me know. I smell trouble for all of us on this, Bobby DeLaughter, do you hear me?"

"Yes, ma'am. Can I read my file now?"

"Don't you lose that file," she ordered, and with that she was gone.

Court files usually don't contain any evidence, transcripts, or anything that reflects what the witnesses know. That information comes from the police report and the district attorney's file—neither of which I yet had. Court files contain papers that are filed with the court, such as the indictment, which sets forth the charge brought against the defendant; any motions that are filed by either side and the orders setting out the judge's rulings on them; the jury instructions, by which the judge tells the jury the legal principles to apply to the facts or evidence in the trial; and the subpoenas issued for witnesses.

Reviewing this court file would, I hoped, shed some light on the legal issues that arose in the case. Also, the subpoenas, while not telling me how a witness fit into the puzzle, would nevertheless produce some names and possibly addresses. Sure, I knew there were probably witnesses who may not have been subpoenaed but nevertheless testified, and that the addresses were old, but it was a start.

I opened the file. It had that musty smell that usually emanates from old books and papers. It hit me that I truly was stepping back in time. I had expected this in a theoretical or logical sense, but I didn't expect it through my sense of smell. Yet, there it was.

John Fox, Bill Waller's ADA, had requested a subpoena seeking three different court files from the chancery court of Leflore County, in Greenwood, Mississippi, Beckwith's hometown. Each file appeared to be for divorce proceedings between Beckwith and his first wife, Mary Louise Williams Beckwith. Fox, in requesting these files, represented to the court that they "bear materially upon the reputation of the defendant for peace and violence in the community in which he lives."

So, he's not only a back-shooting bushwhacker, I thought, *allegations of domestic abuse, too? What a sweetheart.*

Hardy Lott, one of Beckwith's lawyers, had requested access to "all tapes or recordings of telephone calls directed to Television Station WLBT immediately after the appearance of Medgar Evers on May 10, 1963," claiming only that they were "essential to the defense and contain evidence material on the issues." Lott did not say how they were material or why they were essential, and the court, Judge Leon Hendrick, obviously disagreed, as he denied the request.

Next in the file was another request by Fox: for Southern Bell Telephone & Telegraph Company to produce records that "will show that the deceased, Medgar Evers' telephone number was unlisted and that the whereabouts of his residence could not be obtained by examination of the telephone book, but rather that inquiry would be necessary." I wondered how that would be material.

Waller had filed a request seeking, from the *Memphis Commercial Appeal* newspaper, "letters to the editor published or unpublished of the years 1957 through 1963 to said newspaper from Byron De La Beckwith." Their purpose, Waller represented, was "to establish motive." After reading Beckwith's 1987 letter to Ed, I could only imagine what he was writing to the newspaper from 1957 to 1963. I wanted to see those myself.

Waller's next request was for a specific report from the Railway Express Agency in Greenwood. The report sought was "of paid COD Collections Form Number 94-S, and most specifically, Railway Express Receipt Number 05907 dated on or about February 6, 1959, and Record of Delivery Sheets Form Number 510, Sheet Number 0680, dated on or about February 17, 1959." The purpose, Waller said, was for "the establishment of the ownership of that certain .30-06 Enfield rifle as the property of the Defendant." That had to be the murder weapon.

Next was a court order, issued by Judge Hendrick, for the seizure of a white, four-door 1962 Valiant sedan from Delta Liquid Plant Food, Inc. Jerry Mitchell's first article in October said witnesses placed Beckwith's car at the scene the night of the murder. This Valiant was probably it. I had read or heard that Beckwith was a fertilizer salesman in the Delta. Boy, that seemed appropriate.

Jerry's article also mentioned that Beckwith's fingerprints were found on the murder weapon. Such seemed to be the case, as I read a motion filed by Hardy Lott asking the court to make those prints available to the defense and any fingerprint expert hired by the defense. It's a routine request.

The most interesting thing in the file was a document filed by Waller titled, "Suggestion of Insanity and Motion of District Attorney for Mental Examination of Defendant."

The sanity issue, as Tommy had told me during lunch, went all the way to the Mississippi Supreme Court. Judge Hendrick, the Hinds County circuit judge who would preside over the trial in Jackson, agreed with Waller and signed an order committing Beckwith to the State Hospital at Whitfield to be examined.

The defense team did not, however, appeal Judge Hendrick's order. Instead, they waited until their client was physically transported from the Hinds County jail in Jackson (where he had been confined in a cell as any other prisoner) across the Pearl River and into Rankin County, where the State Hospital at Whitfield is located. Not coincidentally, it is also where Judge Hendrick had no jurisdiction.

Gov. Ross Barnett not only had a law partner on the defense team, but, according to an FBI report I later obtained, he also had a relative who was a circuit court judge in the district that included Rankin County. It was to that judge—Judge Barnett—that the governor's law partner and Beckwith's other duo of lawyers ran for help.

Judge Barnett, not surprisingly, sided with the defense and ordered that Beckwith be released from the state hospital. Normally, that would have meant returning him to the jail from whence he came, but that would have sent Beckwith back to Hinds County where he would have been treated as any other prisoner awaiting trial for murder.

So, Judge Barnett simply added to his order that Beckwith await his

Hinds County trial not in the Hinds County jail, but rather in the Rankin County jail in Brandon, Mississippi, under the watchful jurisdiction of Judge Barnett. This ruling definitely had its perks. In stark contrast with his confinement in Jackson, Beckwith's "stay" (indeed it can hardly be called confinement) in Brandon had all of the amenities of home. Beckwith, in a letter to Hinds County sheriff J. R. Gilfoy, bragged that his cell door in Rankin County was rarely closed; he was provided a typewriter and enjoyed little restriction of visitors.

The Mississippi Supreme Court then issued a decision of which Solomon would have been proud, attempting to split the baby down the middle; it held that Beckwith could not be forced to undergo a mental examination, but he should await his trial in the Hinds County jail. He had to relinquish his television and typewriter and smoke one last Cuban stogie before leaving Rankin County.

Also of interest in the court file was a letter, dated January 24, 1964, and typed on the letterhead of Vickers, Incorporated, a division of Sperry Rand Corporation:

> To Whom It May Concern: I would appreciate having Mr. Willard Smith excused from jury duty beginning January 27. Mr. Smith is currently performing functions at Vickers, which if absent from his work for any period of time (over one day), would cause a serious interruption of other people's work. Please use this note as an appeal to relieve Mr. Smith of any jury duty.

That kind of request by an employer to get an employee excused from jury duty is common. The stirring aspect of this letter, though, was the note of four simple words handwritten across it: "Mr. Smith is colored."

I'm surprised it said "Mr." That was part of our informal education in the South. No white should ever, I was taught, say "Mr." or "Mrs." in reference to a "nigra" (which was thought to be a genteel substitute for *nigger* and thus, in the minds of those who used it, should be appreciated by those to whom it referred).

I also learned that Beckwith's case was nol-prossed (dismissed without prejudice to the state) by the court, at Jack Travis's request, on March 10, 1969. My hopes were raised that he had possessed and reviewed Waller's file before making that request and that it would be in whatever boxes bearing his name that Clara had seen in the warehouse at Hood Industries.

The last item in the court file was the capias, or warrant, which is issued after a person is indicted. No indictment was in the file, though. I picked up the phone and called Barbara. She said it was possible that the indictments then were kept separate; she would ask Henry Brinston if he had any idea where it might be. Her office, however, did not have any of the evidence. Henry and she had thoroughly searched her vault, and it was just not there. I thanked her and hung up. Something on the capias caught my eye.

The deputy circuit clerk who had issued the capias was Robert E. Lilley. There was a Bob Lilley who was a county election commissioner. I flipped back through the subpoenas. Most of them as well were signed by Robert E. Lilley. If former deputy clerk Robert E. Lilley was election commissioner Bob Lilley, I thought he might be helpful in discovering what was done with all of the evidence. At least now, one of Barbara's deputy clerks is always on hand at the end of each day of a trial to take custody of the evidence. If that was part of Lilley's job in 1964, he might know something. I made a note to follow up on that hunch.

Barbara soon called back to say that Henry did not have a clue where the indictment was located, but he would be glad to go with Clara and me to the warehouse at Hood Industries, on Friday, to see if we could find Waller's file. Barbara had even checked with the State Department of Archives and History to see what, if any, records and evidence might be stored there—nothing. It was a long shot, but the furniture warehouse was becoming our last hope in the search for evidence.

The time was nearing to go home. Chief of Detectives Bartlett called as I was leaving. The records division at the police department had found the investigative report, and he promised to have a copy on my desk first thing the next morning. I thanked him profusely and headed out.

I was exhausted by the time I crawled in bed. I thought that I would fall asleep as soon as my head hit the pillow, but I didn't. I lay there looking up at the ceiling fan that I could not see but could hear steadily whirring. Even in cool weather, I have to sleep with a fan—not so much for the breeze as for its unvarying resonance.

What would I find in the police report when morning came? Where would all of this lead? Would I come out of it with any kind of career in public office intact? These questions flooded my mind as I slowly drifted into a deep slumber to the soft hum of the ceiling fan.

CHAPTER TWO

THE 1963
POLICE INVESTIGATION

I opened the large, plain brown envelope that I found on my chair the next morning at the office. It contained the report Bartlett had promised: JPD Case No. 0-5695, charge—murder. The victim listed: "Medgar Evers (c/m)" (colored male). I flipped over the cover sheet of the report. One small sketch showed the neighborhood where Evers and his family lived, and another diagram showed the layout of their home at 2332 Guynes Street. It charted where Evers was standing when shot, the bloody trail he left, and the path of the bullet after it exited his body.

Police involvement in the case began at 12:45 A.M., Wednesday, June 12, 1963, when Det. Capt. B. D. Harrell received a call at headquarters that a man had been shot at 2332 Guynes Street. Captain Harrell immediately dispatched two patrol officers to the scene. Officers Joe Alford and Eddie Rosamond did not know until after they arrived that the man who had been shot was Medgar Evers.

Captain Harrell assigned homicide detective John Chamblee and his partner, Fred Sanders, to the case. Arriving at the scene at 12:53 A.M., they found the wife of Medgar Evers, Myrlie, and neighbor M. F. Sarton standing in the carport near a large pool of blood. After speaking with Mrs. Evers, the detectives began inspecting the scene. Two concrete steps led from the carport into the house. Medgar Evers had fallen at the base of these steps, as evidenced by the extremely large pool of blood there.

The bullet had struck Evers in the back, exited his chest, and blasted through a front window of the house. Detectives found that it had torn a hole through the venetian blinds covering the window and traveled fifteen feet nine inches across the living room. It then penetrated a four-inch interior wall separating the living room and kitchen, blowing out a ceramic tile on the kitchen side of the wall. Crossing the kitchen six feet ten inches, it next struck a refrigerator. Turning at a forty-five-degree angle, the bullet traveled five feet ten inches before coming to rest on a countertop in the kitchen.

Working backward from the bullet's trajectory, the detectives determined that the shot was fired from a vacant lot and semiwooded area between nearby Missouri Street and Delta Drive. Heavy dew had formed on the ground, and Chamblee and Sanders did not want to risk disturbing any physical evidence, so they had the area sealed off until daybreak.

Fully aware of the victim's identity, and completely appreciating the social and political pressures that had been building in Jackson that hot and sweltering spring, Chamblee and Sanders were apparently aware that they and the other officers of the JPD were sitting on one helluva powder keg. All that it would take to ignite an uncontrollable inferno was a major screwup such as some cop walking over crucial clues. The situation was delicate, and the world was watching. Whether or not the assassin was apprehended and tried, the JPD and Mississippi were already on trial, as far as Chamblee and Sanders were concerned. If the back-shooting son of a bitch wasn't caught, it wouldn't be because of a lack of effort on their part. Thus, they waited for the silver shadows cast by the full moon to give way to the brilliant rising sun of a Mississippi June morning.

In the meantime, they received word that Evers had died on the operating-room table at the hospital. The detectives' report noted that Evers was admitted by a Dr. Cutcher, an intern, and "worked on by Dr. Robertson, the surgeon." The time of death was 1:20 A.M., approximately thirty-five minutes after Evers was shot.

A coroner's jury was then impaneled, with Detective Chamblee serving as foreman. His report states that Houston Wells, the next-door neighbor of the Evers family who had helped get Medgar to the hospital, testified at the inquest. Wells was in bed asleep when awoken by a gunshot and his daughter's ensuing scream. He jumped out of bed, grabbed his pistol, and looked out the window. Wells said that he could clearly see into the Everses' carport and saw his neighbor lying facedown.

After checking that his daughter was okay, Wells ran out of his front door onto his porch, leaped behind a bush, and fired his pistol once in the air. He then ran to Evers's carport and turned Medgar over on his back, finding a large hole in his friend's chest. Wells ran back home to call the police, but his wife already had them on the phone.

According to Wells, he returned to the Evers house, and about two to three minutes later two uniformed officers (Alford and Rosamond) arrived and helped him and other neighbors get Medgar on a mattress and into Wells's station wagon. The officers escorted him to the hospital.

The verdict of the coroner's jury was "held open pending further investigation," and an autopsy was ordered.

Still waiting for daylight, Chamblee, Sanders, and other officers canvassed the area, interviewing neighbors and people who had seen Evers earlier that evening.

One such person interviewed, I saw from the next page in the report, was "Matthew Blackwell, cm." Approached by Officers W. C. Chance and J. D. Simpson, Blackwell stated that he had been with Medgar Evers earlier in the night at the NAACP office on Lynch Street. After Medgar locked up, the two of them crossed the street and drank coffee at the Smackover Café. Evers and Blackwell left the diner, heading for their homes in separate cars, but Blackwell said that he followed Medgar most of the way. They left Lynch Street, which is just west of downtown, and proceeded north on Delta Drive.

Blackwell remained behind Evers, and as they approached the intersection of Marydell Street, Evers slowed his baby blue Olds and turned right on Marydell. His family would be waiting for him in their home a mere block away. Matthew Blackwell lived on Ridgeway, the next turn to the right off Delta Drive, just past Marydell.

Little did Medgar Evers or Matthew Blackwell know, as they parted ways, that lurking in a nearby thicket was a cowardly assassin waiting with a bullet in his rifle's chamber; a bullet that within seconds would tear through the flesh and major thoracic organs of Medgar's body and end up on a countertop in his kitchen. Little did a nine-year-old boy, sleeping on the other side of town in a white, middle-class subdivision, a boy named Bobby DeLaughter, know that his life, twenty-six years later, would be profoundly affected by that same bullet.

Blackwell said that he had only been home about fifteen minutes when he received a telephone call telling him that Medgar had been shot. Blackwell immediately went to the Evers house to see what help he could offer.

The interviewing officers were evidently impressed with Blackwell's information and willingness to cooperate. They had already attached the "cm" (colored male) to Blackwell's name, and I suppose in an effort to make sure that his information was not just ignored or skimmed over, the officers added that Blackwell "seemed to be very sound-minded about this unfortunate situation." If they thought that they were getting good information from a white person, would the officers have found it necessary to add that the interviewee was "sound-minded," or would that have been considered redundant?

Detectives J. L. Black (who later became police chief) and H. B. Benton interviewed two other neighbors. Thomas Young, who lived directly across the street from the Evers family, and M. F. Sarton, who lived a short distance up the street, had heard the shot and assisted in getting Evers loaded into Wells's vehicle. They had seen nothing unusual earlier. Sarton told the detectives, though, that shortly after the two uniformed officers had left the scene to escort the station wagon, "the two Pittman boys came up in front of the Evers house and Medgar's wife cursed them and ran them away from there." I recalled seeing some Pittmans on the state's subpoenas in the court file the day before.

Another subpoena was for Betty Jean Coley. I reviewed a report stating that Officers Hammond and Magee talked to her on June 12. She told them that a boy named Kenneth Adcock (I had seen his name, as well, on a subpoena in the court file) had rented a room at her house on Marydell Street. They took a walk that night and were returning home about 12:30 A.M. Coley and Adcock were walking east on Missouri Street, she said, about a hundred feet east of the intersection of Missouri and Guynes, "when someone fired a gun from a clump of trees and the blast was so loud that it hurt her ears and the blast seemed very close to her head. She thought someone had shot at them."

Coley said that immediately after the gunshot she heard "a heavy thud" in the bushes "like someone leaped," and then she could hear someone running in the opposite direction, farther into the vacant lot. She told the officers that it sounded as if the person was running on the ground at first, but then she heard something "crunch" underfoot. A black dog ran out of the bushes into the street. Betty Jean and Kenneth kept walking, and then another gunshot erupted, followed by a woman's scream.

Betty Jean said that she wanted to go see what happened, "but that Kenneth was scared that they may get shot and made her go on." She called police headquarters as soon as she learned from the news about Evers's death.

Daylight came, and after getting her statement, Hammond and Magee took her to the scene she had described. She pointed out where she and Adcock had been when they heard the gunshot and showed the police the clump of trees from which she thought the shot was fired. As recorded in the police report:

As we lined up her position with the clump of bushes and the bullet hole in the window of Evers' house, we could see that she was almost in the line of fire when the gun went off. We followed the direction of the running sound she heard and it was across grass at first, then across a concrete slab where a house has been torn down, there was all kinds of debris which is probably what she heard crunching under the person's feet. At the opposite side of the slab is a well-traveled path leading to Joe's Drive-In at the rear of the parking lot.

Det. O. M. Luke helped survey the area. The clump of trees mentioned by Betty Jean Coley was a cluster of sweet gum located about two hundred feet southwest of the Evers house. Her belief that the gun was fired from that spot was buttressed by its being in line from where Evers was shot and the bullet hole in the glass window of his house.

Luke also found that the grass amid that group of trees had been "mashed down" and that "a hole about eighteen inches wide had been cleared in the vines that grew on these trees at the height that the average person would need to shoot a gun from his shoulder. Also on the side of one of these trees, the bark had been slightly scraped at this same height, indicating that something had either rubbed against the tree or a gun had been placed against it using it as a brace to fire from."

The detectives continued their search of the area, proceeding from the sweet gum, past the concrete slab, along the path that led to the back parking lot of Joe's Drive-In, which was best described as a "joint."

While Detective Luke was searching an area about ten feet to the right of where the path neared Joe's parking lot, he spotted what appeared to be the rear end of a gunstock in a thicket of honeysuckle vines. Carefully lifting the vine cover, Luke discovered it was, indeed, a gun.

Capt. Ralph Hargrove, who was the one-man mobile crime lab for the Jackson Police Department in those days, was summoned. He took photographs of the weapon as Luke removed it from the honeysuckle, careful to preserve any possible fingerprints.

At headquarters, Captain Hargrove checked the gun for fingerprints, finding one near the front of its scope. After photographing the print, Hargrove lifted it.

It was a 1917 .30-06 Enfield rifle, a seven-shot, bolt-action repeater, serial #69431. The chamber contained one empty casing, and six live rounds were in the magazine. The ammunition was Super Speed, .30-06 Springfield. Both gun and ammunition were properly marked and tagged.

Luke then began the tedious legwork of taking the evidence to various gun shops, gunsmiths, and pawnshops to see if anyone had ever seen the gun, mounted the scope, or sold the ammunition. No luck.

The path from the sweet-gum trees led past the rifle hidden in the honeysuckle to the rear parking area of Joe's Drive-In. Detectives Hammond and Magee next concentrated their efforts on that dive, seeking information from anyone who may have seen or heard anything.

Lee Cockrell was the new owner and operator of Joe's Drive-In. He had changed its name to Lee's, but the regulars (and the police) still called the place what it had been called for years—Joe's. Lee told the detectives that his place was still open at twelve-thirty the morning of June 12, when he heard the gunshot. Cockrell, however, said that he didn't go outside, but rather kept his attention on a carload of unruly drunks parked at the front door.

Hammond and Magee checked back at Joe's later that same day when the cook returned to work. Ellaweese Cooper said that she had been sitting near the rear door of the kitchen when she heard two gunshots, followed by a woman's scream. The detectives noted in their report that the honeysuckle, where the rifle was found, was behind Joe's, but the weeds and brush were so high, this cook could not have seen anyone hide the weapon on the other side of the hedge and brush. She could have seen someone come out from that area, but, according to Lee Cockrell, Ellaweese Cooper had come to the front of the café, where he was keeping a watchful eye on the drunks, as soon as the shot was fired. The assailant, consequently, could easily have walked out onto the parking lot, got in a vehicle, and driven unnoticed around the back of Joe's, instead of leaving by the front where the drunks were living it up.

The assassin's chances of being noticed (even by drunks) would have been greater if he stepped out of the woods carrying a rifle. So he chose to leave it behind, after wiping off all fingerprints. As criminals normally do, however, he made a mistake—he missed a print, not on the gun, but on the end of the scope.

Ancie Lee Haven, a waitress at Joe's, said that when she left work about 11 P.M., she saw a white Valiant backed in the corner of the lot by the pathway entrance, but she didn't see anyone in it.

Carhop Martha Jean O'Brien worked from 3 P.M. to midnight at Joe's. She told detectives that around 8:30 P.M., or possibly later, a Valiant pulled into the parking lot. She remembered that the Valiant was white, had a long, whiplike aerial on the back, and initially parked behind, but close to, the building. The driver got out and entered the rest room at the café. He then got back inside the car and backed it up to the far corner of the parking lot (by the pathway). The interviewing officers noted in their report that the Valiant was parked as close as an automobile could get to where the gun was found.

O'Brien said that she never went outside to wait on the driver because he never flashed his lights for service. According to her, she did not see the driver leave and did not remember if the car was still there when she left work at midnight. She described the man as a white male, "dark complexion, black hair, mustache, about six-feet to six-feet-two-inches tall and weighed about 160 pounds, slim build."

Detectives Luke and R. Q. Turner also visited Evers's NAACP office. There, they met Gloster Currents, the director of branches for the national organization. According to Currents, Medgar Evers told him the day before he was gunned down that he felt he was being followed. Evers knew that the police tailed him occasionally, but this, he confided in Currents, felt different, and he was a little concerned about it, "as if he had a premonition that something was going to happen."

It was a long, hard day for the detectives of the Jackson Police Department, but finally darkness closed out a dark day in the history of humanity.

On Thursday, June 13, 1963, Detectives Chance and Simpson spent the day in a house-to-house search for anyone in the neighborhood who had any information concerning the rifle that Detective Luke had found. Four pages of Chance and Simpson's report for the day listed all of the addresses to which their search took them. Nobody knew anything.

Detectives Luke and Turner talked to two teenage boys, Robert Don Pittman, age fifteen, and his friend Ronald Jones, age sixteen. Pittman's parents ran Pittman's Grocery on Delta Drive, just south of Joe's Drive-In. The elder Pittmans were out of town when Evers was killed. They had left young Pittman to tend the store, and he had enlisted the help of his friend Jones.

The Pittmans lived in the same building that housed their store, and the two boys were in bed by 12:15 A.M. They were not yet asleep, though, when they heard a shot. They jumped out of bed and ran to the window to see what was happening. They couldn't see anything, so they walked behind the store. They heard a second shot (Houston Wells's) and then a woman screaming and crying. Tracking the mournful sound, the boys soon found themselves crossing Missouri Street and approaching Guynes Street.

Pittman and Jones saw a station wagon backing into Evers's driveway. They watched as neighbors put Medgar in the vehicle and it drove away with the police. Curious, the boys approached the house. Mrs. Evers, they said, called them some names and told them to get away before she killed them. Neighbor M. F. Sarton told the cops the same thing.

The boys took off running back to the Pittmans' store/house and did not come outside again until the police came knocking. According to the detectives' report, when asked if they could think of anything to add to their statement, the boys said only "that the next time that they heard a gunshot, they were not going to see what happened, [but] instead go in the house and crawl under the bed."

Adding to their anxiety, the teenagers were fingerprinted while at headquarters by Captain Hargrove and were released only after their prints did not match the one on the rifle's scope.

Detectives Luke and Turner, after finishing their interview with the boys, spent the remainder of the day traveling to Vicksburg and then north into the Mississippi Delta, going from one gunsmith to the next seeking information about the rifle. They found none.

Meanwhile, back in Jackson, Detectives Rester and Reeves had some better luck. They went to the Trailways bus station on Pascagoula Street around 10:10 P.M., June 13, to see a White Top cabdriver who had called headquarters and said that he might have some information.

Lee F. Swilley, one of the names I had seen on a subpoena in the court file, told them that one day the weekend before the killing, he and another cabdriver, Hubert Speight (another name I recognized from a subpoena), were parked in front of the bus station. A white male walked out of the station and up to them, asking if they knew where "the nigger Evers lived," stating that he had to find where Evers lived very badly. Neither cabdriver knew where Evers lived.

Swilley said the man went back inside the bus station, looked through the telephone book, and came back outside, telling Swilley and Speight that he could not find Evers's address in the phone book. He again asked them if they knew where Evers lived, saying that it was important that he find the house in the next couple of days. Soon after that, both Swilley and Speight got calls for fares and left the bus station.

This explained the subpoena by the prosecution for the telephone records of Medgar Evers's house to show that he had an unlisted phone number. This verified what Lee Swilley had said. The man looking for Evers's house had sought the location from two people whose jobs carried them over every street in Jackson—cabdrivers.

The first link to Byron De La Beckwith began with a telephone call the night of Thursday, June 13, to Capt. Ralph Hargrove. Thorn McIntyre, a young Delta planter of Itta Bena (just outside Greenwood, Mississippi), had seen the photograph of the recovered rifle in the newspaper and the request to the public for any information concerning it. He then did something that would later cause him much grief and harassment, eventually requiring him to leave the state. He picked up a phone and called the Jackson Police Department.

McIntyre informed Hargrove that he had traded a 1917 Enfield .30-06 rifle about three years earlier to a man by the name of "Mr. De La Beckwith, 306 George Street, Greenwood, Miss." He related that Beckwith was a war veteran and "is very radical on this racial problem and he would not be surprised as to what this man might do."

McIntyre wanted to keep his name a secret for the time being, and Hargrove assured him that when Beckwith was contacted about the rifle, he would not be told that McIntyre was the source of the detectives' information.

Back from their fruitless trip to Vicksburg the previous day, Luke and Turner were busy again on Friday. They went to Pittman's Grocery on Delta Drive. This time, they talked to Mr. and Mrs. Pittman. They remembered that the Friday or Saturday before the murder, a well-dressed white male, of average build and weight, parked a white car, which the Pittmans believed was either a Valiant or a Dodge, late model, near Delta Drive and walked to the back of their parking lot, looking around. This stood out in their minds because it was after dark and the man was wearing sunglasses. He looked around the back of the parking lot for a few minutes and then left.

As one looks over the back of the Pittmans' parking lot, one is looking at the trees and brush concealing the pathway found by the police the morning of the murder.

On Friday, Rester and Reeves resumed their lead from cabdriver Lee Swilley and located Hubert Speight, the other cabby. For the most part, Speight gave the detectives the same information that Swilley had given them. Speight added that after the man looking for Evers's house searched through the phone book in the bus station, he came back outside and asked Swilley and Speight if Evers could possibly live on Lexington Avenue or Buena Vista or Hartsfield Streets. The drivers told him no, those were "white" streets.

The detectives then talked to various employees at the bus station to see if anyone else had seen the man who was seeking Evers's address. Nobody else had.

Also on June 14, just one day after Police Chief W. D. Rayfield's request for assistance from the FBI Crime Lab, the detectives had some answers. At 11:10 A.M., they received a telegram from the FBI, advising them that the bullet recovered was a thirty-caliber that could have been fired from the Enfield .30-06 rifle. The bullet, however, was too mutilated to be specifically identified with any particular gun to the exclusion of all others. Further, no record was located in the FBI's National Stolen Property Index that the rifle had been reported lost or stolen.

By 7:36 P.M. that same day, Chief Rayfield had received another telegram, advising that the fingerprint recovered from the rifle's scope could not be identified from the FBI's criminal files.

The next day, June 15, a female who refused to identify herself called the Jackson FBI office and "stated that she heard a rumor that Medgar Evers' wife had gotten jealous of Lena Horne and might have gotten her brother-in-law to kill Evers." The FBI relayed the information to JPD the following day.

Sanders and Chamblee spent the next several days talking to various black ministers who either knew or were associated with Medgar Evers. One was Rev. Robert L. T. Smith. The detectives went to Smith's Grocery on Valley Street around 4:30 P.M., June 19, one week after the murder. Rev. Mr. Smith provided little information but assured Chamblee and Sanders that he would do anything he could to help them in the investigation and that he would "try to find any loose talk that is going around."

The morning of June 21, Chamblee and Sanders went to Wells Furniture Company and talked again with Houston Wells, Evers's neighbor. According to the detectives' report that day, they had a lengthy conversation with Wells and found him to be "a sound, sane Negro not addicted to the demonstrations and he has had no part of this movement."

From this "sound, sane Negro," Chamblee and Sanders learned that Evers's neighbors had expected something like this to happen and had discussed what they would do if it ever came about. They had agreed that the first neighbor outside would give the alarm. That, Wells said, was the reason that he had fired a shot into the air and shouted, "There's a killer in the neighborhood!" Wells said he listened carefully for the sound of a car starting but never did hear one.

Houston Wells provided the detectives, as well as me, the first glimpse at the personal side of Medgar Evers. Wells stated that Evers "was a man dedicated to his work and if given the opportunity he would have helped a white person the same as a Negro. He was a Christian and thought that he was doing the right thing."

Wells had discussed with Evers the possibility of Evers being killed, but Medgar would just "shrug his shoulders and say that if it had to come, he was ready."

As to Medgar's wife, Myrlie, Wells said that she was religious. He said the couple had their family arguments at times, but nothing more than was common between any other married couple. Wells said that Medgar and Myrlie were devoted to one another and often spoke of their disgust with married people who had "friends" on the side.

Chamblee and Sanders went to the Evers home next and talked to Mrs. Evers. She invited them inside, remembering them from the night of the shooting. Mrs. Evers told them that she had thought of going to police headquarters to learn what efforts were being made regarding her husband's death.

John Chamblee and Fred Sanders then told Myrlie Evers something that struck a chord with me. Although it was 1963 Mississippi, and it was the local leader of the hated NAACP who had been killed, the two detectives that day, in Myrlie Evers's living room—the same room traversed by the bullet that would touch so many lives through the years to come—told her that "this is a murder case, and this case would never be closed. And we would do everything possible to find the killer of her husband."

After hearing those words, Mrs. Evers was not as upset as she had been, according to their report. They further eased her mind a little by telling her about the rifle's discovery, the fingerprint on its scope, and the other measures being taken by the police to expose the killer.

Understandably distraught the night of the murder, Mrs. Evers said that she did not remember too much of what had happened. When she ran to the carport to help her husband, she remembered hearing another shot and thought that she, too, was a target in the sniper's sights. She later learned that the second shot was fired by her neighbor Houston Wells.

Mrs. Evers was asked about any threatening phone calls. She told the detectives that such calls had been going on for nine years, both at home and at the office, but she could not recall Medgar ever attaching any names to the calls. Their home phone number, though, had been in the phone book until the previous year when James Meredith entered the Ole Miss Law School. After that, the calls became so regular that Medgar had the number changed and unlisted.

According to Mrs. Evers, about ten days to two weeks before Medgar was shot, he received a call from Dr. Felix Dunn, a close family friend and confidant who lived in Gulfport, on the Mississippi Gulf coast. Dr. Dunn told Medgar that he had heard, through his attorney, of a death threat against Medgar.

The conversation ended with the detectives assuring Mrs. Evers that they would keep her posted, but for her to call anytime and they would do all they could to help her.

Thus far, the only mention of Beckwith's name in the police report was in the tip called in by Thorn McIntyre. The FBI's telegram of June 14 said it had not matched the fingerprint found on the scope with anybody's prints, and no person other than McIntyre had mentioned Beckwith's name anywhere in the report.

Yet, the next page was a report by Detectives Chance and Simpson, which stated:

This date [June 23, 1963] at 1:40 A.M., Special Agent Waltser Prospere and Thomas Hopkins, Agents of the Federal Bureau of Investigation, delivered to the Police Department, Byron De La Beckwith, w.m., age 42 yrs. Address, 306 George St., Greenwood, Mississippi, to be held on a charge of violating Sec. 241, Title 10, of the U.S. Code.

The FBI made the initial arrest of Beckwith for violating Medgar Evers's civil rights—not for murder, which is a state charge. Something was missing, though. Thorn McIntyre was the only one who had mentioned Beckwith's name, and I had not seen any report yet of any detective interviewing McIntyre about the recovered rifle.

If, indeed, the police department was informed of the arrest only after the fact, it had one helluva hot potato tossed into its lap. News of the FBI's arrest was published and broadcast by media outlets spanning the globe; but what were the local and state authorities going to do about murder charges? They now had to formally charge Beckwith with Evers's murder, even though they may not have been informed beforehand that the FBI would be making an arrest. Then, astonishingly, the Justice Department dropped the federal charges, leaving the State of Mississippi and the Jackson Police Department with the burden of proving a murder case before their investigation was complete.

Suddenly having an arrested defendant shoved at them, police detectives conducted a lineup later that same day (June 23, 1963) at headquarters. Cabdriver Lee Swilley was unable to make an identification. Hubert Speight, the other cabby, positively identified Beckwith as the man seeking the address of Evers at the bus station a few days before the murder. Mr. B. L. Pittman picked out Beckwith as the man wearing sunglasses after dark, walking around the back parking lot near the area where the gun was later found. Mrs. Pittman was unable to make any identification.

While Detectives Luke and Turner conducted the lineup, Detectives Black, Benton, Rester, and Reeves were assigned to check hotels and motels in the area to see if Beckwith had checked in at any of them at any time from June 1 to June 12. There were no such records.

After they finished with the lineup, Luke and Turner drove to Greenwood, armed with a search warrant for Beckwith's house. This two-story structure of ten rooms, two baths, and several closets was in dire need of repair. In Beckwith's bedroom, the officers found many newspaper clippings concerning integration as well as copies of numerous letters that he had written to newspapers and other people on the subject. Luke and

Turner noted in their report that Beckwith "seemed very much disturbed over it."

Also found in Beckwith's room were three guns: a Remington Model 03-3A bolt-action repeater, a Stevens double-barrel sixteen-gauge shotgun, and a Galesi .25-caliber automatic pistol. Several hundred rounds of various ammunition—.22, .45, .03, and .25 caliber—were found; but no .30-06 caliber. There was, however, a booklet advertising Peters ammunition on which the power of .30-06 ammunition had been circled.

A pair of gloves was found with these items. Found in a closet behind the stairs was a twelve-inch wood rasp. It was new and had wood particles on it similar to the wood of which the murder weapon's stock was made. The wood piece extending under the barrel had been cut off, and something resembling a wood rasp had been used to round off the edges.

Monday, June 24, Chamblee and Sanders, with a court order in hand, traveled to Greenville, Mississippi, to locate and seize the white 1962 Valiant described in the order that I had found in the court file. The car was owned by Beckwith's employer, Delta Liquid Food, and was assigned to him.

The two detectives found the car at the fertilizer company, took possession of it, and drove it to police headquarters in Jackson. It certainly fit the description of the car seen in the back parking lot by the pathway the night of the slaying, including a long, whiplike aerial on the rear. Captain Hargrove photographed the car on the police impound lot.

Luke and Turner conducted another lineup that same day. Ancie Lee Haven and Martha Jean O'Brien, two employees of Joe's Drive-In, viewed this one. Neither girl could identify anyone in the lineup.

During the lineup, Chamblee and Sanders drove Beckwith's Valiant to Joe's Drive-In and parked it in the approximate position that Haven and O'Brien said the car they had seen the night of the murder was parked.

Following the lineup, Luke and Turner drove the two girls, Haven and O'Brien, to Joe's to look at the car parked there by Chamblee and Sanders. Ancie Lee Haven could not identify it as being the one she had seen, "as she had only gotten a fleeting glimpse of the car as she was preparing to leave the drive-in to go home."

Martha Jean O'Brien, however, said the car was "definitely the same car that was on the lot that night," saying that there was no doubt in her mind.

Chamblee and Sanders interviewed Thorn McIntyre on Tuesday, June 25, twelve days after he first called Captain Hargrove and two days after the feds snatched up Beckwith. McIntyre told the detectives that he could not be certain that the recovered rifle was the one that he had traded to Beckwith, as he did not keep any of the paperwork when he had purchased it. If the authorities could obtain copies of these documents, then the serial numbers could be compared. If the numbers matched, the gun recovered would have to be the one that McIntyre traded to Beckwith because it was the only .30-caliber rifle he had ever owned. The gun, according to McIntyre, did not have a scope on it at the time of the trade.

The detectives, while in Greenwood, talked to Hugh Warren, a Greenwood farmer who had seen and talked to Beckwith the day before the killing. Beckwith, Warren said, had a semicircular scar over his right eye. Warren had asked him about it, but Beckwith "just laughed and let it pass."

Upon their return to Jackson that night, Chamblee and Sanders learned that the FBI Crime Lab had identified the fingerprint found on the scope as that of Byron De La Beckwith's. They had not identified it earlier because a search was made only of the Bureau's criminal records. After his arrest, his prints taken as part of the booking procedure and those in his military records were compared with the print on the scope. Matches were made all the way around.

The next day, Wednesday, June 26, Detectives Luke and Turner removed Beckwith from his jail cell to question him. He talked about everything except the case. When asked anything about it, Beckwith replied that he did not care to make a statement. He "would get rather carried away when you engaged him in conversation about the Citizens' Council or things like that," and he insisted "that we definitely needed a Ku Klux Klan at this time, that it could do a lot of good. This subject is also way overboard when Masonry is mentioned." Beckwith never mentioned an alibi—neither then nor during the ensuing seven months of incarceration leading up to his first trial.

Meanwhile, Detective W. L. Allen and Assistant District Attorney John Fox met FBI agent Sam Allen in Grenada, Mississippi, approximately a hundred miles north of Jackson and thirty miles northeast of Greenwood. The three men paid a visit on John Goza, whose name I had seen on a subpoena in the court file. Beckwith had obtained the scope from Goza in a trade.

Goza provided the men with the invoice that had come with the scope when he obtained it from United Binocular. The serial number on the invoice matched that on the scope.

Reading between the lines, I guessed that someone (probably with the FBI since it would be a nationwide search) had already traced the scope from United Binocular to Goza. I seriously doubted that John Fox, Sam

Allen, and W. L. Allen picked Duck's Tackle Shop in Grenada, Mississippi, out of thin air to ascertain where and how Beckwith had obtained the scope. I was getting much information out of the police report, but I knew there were some gaps in the progression of the investigation.

After their futile attempt to get a statement from Beckwith, Detectives Luke and Turner were assigned to go to the NAACP office to follow up on some information that several of Evers's coworkers had phoned in to Chief Pierce, the department's chief of detectives. Luke and Turner went to the Masonic Lodge on Lynch Street, which also housed the NAACP's office.

Lillian Louie, Alphanette Bracey, and Pearlene Lewis told the detectives that on June 11 (the day before Evers was killed), around 1:30 P.M., a white man came to Medgar's office and stayed about two minutes looking around. Ms. Louie had seen the man before he came inside. He had been across the street talking to some police officers for about an hour. After seeing Beckwith's picture in the newspaper following his arrest, all three women said that they were certain that he was the man they had seen in the office the day before Evers was shot.

Bracey and Doris Allison told Luke and Turner that, upon seeing Beckwith's photo in the paper, they recalled seeing him on the night of June 7, at a mass meeting. These meetings had started on May 21 and continued every night until June 11, as Evers attempted to rally support for the sit-ins, demonstrations, and boycotts in what became known as the Jackson Movement.

The two women remembered that they had seen Beckwith at the June 7 meeting because that was the night Lena Horne had spoken to the crowd. The women said that Beckwith walked in the auditorium from the rear with two other white men. The two men with Beckwith stopped just inside, but Beckwith proceeded down the east side and found a seat. Other white men were there with the press corps, but the man who they said was Beckwith neither sat with nor appeared to belong to that group. Bracey approached him and asked if she could sell him a NAACP membership card. The man told her that he already had one. Still not satisfied, Ms. Bracey told Evers's close friend Sam Bailey to ask him who he was. As Sam started walking toward him, the man "got up and left in a big hurry."

The next day, Thursday, June 27, Detective Turner contacted Lt. William Bennett, the Jackson police officer on duty watching the Masonic Temple on Lynch Street on June 11. Turner asked Bennett if he recalled talking to anyone at length outside the temple that day. Bennett remembered talking to a white man for about an hour "and found that he was a nut." Bennett said it was a man from Flint, Michigan, who worked at one of the automobile manufacturers there. Bennett said the man had started talking to him at about 1 P.M. At the end of their conversation, this guy asked Bennett if he thought it would be all right to go inside the Masonic Temple. Bennett replied that he did not care but advised the man to leave if anyone inside asked him to do so. While the Northerner was inside, Lieutenant Bennett verified the personal information that he had been given.

By Saturday, June 29, Detectives Chamblee and Sanders were back in Greenwood. They had the .30-06 rifle and scope in their car and were beating the bushes trying to find anyone who knew anything about Beckwith or the rifle. The brick wall they ran into there in trying to obtain any useful information can be gleaned from this paragraph in their report:

> We then went to Greenwood where De La [pronounced "Deelay," as Beckwith was called by his friends] is known by just about everyone in town. We found the general nature of this town to be CLANNISH [I wondered if the detectives meant to spell that with a *K*], from the bankers to the drunks, about anything pertaining to this subject [Beckwith]. Everyone that we talked to seemed to know that we were in town and what we were after. Many of them, on showing our credentials, showed us their Citizens' Council cards.

Citizens' Councils had sprung up throughout the state to supplement the work of the Sovereignty Commission in resisting integration. Medgar Evers referred to them as the "uptown Ku Klux Klan." The Citizens' Councils had begun in Indianola, a small Delta town not too far from Greenwood. In fact, the state headquarters was subsequently moved to Greenwood.

Chamblee and Sanders turned to local law enforcement officers for help, paying a visit to one particular county sheriff in Beckwith's home county on Monday, July 1. The deputy quickly informed the Jackson detectives, in so many words, that no assistance should be expected from anyone in Greenwood. He told them that the Evers killing was similar to an earlier shooting in Greenwood and that neither the FBI nor any "outsider" ever found out anything about it and never would.

The previous shooting, he said, was well planned, and others were in on it in addition to the man that was charged. According to Chamblee and Sanders's report, the deputy also said that no one would be prosecuted in the other case, and the shooting of Medgar Evers would be no different. Chamblee and Sanders noted, "In short, [the] Deputy . . . let us know that they run the Delta and that no outsider would come into their section and find anything or tell them what to do."

With that bit of encouragement and assistance from a brother officer of the law, Chamblee and Sanders headed west for Greenville. They found John Book at the fertilizer plant where Beckwith had worked. Book told them that on June 10, the Monday before the shooting, he had worked with Beckwith all day. Book and Beckwith met at the plant that morning, and Beckwith rode with Book throughout the Delta. Book was to teach Beckwith about their product and the ropes, so to speak, of selling fertilizer.

The teacher, however, had a problem maintaining the pupil's attention. Book said that Beckwith's mind was not on the job, that all Beckwith wanted to talk about (to customers and Book alike) was segregation and guns. Although Book told the detectives that he knew little about Beckwith, he knew that Beckwith "was a gun nut and traded guns all over the Delta."

Book and Beckwith returned to the fertilizer plant in Greenville after dark. Beckwith entered the office, talked, picked up some material, and left in his company's white Valiant.

On Tuesday, July 2, Chamblee and Sanders were on the road to the Delta again. This time, they were under orders from Chief Pierce to return the Valiant to Beckwith's employer and to return everything seized from Beckwith's home pursuant to the search warrant of June 23, as the items "were of no value and were released on orders of the district attorney."

I was surprised that the wood rasp, gloves, and ammunition booklet were not kept. The stock of the .30-06 rifle had been modified, and Detective Luke had seized the rasp for that reason. He had even observed fresh wood particles on the rasp of the same type of wood as the gun's stock. I wondered whether the FBI Crime Lab had compared the two.

Waller could certainly have waved the gloves around at trial, it seemed to me, to offer the jury an explanation as to why none of Beckwith's fingerprints were on the rifle, and only one was on the scope.

The presence of a booklet with the power and velocity of .30-06 ammunition marked indicated that Beckwith had an interest in a weapon that would fire that type of cartridge; yet, there was no .30-06 rifle among the firearms in the house nor any .30-06 ammunition found. That there was no such ammunition struck me as odd. What had happened to the .30-06 he had obtained in his trade with McIntyre? It did not appear to have been stolen, for several reasons.

First, other guns were found in the house. Any thief would have taken all of the guns, not just one. Also, the FBI found no report in the National Lost and Stolen Property Index wherein the gun had been reported lost or stolen. If Beckwith was the gun nut that everyone said that he was, he would immediately have reported any loss or theft of the weapon if, in fact, that is what had happened to it.

While Chamblee and Sanders were taking the car and other items back to the Delta, Detectives Benton and Black returned to Joe's Drive-In and talked to Barbara Holder, a waitress there. Although she was not working on June 11 and 12, Holder told Benton and Black that she was there the night of the killing, and she saw a white Valiant parked near the back of the lot. She could not see if anyone was inside. It was still there when she left about 11:45 P.M. What stood out most was the long antenna on the rear of the car. That had made her pay attention because it might be a Mississippi Highway Patrol car.

On July 5, Chamblee and Sanders went to the NAACP office to talk to Lillian Louie, Alphanette Bracey, Sam Bailey, Doris Allison, and Pearlene Lewis, the people who claimed to have seen Beckwith at the June 7 mass meeting.

As the two detectives entered the office, they were met by Doris Allison, who again stated that she was sure that the man she had seen at that meeting was Byron De La Beckwith. However, when shown a photo of one Billy McPhail, Ms. Allison stated that it was, indeed, the man whom she had seen. After being advised that the man in the photo was not Beckwith, Ms. Allison changed her mind and said that McPhail looked similar to Beckwith, but that she was positive she had seen Beckwith at the meeting.

After learning from Doris Allison that Lillian Louie, Alphanette Bracey, and Pearlene Lewis were in Chicago attending the NAACP's National Convention, Chamblee and Sanders left to question Sam Bailey. Ms. Allison told them that he could be found at Universal Life Insurance Company.

Sam Bailey insisted that it was Beckwith, and not Billy McPhail, whom he had seen at the June 7 mass meeting. The detectives noted, however, that Ms. Allison had had sufficient time to phone him, while the detectives were en route, and advise Bailey as to what was going on.

It was already past 5 P.M. when I finished reading the report.

Clara Mayfield was still at her desk, so just before stepping into the elevator, I reminded her of our plans to search the Hood Industries warehouse the next morning. It was then that she informed me that the building had no electricity.

CHAPTER THREE

SEARCHING AND RESEARCHING
TO A NEW HEIGHT

I needed to find Waller's file. The information contained in the police report would not be enough to get a conviction. A third jury, psychologically at least, would insist on something over and above the evidence presented to the two 1964 panels. Something new might even be necessary to overcome the speedy-trial challenge that was sure to follow any reprosecution of the case.

If a court could be convinced that the involvement of the Sovereignty Commission had tainted the prior trials, then maybe, since evidence of that blemish was only now coming to light, a third trial after twenty-five years would not be barred. What a challenge it would be for a prosecutor to rebuild a murder case after a quarter century.

It was imperative that I learn firsthand what information lay hidden in the Sovereignty Commission files that might pertain to the Beckwith case. Steve Kirchmayr, of the state attorney general's office, represented the state in the federal lawsuit filed by the ACLU to gain access to all of the commission's records. U.S. district judge William Barbour Jr. had earlier ruled in favor of the ACLU, but his ruling was appealed by the state to the Fifth Circuit Court of Appeals in New Orleans. I decided to fire off a letter to Kirchmayr the next day, telling him of our investigation of possible jury tampering and getting his advice on what steps I could take to review the commission's records or have them subpoenaed for a grand jury to do so.

On Friday morning, November 10, 1989, Clara typed my letter to Kirchmayr. I signed and dropped it in the office outgoing-mail basket. She and I took the elevator down to Barbara Dunn's office, where we found Henry Brinston waiting for us. The three of us headed to the Hood Industries warehouse.

The building was an enormous brick structure that reminded me more of a dungeon than a warehouse. It was dark, dank, and pungent with the smell of mildew. The few windows were painted over, and but for the chipped portions in the paint and the slightly ajar door, no sunlight penetrated the murkiness.

Clara flicked on her flashlight and slowly brought its beam across the gargantuan room, unveiling canyons of cardboard boxes in the ghostly narrow light. Some stacks were only two or three boxes; others were at least ten or fifteen feet high.

Hour after hour passed, and the only thing that we collected was dust. I managed at times to appropriate Clara's flashlight, but only when I had to climb ten or fifteen feet to reach a box. At one point, using both hands to speed up the process, I crawled, box to box, holding the flashlight in my mouth. I remember thinking at the time that they didn't teach me this in law school.

Hopes of finding the file waned along with the fading of the little sunlight we had when we began. It was time to leave, and we had struck out.

On Saturday, the next day, Doc interviewed the former head of the state Sovereignty Commission. That evening Doc called and told me all about his visit with Erle Johnston in Forest, Mississippi, a small town about forty-five miles east of Jackson. Benny Bennett, another investigator in our office, had gone with Doc on the interview. Benny had been with our office only a short time, but it didn't take long for us to become good friends as well as coworkers. He was actually a detective with the Jackson Police Department on loan to the DA's office as an investigator. They had talked to Johnston at his house on Third Street in Forest.

Johnston told Doc and Benny that he had been the director of the state Sovereignty Commission from April 1, 1963 (only a couple of months before Medgar Evers was killed), until July 1, 1968. The commission had been in existence for seven years before he assumed the post. The offices housing this agency were located on the fourth floor of the state capitol and employed three investigators: Tom Scarborough, Andy Hopkins, and Virgil Downing. The state was divided into three geographical districts, with an investigator assigned to each one.

Doc asked Johnston just how the commission became involved in investigating prospective jurors for Beckwith's second trial in 1964. According to Johnston, commission investigator Andy Hopkins approached Johnston and told him that Stanny Sanders, one of Beckwith's lawyers, had asked Hopkins to "check them out." Hopkins, in turn, was seeking permission to do so from his boss, Johnston.

"Surely," I asked, "Johnston didn't admit to giving Hopkins the green light, did he?"

"Well, that was interesting. Let me look at my notes and read his response to you. He said, 'I told him to go ahead; I knew he could go to the governor and get it approved, but he was told not to talk to any of the jurors.'"

"Wouldn't you say that was a rather slick answer?"

"Ol' Erle is getting on up in years, but he's nobody's fool. He was definitely ready for us. In fact, when I called him on the phone to see if he would talk to me, he said that he had been expecting to hear from us."

"So, assuming that Johnston did instruct Hopkins not to talk to any of the jurors, and assuming that Hopkins followed those instructions, how did he go about 'checking them out'?"

"Johnston said that Hopkins got a lot of information about them from the city directory, including where they worked. Then he called their employers and neighbors on the phone and questioned them about the jurors."

"That was an awful lot of calling for one person. Was anyone helping Hopkins?"

"I don't know, and I don't think we will ever know for sure. I asked Johnston that very question. Get a load of this answer and tell me if this guy hasn't been thinking about all of this: 'No, he was the only one who did it and this was the only instance of it happening.'"

"Yeah, right," I said. "So, the information, papers, or whatever it was of the Sovereignty Commission that Jerry Mitchell got his hands on just happened to be the one and only case that only one investigator, in the entire sordid history of the commission, who just happens to be dead, 'checked out' jurors in a racially charged case. You don't buy that bullshit, do you?"

"It's not what I 'buy' or don't 'buy,' Bobby; it's what we can prove, and I'm telling you ol' Erle has all the right answers."

I knew Doc was right, but Hopkins's actions and Johnston's blessings to those actions left a bad taste in my mouth. No law may have been violated, but something about all of this smelled to high heaven.

"Who," I asked Doc, "had access to Hopkins's information on the jurors, and when did they have it?"

"Johnston said that Hopkins prepared a complete report on every person that received a summons for jury duty, which Beckwith's lawyers had before the trial even started."

"And I'm sure that Hopkins, being employed by a state agency, also provided a copy of his report to the state's lawyers—the prosecutors," I said in a more than slightly sarcastic tone.

"No, Johnston said there was no contact made by Hopkins with the state. He said, without any prompting from Benny or me, that it was probably unethical."

"No shit."

"You know," Doc said, "I got the feeling that Erle mellowed some over the years; had a change of heart of sorts."

"What do you mean?"

"I don't know. He just seemed almost apologetic about it all and admitted that it was probably unethical. He evidently kept copies of some commission documents because he gave us a copy of Hopkins's commission report—the same thing he says that Jerry Mitchell has."

"Did he say anything about Evers?"

"Yeah, Erle said that he was truly surprised at the assassination—not that a civil rights activist was killed, but that Evers was the target. He said Evers was trying to work within the system to bring about change; that there were several militants in the movement that it wouldn't have surprised him if one of them were shot, but I think it really did surprise him about Evers."

"That is interesting. It's almost like he is trying to make amends and give you all the information you asked him about, short of telling you everything that would implicate him or any other living person of a crime.

"Doc, I know we don't have anything in hand, and probably never will, but there's enough of a stench permeating all of this that we at least need to do some more digging."

"Which means you still want me to talk to the jurors."

"Yeah, I do." I knew if anyone could find them, Doc could.

On Tuesday, November 14, 1989, I received a call from Eric Lowery, an old acquaintance whom I had first met some years back when I was still in private practice. Eric, in those years, was working his way through the Mississippi College Law School in Jackson as a deputy court clerk. I had lost touch with him after he graduated and established a practice in Hattiesburg, a growing college town about ninety miles southeast of Jackson.

According to Eric, some well-funded and respected people, whom he would not identify, had been in touch with Myrlie Evers. They wanted to get involved in the case and were willing to serve as special prosecutors at no expense to the State of Mississippi. Eric was serving as an intermediary of sorts. I told him that District Attorney Peters had already asked that I try to set up a meeting with Mrs. Evers and Medgar Evers's brother, Charles. I explained that involving whomever Eric was referring to might come as a result of that meeting, but I did not want to proceed until we could talk to the Evers family. Eric was kind enough to provide me with Mrs. Evers's address in Los Angeles. Letters went out that day, over Ed Peters's signature, asking Myrlie and Charles if it would be possible for us to sit down in our office and "advise the two of you, firsthand, of what we have done and steps we plan to take in the investigation, as well as receiving feedback and information from you that might be helpful."

We were still trying to locate Bill Waller's file on the Beckwith case. Waller said that he had talked with John Fox, who had been one of his assistants. Fox also insisted that the file had been turned over to Waller's successor, Jack Travis. Waller was as pessimistic about us getting anything useful from Travis as we had been. Communication would be difficult, as Travis was aging and had suffered a stroke.

Waller had no doubts that he had prosecuted the right man, but after two hung juries he had decided that a conviction was not on the horizon for him.

Waller worried about the outcome of any reprosecution if we did not have new evidence. As a former governor, he was concerned (and rightfully so) about the damaging blow that would be dealt to Mississippi's improving image if we reprosecuted Beckwith and lost. Ed and I assured him that we felt the same way.

I wanted to speak with Robert Lilley, whose name was on most of the documents in the court file. I called the Election Commission and determined that he had indeed been a deputy clerk in the 1960s. I asked if he knew where the evidence introduced at the 1964 trials was. Though friendly and cooperative, he said he had no firsthand knowledge of what might have happened to it. He had heard, though, that the judge eventually got the rifle. "Once cases were disposed of back in those days," he said, "it wasn't unusual for things like that to be taken."

The judge? I thought.

I had never appeared before Judge Leon Hendrick, but everything that I had ever heard about him was inconsistent with the notion that he had taken the murder weapon.

I thanked Lilley for his time and picked up the phone to call one of Judge Hendrick's grandsons, who is a lawyer in town.

I explained the reason for my call and assured him that I really did not expect that the rifle had been in his grandfather's possession, but that I needed to go through the motions and check out this hearsay. As I had anticipated, he had never heard Judge Hendrick mention any such rifle and had never seen one like the .30-06 I was describing to him around his grandfather's house. I thanked him and hung up.

Waiting in the courthouse basement for an elevator the next morning was Barbara Dunn. "There you are. I was on my way up to see you," she said.

"Good morning, Miss Barbara, what's going on?"

"Peters told me yesterday that he would like to have a letter from me confirming that I cannot find the Beckwith evidence. He said that he just wanted it for the file, so for me to give it to you, since you were keeping up with everything."

She handed me the letter. It was short and sweet: "Dear Mr. Peters: After a diligent search of our evidence vault and inquiring with retired employees of this office, I have been unable to locate any evidence dealing with [the Beckwith case]."

Barbara told me that she had also been talking with Dwight Harris at the State Department of Archives and History. He was looking through that department's records to see if the file or any evidence had found its way there.

The kids stayed with my mother that night while Dixie and I went out to celebrate our sixteenth anniversary. We exchanged gifts and then had a nice dinner. Things were a little strained, though, and our efforts to mask our feelings were not successful. I did not understand why she was away from home as much as she was, and Dixie seemed less than happy about my involvement with the Beckwith investigation.

Dixie had told me about some derisive comments made to her by friends and coworkers at the paper (ironically, the same newspaper that was promoting the investigation). So, I attributed the uneasiness that I detected to her embarrassment. I couldn't think of anything else that it could be, but, yet, in my gut, I sensed that there was some deeper reason.

As I was sitting in my office the next morning, Friday, my phone rang. Steve Kirchmayr of the attorney general's office was calling in response to my letter of the previous Friday.

Steve brought me up-to-date on the federal litigation regarding access to the Sovereignty Commission files. I would, he felt, need a court order from the federal courts granting our office access to the files. Consequently, I spent the balance of the day preparing a motion seeking such access under any appropriate guidelines established by the court, or alternatively for the court to examine the files to ascertain if they included any information that would be useful to our investigation of jury tampering.

Ed reviewed the motion and made a few changes before signing the finished product. I arrived at the federal court clerk's office shortly before it closed for the weekend and filed the motion. I mailed copies to the attorneys representing the parties in the case as well as a copy to Judge Barbour.

Monday, November 20, 1989, I began the week with a visit from Jerry Mitchell. In the privacy of my office, he wanted me to review a rough draft of an article on the progress of the Beckwith investigation that Jerry said would appear in the *Clarion-Ledger* the following week. I did not have to read far to see the not-so-subtle message that Jerry was giving me.

I read with interest a quote attributed to Aaron Condon, one of my law professors at Ole Miss, stating that speedy-trial considerations should not be any obstacle to clear the way for reprosecution of the case. The statement initially appalled me, since it was my opinion at the time (and that of every other lawyer I had talked to) that constitutional speedy-trial issues were going to be a big problem.

I held my tongue, though, as I felt that Jerry was looking for a negative reaction or comment. That the *Clarion-Ledger* would like nothing better than pitting the Hinds County DA's office against a well-respected law professor and ex-prosecutor, I had no doubt. I just told Jerry that the article was interesting and that I would have to confer with Condon.

As soon as Jerry left my office, I fired off a letter, basically asking Condon what the hell he was doing making such a sweeping declaration that the biggest legal issue on the horizon in this emotionally charged case was not a problem at all.

Doc, true to his word, came into my office and laid on my desk a typed statement of the first 1964 juror he had found, whom I will call Adams. Not wanting to cause any of these jurors problems, I am not publishing their names.

Adams vividly remembered that it was the second Beckwith jury in 1964 on which he had served—April, as he recalled, because his wife had had to prepare the family income-tax return during the twelve nights that Adams was locked up with the other jurors.

Adams was retired from the State Highway Department and was still living in Jackson. He had not known that the Sovereignty Commission had investigated any of the jurors until he had read Jerry Mitchell's article in the October 1 *Clarion-Ledger.* Further, Adams stated that he was not approached by anyone—whether associated with the defense, the Sovereignty Commission, or otherwise—who attempted to influence him in the case.

Doc went further with Adams, though, just as I had asked him to. Evidently, Adams did not think too much of Waller's case, including the rifle and the fingerprint. To Adams, it was a trial where "the state said one thing and the defense witnesses said another. . . . He [Beckwith] had some witnesses who said he was in Greenwood about the time it happened. I think they were policemen."

Policemen! If a cop testified that he had seen a defendant ninety miles away from the scene of a crime at the time of the crime, I could see how a jury would be reluctant to convict. Knowing what I had learned from the Jackson Police Department's report, though, the alibi just did not ring true. Jackson detectives John Chamblee and Fred Sanders, not to mention Lord knows how many FBI agents, spent months in Greenwood, Mississippi, from late June 1963 until the trials in 1964, interviewing everyone they could to learn more about Beckwith. They were a common sight in the Greenwood Police Department (which could not have been that big in 1963), interviewing people, including Greenwood police officers. I doubted that there was a single adult person in the United States who was not aware that the Jackson Police Department and the FBI were investigating the Evers assassination, that Byron De La Beckwith had been arrested, and that he was in jail without bond for some eight months before his trial.

Under those circumstances, if a Greenwood policeman truly knew that Beckwith could not have possibly committed the murder because that cop had seen him in Greenwood at or near the time of the murder, would it not stand to reason that the cop would pick up the phone and call the Jackson Police Department or the FBI, or tell Chamblee and Sanders when they were in the Greenwood Police Department building, "Hey, guys, as a brother officer of the law, I need to let you know that you have the wrong son of a bitch locked up down there"? If a cop truly felt this man was wrongly accused, would the cop allow him by silence to languish in a jail for eight months? I didn't think so.

Adams finished by making sure that Doc knew his opinion about our reinvestigation: "It looks like foolishness to reopen it. You can't reincarnate something that is twenty-five years old."

That night I looked up the word *incarnate*. According to Webster's, it means "personified; to give bodily form to; to be the type or embodiment of." I closed the reference book, replaced it in its proper place on the shelf, crawled back into bed, and turned off the light.

Twenty-five years ago, a back-shooting coward had inflicted a terrible wrong. It was a wrong dealt to the Evers family, to be sure, but it was more than that. Mississippi's honor and reputation had been smeared by the assassin's bullet, as well. Even those people who did not necessarily agree with Medgar Evers or his work should have been outraged at the *act* and the kick-in-the-balls blow that it delivered to Mississippi's already tarnished image.

Dr. Martin Luther King Jr. once said, "Injustice anywhere is a threat to justice everywhere." Bill Waller, John Fox, John Chamblee, Fred Sanders, and others obviously felt that way and made a stand twenty-five years ago for society, for Mississippi, and for what is right. *If it was for the good of mankind, for the good of our state, and for what was right twenty-five years ago,* I thought, *if the courts allow it, and if I ever get enough evidence, a similar stand would still be right today. Does that which is right and just wane with the passage of time?*

The answer for me was a clear no. It is never too late for that which is right, just, and brings honor to one's home state, to the human race itself. Waller, Fox, and the others personified those qualities twenty-five years ago. Thus, the reembodiment of those worthy attributes—our efforts to pick up, in 1989, where Waller and company had left off—constituted the "reincarnation" of what is right, just, and honorable. With these thoughts, I began to feel challenged by the case, as opposed to merely curious. I needed good, hard evidence (and a lot of it) to go along with my philosophical musings.

Consequently, the following morning, Tuesday, November 21, 1989, I wrote to Wayne Taylor, the FBI's special agent in charge (the SAC, in Bureau lingo), of its Jackson office. I informed Taylor that our office was "conducting a multifaceted investigation" of Medgar Evers's assassination, including "efforts to locate any and all evidence that may have been introduced into evidence at either of the trials held in early 1964."

I explained to Taylor that neither the county circuit clerk, the State Department of Archives and History, nor the Jackson Police Department could find any of the evidence.

On the day before Thanksgiving, I wanted to leave early, but I learned from Cynthia Hewes that Doc had found another juror and was out of the office interviewing him. I did not want to leave until Doc came back. When he returned, he relayed his conversation with a juror I refer to as Baker.

Mr. Baker was retired from Shell Oil and living in a small town not too far from Jackson. He informed Doc that his boss had been contacted prior to the second Beckwith trial and was asked, "If your son was being tried under similar circumstances, would you want Baker on the jury?"

Baker's boss told the caller no, he would not want Baker on the jury under those circumstances.

Baker did, however, get on the jury and evidently was one of the jurors who voted guilty and stuck to it.

Doc asked him what he thought were the strong points of the case.

"I guess the fingerprint was the strongest. He said the rifle was stolen and the state never proved it wasn't," Baker answered. "When the state finished its case, I was surprised that Waller was through. I was convinced at that point that Beckwith wasn't guilty. I remember saying to myself, 'They haven't proven anything.'"

Baker then shared something noteworthy with Doc, and from which Ed and I later drew part of our trial strategy.

"If the defense had rested at that point, he probably would have been found not guilty."

"What happened to change your mind?" Doc asked.

"Beckwith hurt himself when he testified." Also, the policemen from Greenville, or wherever. "I don't think anybody believed them."

"How," Doc asked, "did Beckwith hurt himself?"

"He was real argumentative and combative on cross-examination. He acted as if 'I did it, but you can't prove it.' Of the three who voted guilty, one was a lawyer from the VA [Veterans Administration] and the other was a construction foreman. He was adamant about conviction."

Beckwith claimed that the gun near the murder scene had been stolen, but according to the police report, Beckwith had never reported it stolen. More important, Beckwith was the only person who could claim to a jury that it was stolen, which meant that if a third jury was to hear that excuse, they would have to hear it from Beckwith's lips. He would have to make a choice. He could take the stand and make his claim that the gun was stolen, but then he would be cross-examined by Ed Peters. If Beckwith had hurt himself by being combative and argumentative with Waller, I was confident the Silver Fox could provoke the same reactions—or worse.

Beckwith could, of course, choose not to testify and thereby avoid such a prejudicial outburst, but the jury would never, in that event, hear his claim that the murder weapon was stolen.

Baker's negative impression of the alibi offered by the Greenwood cops was also comforting.

Lastly, Baker said that nobody had contacted him about the case.

Thanksgiving Day the kids and I went to my parents' house for dinner. Dixie was to join us there after finishing her newspaper route. Inevitably, the conversation found its way to the case.

"What's going to come of this Beckwith thing?" Mama asked.

"I don't imagine anything," I said.

"Have you got anything yet?" my brother, Mike, asked.

"Just some old reports, really."

"The *Clarion-Ledger* sure is pushing this, isn't it? Something will come of it if the paper gets its way," observed Mama.

"Well," I said, "no matter how much the *Clarion-Ledger,* or anybody for that matter, wants the case reprosecuted, it ain't going to happen without evidence, and we are light-years from that."

"For your sake and the children's, I would just as soon that it stay that way," Mama said.

"Why?"

"There are all kinds of kooks out there, and Beckwith is one of the kookiest."

"Really?" I asked. "Did you think so at the time?"

"Sure I did. He's just as crazy and dangerous as he can be. Most people, even back then, felt the same way about him. Everybody, or I should say most everybody, thought he was guilty, but they didn't think Waller proved it."

"Yeah," I said, "I have heard the same thing."

"I firmly believe that a man ought to pay for whatever he has done; to be held responsible. I just really hate that you have to be the one to get involved in this."

"I know, Mama. I'll be careful, but I really don't think that it's going to go very far."

We started picking up the dishes from the table. I picked up the unused plate in Dixie's place. It had been a long time since she had joined us at Mama's house for dinner, but Mama still prepared a place for her.

Friday, November 24, 1989, was also a holiday for state employees. The DA's office did not reopen after the Thanksgiving holiday until Monday. Nevertheless, Doc spent a good portion of his Friday off working on the case. He had found a third juror (whom I will call Clark) and traveled that day to talk to him. Robyn Reynolds, one of our legal interns, went with Doc. They drove to the small town south of Jackson where Clark had moved.

Like Adams and Baker, Clark had not been contacted by anyone attempting to influence him as a juror. His view of the case and of Beckwith, however, was the converse of Baker's. Clark told Doc and Robyn that, at first, he thought Beckwith was guilty, but was later convinced that he was innocent. To him, Beckwith stood up well on cross-examination and seemed to be telling the truth. Clark also said that he believed the alibi testimony of the Greenwood policemen.

The report that Doc handed me first thing Monday morning prompted another decision that I made early in the investigation. Through Baker and Clark, it was clear that the testimony of the cops, providing Beckwith with his alibi, could be perceived in different ways by jurors. If we ever got far enough along in our investigation that we actually had evidence to present to a grand jury for a possible indictment, I would have grand-jury subpoenas issued for the cops (assuming they were still alive).

Having them testify under oath before the grand jury would be beneficial in several ways. It would "lock" them into their testimony, providing us with possible impeachment material if they deviated later at any trial. It would provide Ed and me with an excellent opportunity to see how they would likely stand up to cross-examination. And, of extreme importance, it would afford us a glimpse of what jurors in contemporary Mississippi would think of their testimony and credibility. Would it be the same view as Baker's, or would it be that of Clark? Grand jurors are a cross-section of eighteen citizens who meet the same qualifications for jury service as trial jurors. Their input can be valuable in trying to assess the strengths and weaknesses of a case through the eyes of a jury.

Later that Monday, Doc found two other jurors—"Daniels" and "East." Daniels, who worked for the State Highway Department, said that nobody ever contacted him concerning his jury duty, nor did any friends or coworkers ever tell him that they had been questioned about him. It was, however, clear to Daniels that the lawyers had talked to someone about him.

Daniels was not swayed by the police officers' alibi for Beckwith and considered Beckwith's fingerprint on the rifle's scope the strongest evidence against him. It bothered Daniels, though, that the fingerprint was "facing the wrong way," as he put it. The print was pointed toward the shooter, rather than the target, and the rifle appeared to have been wiped off, since no other fingerprints were found on the gun.

I didn't see how that was such a nettlesome problem. Detectives had found a pair of gloves stored with the guns and the ammunition that they had seized from Beckwith's house. That Beckwith had wiped off the rifle before the murder and wore gloves, or did not wear gloves but wiped the rifle down before placing it in the honeysuckle thicket, were both plausible. Like legions of criminals, then and now, he had made a mistake—he missed a print at the tip of the scope. It had not been visible to the naked eye. Captain Hargrove did not see it until he processed the rifle at police headquarters.

Daniels did not think that the result would be any different if the case went to trial a third time. He told Doc that "the climate is different now, but the result would be no different. The whole thing is an insult to the jurors and their integrity. Not meaning you and your office—the papers have put you between a rock and a hard place—but the ones who want the case reopened. They just didn't prove their case."

Mr. East, the second juror Doc interviewed that day, was retired from the IRS. He had not been contacted by anyone concerning his jury service, and, he told Doc, if Andy Hopkins or anyone else from the Sovereignty Commission had tried to garner any information about him from his employer, he doubted they were given the time of day. That, I believed.

East was impressed with the policemen who testified on Beckwith's behalf, but was not impressed with Beckwith.

"Anything else about the case that you want to say?" Doc asked.

East responded, "Even though the jury was white, the defendant was white, and the victim was black, I honestly don't believe race entered into the decision at all. The state simply didn't prove its case. I have been an investigator a long time and can appreciate good circumstantial evidence, but they needed more."

"Do you think it would be possible to get a conviction today, if all of the evidence and witnesses were available?" Doc asked.

"No, not unless there is some new and strong evidence."

The feedback that Doc was bringing to me from the jurors confirmed my gut feeling. We had to have something new.

Doc found another juror and spoke with him on the telephone just long enough for the guy to tell Doc that he was not going to talk to him and what we could do with our investigation. What really chapped Doc was that the guy had been interviewed by Jerry Mitchell, yet refused to talk with us.

"Okay, Doc, if he wants to play hardball, fine. Have a grand-jury subpoena issued for him, and we will let him tell the grand jury exactly what he told you. He may learn a lesson about contempt. Find out from Clara what date will be good and let me know. Oh, and Doc, regardless of the time he is to testify, have him subpoenaed for eight-thirty A.M., and he can just sit for a while. Maybe the next time an officer goes to talk to him, he will have learned that it's a lot easier and convenient to cooperate instead of being a horse's ass."

Before I left Monday afternoon, I received a call from Glenda Bond,

Judge Barbour's court clerk. He had ruled on our motion to gain access to the Sovereignty Commission records, and Glenda said that I could come over and pick up a copy of the order.

It was a good thing for us that Erle Johnston had kept, and given us, copies of what we were looking for from the Sovereignty Commission records. Judge Barbour denied our request. Under the circumstances, the loss was not that big of a deal.

The next morning, Tuesday, Doc stopped by my office to tell me that he and Benny had just interviewed another juror from the second 1964 trial. That made six that Doc had found and talked to so far. "Mr. Grant" worked in downtown Jackson only a few blocks from the courthouse.

Mr. Grant had not been contacted by anyone about the case in 1964. Somebody wanting to know what sort of person Grant was, though, had questioned someone at his office, over the phone. Grant did not know of that call until after the trial, and it irritated him. According to him, "The state didn't have any strong points. There was no evidence to prove he did it."

"What about the policemen from Greenwood?" Doc asked him. "Were you impressed with them?"

He must not have been influenced one way or the other. Grant did not remember any policemen.

I was still scratching my head over that critique when the phone rang. It was Aaron Condon, my former law professor. He had received my letter and wanted to clarify his position regarding the speedy-trial issue.

Condon agreed that we had an uphill battle, but he said that in his mind it was more of a "due-process" problem than a "speedy-trial" problem.

To me, a problem was a problem, regardless of the label attached to it, so I asked him what the difference was.

"It is a distinction with no difference," he said.

Boy, was I glad that he called to clarify that.

Wednesday, November 29, 1989, was the eighty-fourth birthday of 1964 juror "Holmes." He was the construction worker that juror Baker had described as being adamant for conviction. Although Mr. Holmes had a severe hearing problem and did not remember a lot about the trial, he had little trouble recalling the obduracy of his position.

"Did you think Beckwith was guilty?" Doc asked him.

Holmes's answer was a simple three-word sentence: "He killed him."

As with all of the others that Doc had interviewed, Holmes was not contacted by anyone who attempted to influence his decision in the case. I noticed, as I read Doc's statement, that the third investigator in our office had gone along with Doc to the interview. Charles Morris Crisco retired from the Homicide Division of the Jackson Police Department on Friday, September 29, 1989. He reported to work as an investigator in the Hinds County DA's office the morning of October 2, 1989—the day after the article regarding the Sovereignty Commission's involvement in the Beckwith trial appeared in the *Clarion-Ledger.*

Crisco's appearance is deceiving. He is every bit as wiry as Benny Bennett is massive, but equally capable of taking care of himself on the streets. The only major difference between the two veteran cops, who were also members of the police department's SWAT team and were partners at one time, might be their respective weapons of choice. Benny preferred a blade of some unique configuration in close combat; Crisco would probably just prefer to shoot and be done with it. I never saw him shoot, but his reputation as a crack shot preceded him.

On several occasions, Dixie's stepfather, Judge Russel Moore, told me two things about Charlie Crisco: he was an expert marksman, and he was the best police witness Judge Moore had seen on the witness stand in the twenty years he had presided over criminal court in Hinds County. While I cannot vouch for the first observation, I can for the second.

Whenever I saw the names of C. M. Crisco and his last partner, Robert Jordan, on a police report, I breathed a small sigh of relief. I knew that all of the *t*'s were crossed and the *i*'s dotted, and that little preparation would be necessary for their trial testimony. My first capital-murder conviction after going to work at the DA's office, in fact, was a Crisco-Jordan case.

Another juror whom Doc located that Wednesday was "Mr. Ivy," who had moved out West. Doc talked to him on the phone and learned that nobody had made any contact with him. Ivy assured Doc that he would have notified the authorities if any such attempt had been made. Doc tried to get Mr. Ivy to talk about the case and was tersely told, "I do think the state must have better and more pressing things to do than trying to dig up a case twenty-five years old." The conversation ended.

Doc located a third juror toward the end of the day. Juror "Jones," as it turned out, did not live too far from Doc, who made arrangements to visit with him on the way home that afternoon. Again, no contact had been attempted. Mr. Jones was impressed with the prosecution. "The state had a good case and Waller presented it well. He had Beckwith's car, rifle, and fingerprint."

"Did Beckwith help his case with his testimony?" Doc asked.

"No," Jones said. "He hurt himself with me."

"What," Doc continued, "was your impression of the two policemen who testified that Beckwith was in Greenwood on the night of the murder?"

"I didn't believe them."

"If the witnesses and evidence were available now, do you think the state could get a conviction?"

"Things are different now," Jones said. "I believe you could convict him now."

Notwithstanding his favorable impression of Waller's case, Jones, like Ivy, thought "the state ought to spend the taxpayers' money doing something else. Unless some strong, new evidence comes up, I don't think it ought to be reopened."

Even if it was not required legally speaking, I was now even more certain that new and strong evidence was essential before going after an indictment. I was, in a way, living in dreamland, thinking in terms of new evidence when I did not even have the old stuff.

Some significant news came the next morning. John Henry, a special assistant attorney general, called with some research assistance on the speedy-trial issue. Interestingly, while he indicated that he was authorized to discuss the issue and his research, he was not authorized to put anything in writing.

I was in the mood to settle for any assistance I could muster, so we discussed the case law that John had found. Before hanging up, he gave me the names and citations of the cases. I immediately pulled them, engrossing myself in the legal technicalities. For the first time, I began to understand what Professor Condon had tried to explain regarding the speedy-trial versus due-process "distinction with no difference." It did make a difference, however, and a big one.

The right of an accused to a speedy trial is based upon the guarantee of the Sixth Amendment, which is applicable only when formal criminal proceedings are pending. While such charges are pending, the burden is on the prosecution either to put the defendant to trial in a speedy manner or to provide an acceptable reason for any failure to do so to the court. In that context, prejudice or harm caused by any lengthy delay is presumed by the law and need not be proven by the defendant.

On the other hand, and of extreme importance, once formal criminal proceedings are no longer pending, the speedy-trial right under the Sixth Amendment is likewise no longer relevant. The defendant is no longer an "accused." Instead, any lengthy delay in instituting formal criminal proceedings is tested by the court applying the "due-process" guarantees of the Fourteenth Amendment. The famous Jeffrey MacDonald case is the landmark decision on this point. What is the difference? A lot.

Based on cases decided by the federal courts and the Mississippi Supreme Court, the burden is different when the due-process standard is applied. The onus is not on the state, but rather it is on the defendant to prove to the court two things: (1) the delay was created by the state with the specific intent *at the time* to gain a tactical advantage over the accused (it is not sufficient to merely show that the state ultimately benefited from the delay); and (2) the defendant has been prejudiced to such an extent by the delay that he cannot be afforded a fair trial, i.e., that he has been deprived of a defense that he would have been able to present to a jury had the delay not occurred.

If we could get enough evidence, there was hope. Beckwith could never satisfy the first burden, and if I could get my hands on a trial transcript that had the testimony of his alibi witnesses, he could not meet the second prong of the due-process test either. I preferred, of course, the live witnesses, so Ed could tear their testimony to shreds, but I had no idea if they were alive or what kind of health they were in.

I did not have much as November was winding down. I did, however, have a glimmer of hope, thanks to John's research, and I had a challenge.

Arriving at the office the morning of Monday, December 4, I noticed that Clara and the secretaries had unpacked our office Christmas decorations. I was pouring coffee when Ed approached me. "Myrlie Evers called while you were out Friday. She is taking us up on our request to meet with her here and is coming in about an hour."

"Today?" I asked, spilling hot coffee over the cup, my hand, and the floor.

"Yep. And, oh, by the way, she will have her lawyer with her."

I thought, *Great. Just great.* As I was wiping up the mess that I had made, I pictured an in-your-face confrontation and dreaded the prospect. I expected Mrs. Evers to join the ranks of those local blacks, such as city councilman Louis Armstrong, who had been publicly hammering us for not immediately going after Beckwith, notwithstanding that we had no evidence. Everywhere I turned there was the attitude of "This is how I feel and don't confuse me with the facts." Now, the final kick in the ass would be from Myrlie Evers. Merry Christmas.

I thought that a few of the black politicians voicing the loudest criticism of our office could not have cared less if there was no evidence with which to obtain a conviction. If there was, so be it. If there wasn't, I suspected that they would just scream "racism."

I expected the voice of Myrlie Evers to join in. I had not really believed she would come to us. More political mileage could be achieved by her and the NAACP, I thought, if no meeting took place than if we sat down in a genuine spirit of cooperation to see where we were realistically and determine what, if anything, could be done.

When they arrived, I picked up my file, which, at that time, consisted only of the partial police report and statements of the jurors whom Doc had interviewed. Walking from my small cubicle to Ed's office was much the same as I imagined a condemned prisoner's march to be as he headed for his firing squad. All I could think was *Let's get it over with.*

The first person I saw as I entered Ed's office was Morris Dees. I had no idea who he was, but I could tell from the tone and inflection of Ed's voice this was not someone I could expect to like.

I was then introduced to Myrlie Evers. The eyes. As we met and I shook her hand, her eyes drew my attention and touched my soul. They were haunting, sad and hopeful; burdened by the knowledge that her husband's killer had not just escaped justice with the help of a state agency, but had also openly mocked it for over twenty-five years.

Ed has been in office longer than any other prosecutor in Mississippi, has served on the Board of Directors of the National District Attorneys Association, and has put more murderers on death row at Parchman Penitentiary than anyone else in the history of the state. He had come under fire for several years by various anti-death-penalty groups, and when Morris Dees identified himself as the director of the Southern Poverty Law Center in Montgomery, Alabama, Ed bristled. Just as the breaking point was about to be reached, Mrs. Evers defused the situation.

"Mr. Peters, your letter mentioned that you have already begun investigating any possible jury tampering. What have you found in that respect?"

"Okay, one of our investigators has been tracking down and interviewing all of the jurors from both trials that he can find. Remarkably, he has found most of them and will keep looking for the few remaining. Also, he has talked with a guy by the name of Erle Johnston, who was the head of the Sovereignty Commission back when all of this was going on. We obtained a copy from him of the report that we believe is the same report on which Jerry Mitchell based his story concerning jury tampering. The actions of the investigator for the Sovereignty Commission, a guy by the name of Hopkins, according to his report and all accounts of the jurors we've talked to, fall short of the crime of jury tampering. To bring those criminal charges, we would have to prove some contact with the jurors themselves, directly or indirectly.

"Besides, Hopkins is dead. He did background checks on the jurors without their knowledge. That's done in hundreds of courtrooms across the country every day now. The part that leaves a bad taste in your mouth is the fact that he fed his information to the defense attorneys. So, you had one representative of the state, Bill Waller, trying to convict this guy for murder, and another agent of the state, Sovereignty Commission investigator Hopkins, helping the defendant get a 'friendly' jury. Unethical? Yes. Illegal? No."

"So," Mrs. Evers said, "where does that leave us with the case itself? I had hoped that we could use the jury-tampering issue to get our foot in the door to reprosecute the case."

"Mrs. Evers, there is no case. We have no physical evidence at all from the 1964 trials: no gun, no bullet, no photographs. Lord knows where the witnesses have scattered to, if they are still alive."

A look of openmouthed shock came across her face. Ed was not yet through, though.

"Jerry Mitchell didn't tell you that, did he? I bet he also neglected to tell you that no transcript is on file in the court clerk's office, either. We don't even have Bill Waller's old file. He insists that he left all of his files to his successor, Jack Travis, who has suffered a series of strokes that have left him useless as far as getting any information. I became DA after him, and I can assure you that my office has never had the file. The only file we have is what Bobby's got there, which is the Jackson Police Department's report."

"May I, Mr. DeLaughter?"

"Mrs. Evers, I really don't think I'd look at that if I were you."

"Please?"

I reluctantly handed her the report. While I truly believed that all of the officers of the Jackson Police Department had done all they could to investigate the case, the report included every possible rumor that had come their way in the ten days prior to Beckwith's arrest. Much of the report was written in vintage 1963 white "Southernese."

Mrs. Evers read aloud: "June fourteenth, 1963. A female who refused to identify herself stated that she had heard a rumor that Medgar Evers' wife had gotten jealous of Lena Horne, who'd appeared with Evers at a rally, and might have gotten her brother-in-law to kill Evers."

There was a dead silence in the office as Mrs. Evers handed the file back to me. Then she did something that I did not expect. She laughed.

"Well, who wouldn't be jealous of Lena Horne? God, what a beautiful woman."

I had to smile at her good humor, particularly in the wake of the news Ed had just given her. He still was not finished.

"And, Mrs. Evers, even if we located all of the evidence and all of the living witnesses, even if we had a transcript for a jury to hear the testimony of those who are dead, we still have the slight problem posed by the constitutional guarantees of a speedy trial. I suspect that your lawyer here would have to agree that there is nothing too 'speedy' about twenty-five years."

Surprisingly, Dees agreed, unless, in his opinion, the cops from Greenwood who had provided Beckwith's alibi could be persuaded to testify that they had lied in the earlier trials. Dees was dreaming, and Ed told him so.

I had expected Myrlie Evers, black political activist, to speak at this point. I listened, however, as *Mrs.* Evers, wife and mother, spoke of her dream that justice would one day be done. There was strength there, but it was not only in her words. This was inner strength—rooted in her soul and built over the years of loving, grieving, working, and enduring. Rather than demanding retribution against the racist who killed a civil rights martyr who happened to be her husband, she made a plea for justice in holding accountable the cowardly bushwhacker who had shot in the back her unarmed husband who happened to have been a civil rights leader. I was mesmerized as her narrative came to life before my eyes.

"I opened the door and saw Medgar lying in a pool of blood, pulling himself across the carport toward the door. His keys were still clutched in his hands. The children had gotten to the door by that time and were crying, 'Daddy, get up! Get up!'"

Images of my own three children and wife flashed in my mind. Wouldn't any man visualize the same thing? Wouldn't any mother or child want the same thing the Evers family wanted? How many years would have to pass before a wife or child would say that it's just been too long, forget it? If I were in that position, God forbid, it would be exactly one day after hell froze over.

It happened twenty-six years earlier, but I was hearing it as if it were one of the many 1989 homicides that I would eventually prosecute. I was sickened and repulsed by what had happened to Medgar Evers and his family the early-morning hours of June 12, 1963. It was driven home to me then that what had occurred was timeless, whether it was in 1963 or 1989. I also realized that the case, if it was ever to be successfully reprosecuted, would have to be reinvestigated and presented to a jury just as it was to me that December morning by Mrs. Evers in Ed's office.

Medgar Evers's civil rights activities and Beckwith's reaction to those activities were no doubt the motive for the murder, but the murder itself, and the dastardly circumstances surrounding it, had to be the focus. It could not be tried as a civil rights case. I could not put the civil rights movement and the reaction of the State of Mississippi on trial—not if I wanted to win.

Mrs. Evers wanted the case reprosecuted, but it was not the in-your-face confrontation that I had expected. There were no demands, no threats of lawsuits. Nor was there a desire by Dees to "take over" the investigation. If Dees had indicated *any* willingness to personally pursue the case, Ed would've immediately had him appointed as a special prosecutor and turned this tar baby of a case over to him on the spot.

But Mrs. Evers seemed to realize that if we had any window of opportunity to do anything, it was going to be a narrow window and would not stay open long. She knew that there would only be one more chance, and then it would be gone forever. If the time ever came for the trap to be sprung, she wanted no wiggle room for our prey. Myrlie Evers wanted the case prosecuted to win, and not to make a political statement. That is what set her head and shoulders above everyone else, and that is what got my attention.

My thoughts drifted to my phone conversations with Professor Condon and with John Henry about a legal argument dodging the Sixth Amendment roadblock, as Mrs. Evers explained how long she and her family had waited for justice, how badly they needed it, as did the State of Mississippi. She then turned from Ed, looked me straight in the eye, and asked that we keep trying and digging. I assured her that we would and told her that we might even come up with an argument getting around the speedy-trial problem. Ed gave me one of those "Yeah, right, sure" looks, and said good-bye to Mrs. Evers. I followed her and Dees out of Ed's office.

I had hardly spoken a word during the meeting. I learned much by listening. Yet, in the lobby, as they were waiting for the elevator, Dees commented, "Your boss is a real fighter in the courtroom, I hear. He didn't give me a chance to say it in there, but if this thing ever goes to trial, we want him in there, and it's you we want with him. I've done my homework on you, young man. You're one hell of a researcher, I understand. You may not be flashy, but I hear that you are always prepared. Most of all, though, I believe your heart is in the right place. The two of you are the team that we want. I'm not interested in trying this case. I'll be there if you or Mrs. Evers want, but I think it's important from the jury's perception to see the two of you prosecuting the case on behalf of the State of Mississippi."

The elevator door opened, and as Mrs. Evers and Dees stepped in, she turned, grasped my hand, and said, "Mr. DeLaughter, just try, and please keep me informed."

It was almost Christmas, and the next day, December 5, was my son Burt's birthday. I had presents to buy. I took the afternoon off, and as I strolled through the malls, buying a birthday present and Santa's gifts for my three children, I could not help thinking that they were the same sexes and about the same ages as Medgar Evers's three children when he was taken from them by a sniper's bullet.

I thought of how many Christmases they had missed with their dad. A fire began to burn within me. The reason to pursue the case had risen to a new height. It was no longer a curiosity, nor a mere legal challenge. It certainly was not political. It was simply the moral and decent thing to do, and I kept asking myself, *Is it ever too late to do the right thing? For the sake of humanity and as a civilized society, I sincerely hope and pray that it is not.*

So strongly did I feel about this, I thought about it over and over. Soon, I made a note of it. Various other thoughts that I would have over the next four years would likewise be committed to those notes and ultimately fashioned into my closing argument to the jury.

That night after I tucked the kids in bed, I sat in the den, lights out with the exception of the warm glow in the fireplace.

I couldn't get my mind off the Evers children: two young boys, Darrell and Van, with a girl, Reena, wedged between them; the same as my three, and even the same ages, almost. However, the life they had lived was so different from that of most kids, including my own. I recalled Myrlie Evers's statement to the police that when the shot rang out, the children hit the floor and lay still for a moment, *just as their daddy had taught them to do.* The image was in stark contrast to the warmth, security, and satisfaction that I felt, and that I believed my children felt, as they lay in a deep slumber, snug in their quilts, probably dreaming of what they would find under the twinkling tree on Christmas morning. Baseball, dolls, fishing, and cartoons; those are the things that should occupy children's minds, not what to do when gunfire erupts.

I was also thinking about what Mrs. Evers had said earlier that day. Mississippi needed justice in this case as much as her family. It was true. A lot had changed in Mississippi since 1963, and what better way to show that to the world than to pursue justice in this case—if we had the evidence and if the courts allowed it?

We were living in a new era of Southern leadership with the opportunity of a fresh, bold start without repeating the irresponsibility of our top leadership for the past 130 years. It amuses me when I hear Southern history buffs proclaim that secession and the ensuing war, which they usually refer to as the War of Northern Aggression, didn't have anything to do with slavery, that it was for "states' rights." I ask myself, *The states' right to do what?* Lincoln did not even come out for abolition at the war's start, just against the *expansion* of the institution in the new territories of the West.

The bottom line is that we seceded and fought the bloodiest war in the nation's history due to fear that we couldn't expand slavery. Southern leaders didn't want to give up power in Congress, which would inevitably have happened as free states began to outnumber the slave states. If slavery was not the core issue, then it wouldn't have mattered that the new states entered the Union as "free."

With rights goes responsibility to mankind and to civilization itself. Because our leaders in the South were not responsible enough to refrain from expanding human bondage on their own initiative, they allowed Lincoln and the North, with the Emancipation Proclamation in 1863, to seize the moral high ground.

Similarly, just twenty-five years ago, our Southern leaders demonstrated the same irresponsibility by refusing to abolish Jim Crow laws and follow decisions of the highest court in the land. While that disregard of the law and basic human dignity did not result in a full-scale war, it brought about the 1965 Voting Rights Act. Even today every law that we pass concerning elections must be approved by the Justice Department. Southern leaders still bitch about the act, but it was a direct result of the callous disregard of the law by our former leaders.

The leaders are no longer "they"; they are *us*. And if we just sit on our butts paying only lip service to our laws, such as the one that says there is no statute of limitations for murder, would we not be showing the same irresponsibility as our forebears? Does our conduct, rather than our claims, not judge us? Mississippi has changed much since 1964. So why not show it, rather than just say it?

More important, the action we took, or failed to take, would set an example for future generations.

I love Mississippi. My roots run deep here, and I have never planned on living anywhere else. That December night I thought about how I wanted Mississippi to be known as a place where God-fearing, law-abiding people, no matter what race, live and raise their families in peace and safety. I want it to be a place that does not need to be under the watchful eye of Uncle Sam, because we can be trusted to do the right thing and tend to our own house. That is the heritage I want to leave my children as a legacy. I couldn't look myself in the mirror if I looked the other way after getting the goods on a back-shooting son of a bitch. Every decent person in the state, I felt, ought to have been sickened by what Beckwith did, and for twenty-six years had gotten away with, but it was evident to me they weren't. Ed and I were considered the outlaws.

Saying that I felt the weight of the world on my shoulders would have been an understatement. Some people were screaming for an indictment with no evidence. Others were making phone calls and writing letters, castigating Ed and me for investigating what could be done legally if we had sufficient evidence. These were two small groups, but vocal ones. The *Clarion-Ledger* was steadily fanning the flames. No matter which way I turned, I lost. If any supporters were in our corner, they certainly didn't let us know about it. The only one who had instilled in me a genuine desire to do anything for the right reason was Myrlie Evers.

My heart was stirred and my spirit willing, but I still had no evidence. All that I had was pressure from all sides and no relief in sight.

Frustrated, I opened my Bible and began thumbing through the pages, hoping my eyes would fix on some passage relating to my plight. I went straight to Proverbs, written by King Solomon, who prayed for wisdom and became the wisest man ever, short of Christ. I needed some sage advice. Shortly, in the third chapter, verses five and six hit their mark:

> Trust in the Lord with all your heart, and do not rely on your own insight. In all your ways acknowledge him, and he will make straight your paths.

That was my mistake. I had been relying on my own insight. No wonder everything seemed so useless to me. I needed to turn the case over to the Lord and trust in Him to handle it. After all, are we not told by Christ in Matthew 19:26 that for mortals some things are impossible, but for God all things are possible? Add to that our assurance from Jesus in John 14:13–14: "I will do whatever you ask in my name, so that the Father may be glorified in the Son. If in my name you ask me for anything, I will do it."

Would asking God, in Jesus' name, to guide me in this unfinished murder case qualify as glorifying Him? I wondered. I looked up the word *justice* in the concordance section of my Bible and found my answer in Isaiah 5:16: "The Lord of hosts is exalted by justice."

Excitedly, I turned the pages to see what else the Bible had to say about the words *justice* and *commitment.* From Isaiah 56:1 and Proverbs 16:3 and 9:

Maintain justice and do what is right. . . . Commit your work to the Lord, and your plans will be established. . . . The human mind plans the way, but the Lord directs the steps.

That was it. I typed the words on a piece of paper and later hung it on the bulletin board in my office. It remains there to this day.

CHAPTER FOUR

THE PIECES COME TOGETHER

Hope is the lifeblood of the heart, writes author Michael Connelly. It's what had kept Myrlie Evers going all those years since her husband's murder. Medgar deserved to rest in peace, and Mississippi deserved to continue the great strides it had made since 1963. Only in justice, though, could the Evers family and Mississippi find that peace, because as Connelly also writes, without justice there is no hope. It was thus time to begin a journey to justice.

The investigation that spanned the next nine months as part of that journey, like many criminal investigations, was akin to piecing together a jigsaw puzzle. This was not one of the whodunit variety, but rather one of finding lost pieces of a puzzle assembled long ago, then scattered in the winds of time. We turned up a piece here and there, but I was amazed at the crucial portions that were seemingly handed to us. The first came a couple of days after Myrlie Evers's visit.

On Wednesday, December 6, Doc came in and told me I'd received a call the previous afternoon from David Adams, the police photographer.

"He asked if you were the one involved in this Medgar Evers thing. When I told him that you were, he said he had something to show you ASAP. I told him that we would be over first thing this morning. Is that okay?"

"Sure," I said. "Let's go."

Doc knocked on the door of David's workroom at headquarters. David opened the door and waved us in. "I want to show you something." He flipped the switch to a large light box on which he had affixed an array of negatives.

My heart began to race as I moved in for a closer look. The first negative showed the front of a ranch-style house bearing the address 2332 on the front. The Evers house was at 2332 Guynes Street. As I looked at each of the other frames, the reality began to sink in. I was viewing all of the crime-scene photographs from 1963: the house (inside and out), the vacant lot from which the shot was fired, aerial photos of the neighborhood, Joe's Drive-In, Beckwith's car, the honeysuckle thicket where the murder weapon was found, and photos of the gun itself. Some showed it being pulled from the honeysuckle, and some showed it on Capt. Ralph Hargrove's desk. I was awestruck.

"Where did you find these?" I asked David.

"In here." He picked up a Kodak slide-carousel box, unmarked except for the words *Mr. Hargrove's pictures* scrawled in pen across the top. "It was in the bottom of that closet over there. The closet hasn't been used in years and was crammed full of stuff. I was cleaning it out yesterday to make room for some of my equipment. Look inside the box. There's more."

I opened the nondescript Kodak box and found enlargements that Captain Hargrove had made of the fingerprint from the rifle's scope and comparisons with Beckwith's fingerprints. Each point of identification was marked and numbered.

"I assume you want prints of everything," David said.

"Just as fast as you can get them," I assured him.

Doc got a kick out of that. "It's not like you're going to be needing them anytime soon, is it?"

"No, but I'm just too damn excited." But I was also mindful that Bill Waller had the photos and fingerprints in 1964 and came up short.

Mid-December yielded three more juror interviews. On December 13, Doc spoke with juror "Keyes" by phone. Keyes, an Ole Miss Law School graduate, was an adjudicator in the Claims Division of the Veterans Administration. He had left Jackson in 1968. After working in Illinois and Washington, he and his wife had retired in Austin, Texas. That's where Doc found him.

Keyes was very open. He was the foreman of the jury in the second trial and one of those who'd voted to convict Beckwith. Baker had said that there were three of them. Keyes said there were four. Nobody had contacted him before or during the trial, but shortly after arriving home, subsequent to the hung jury and mistrial, he had received a phone call from someone who he felt was a Klansman. Keyes had heard that one of the jurors "was in the pocket of the Klan," and that juror, Keyes believed, had quickly let it be known which panel members had voted to convict. Keyes hung up on the caller.

Keyes told Doc, "If you were very careful in your jury selection, you could convict him." Quizzed about his assessment of the case in 1964, he stated, "The fingerprint was the strongest. There was just no way to get around it." The most interesting part of his analysis, though, dealt with Beckwith's alibi cop-witnesses: "I don't think their testimony was even brought up in the deliberations. I don't think anyone paid any attention to them."

Doc concluded the interview by asking Mr. Keyes if he wished to add anything else. "I was bitterly resentful about Kennedy sending the FBI into the case. They arrested Beckwith too soon. If they had waited forty-eight more hours, the police would have had an airtight case against him," he declared.

The grand jury was in session and the following day juror "Ferguson," the one who had refused to talk to Doc, was to appear. He showed up, briefly testified, and gave a statement to Doc. He had served on the second jury along with Keyes. He was never contacted by any outside person and, when asked his opinion of Beckwith's cops, stated he didn't remember them testifying. It appeared Keyes was right. The alibi witnesses were a nonfactor, at least to some jurors.

On December 22, Doc filled in the last piece of the puzzle regarding the jury in the second 1964 trial. The ex-wife of juror "Lindsey" informed Doc that she and Lindsey had divorced in the early 1970s and thereafter he moved to Houston, Texas. He had died of cancer earlier in 1989.

Toward the shank of the afternoon, Doc laid a large envelope containing the Evers photos on my desk. Christmas was at hand, and everyone in the office was engrossed in the holiday season, shopping and going to open-house parties at sundry offices; well, almost everyone. I took advantage of the quiet to study the photos without interruption.

Examining the black-and-white prints, I again realized just how far back in time the case was taking me. This sensation was underscored as I noticed the attire of the detectives in the snapshots. Picking up one of a detective pointing toward the honeysuckle thicket where the gun had been found, my thoughts were broken by a slow, deep voice behind me. "That's my daddy."

I turned. It was Benny Bennett. "What?"

"That's my daddy. He was with the department back then, but I didn't know he was involved with this case."

"Well, Benny, I'll tell you what. I'll get a few more prints made from the negative for you and your dad."

Benny told me how much he would like that and how much it would mean to him to continue helping on the case. I told him I wouldn't have it any other way.

I was amazed. Not only were we going back a full generation in our investigation, but here was the son of one of the detectives originally on the case now picking up where his dad had left off over a quarter century earlier. The ripples emanating from that stone tossed, that shot fired, a generation earlier were touching the offspring of those people first involved. How ironic, I thought. But I hadn't seen anything yet.

Sharing a love of the law and trial work, Judge Russel Moore and I spent many an evening in his den discussing cases, particularly those that dealt with novel legal issues. Russel was a fighter, unafraid to tackle unique challenges. I really wished that he had been around to discuss the Beckwith case with me. It would have been just the kind of challenge that would have appealed to him, and I would have welcomed his advice. He was not around, though, having lost a long and often painful battle with cancer.

Christmas that year was the first without Russel, and I thought of him often, whether I was working on the Beckwith case or was at a family gathering. Russel and Beckwith—the two occupied my mind almost constantly. It was nearly impossible to think of one without the other. I did not associate the two in any specific way, but as Christmas approached and the investigation intensified, I felt Russel's absence more keenly, both personally and professionally.

I was in my office late in the afternoon one day during the week between Christmas and New Year's Day. Everything was dead around the entire downtown area that week. It was the perfect time to study the evidence we had accumulated thus far.

Russel and Beckwith, Beckwith and Russel. It was inevitable that these parallel thoughts would eventually collide.

As I turned over one photo after another on my desk, I came to those of the 1917 Enfield and scope. A local gunsmith had told the police that the stock on the rifle was not the one produced by the manufacturer. Someone had replaced the standard long stock with the shorter one on the murder weapon. It did not, therefore, look like most rifles of that type.

Was it really that unusual? Hadn't I seen guns that looked like the one in the photos? I knew in the back of my mind that I had, but where? Plenty of family and friends had guns, but I couldn't think of anybody offhand who had anything that old. Nobody but Russel.

The confluence of my ruminations about Russel and the Evers murder weapon triggered something in my memory. I thought hard about the guns I had seen over the years at Russel's house. I remembered a deep drawer in his bedroom dresser where he had a collection of old firearms, but those were all pistols. My brother-in-law, Matthew, had a shotgun when he was growing up, but I did not recall Russel having a rifle.

A long-forgotten memory slowly seeped from my subconscious. I had once seen a rifle in Russel's bathroom. He had used it as a prop to hold the door closed on the towel closet. The hinges had worked loose and that was Russel's way of fixing it. Laughing about his repair job, I had asked Russel about the gun.

What was it he had said? It had been in an old civil rights case. That's all he would say. At the time, his reticence was not unusual. I had seen the gun only that one time, and it was soon after Dixie and I had married in 1973. Russel had not yet warmed up to me. The subject never came up again, nor, during the remainder of Russel's life, did I again see the gun.

Russel, I knew, did not have any involvement in the Beckwith case. Judge Leon Hendrick had presided over the 1964 trials. Then I remembered what former deputy clerk Lilley had told me: "I heard the judge got it." I had assumed at the time that he was talking about the judge in the case, Judge Hendrick. "The judge" got it. By the time I'd graduated from law school and begun practicing, Russel had become the senior circuit judge in the county. Those people who didn't refer to him as "Judge Moore" referred to him simply and respectfully as "the Judge."

"Oh, shit," I found myself mumbling. "Surely not." But I couldn't shake the nagging thought that it might just be the gun I was looking at in the black-and-white photos.

I picked up the phone and called the Election Commission office. Mr. Lilley was out. The next call should have been to Dixie. After all, she was my wife, and Russel's stepdaughter. I decided against it. Dixie was too excitable, and she was unhappy about my involvement in all of this, anyway. I didn't really believe that the rifle I had seen at Russel's house sixteen years earlier was *the* gun (that would have been too incredible), and I saw no need in stirring up Dixie over nothing, especially during the holidays. Instead, I called Matthew, my brother-in-law, who was also a young lawyer in Jackson.

I told him about having seen a rifle in his parents' bathroom years ago that his dad had said was from an old civil rights case. I asked Matthew if he had ever seen the rifle or been told anything about it by his father. He had not. But he told me that he was sure his mother had kept all of Russel's things and that she would not care if I looked through the guns if it would relieve my mind. I thanked him and called Carolyn.

I told her what was nagging me and asked if I could come over that night after work and see for myself. Carolyn said she had put away several "long guns" (she didn't know if they were rifles or shotguns) of Russel's. She did not know what they were or where they had come from, but certainly I was welcome to look at them. I hung up the phone and pulled out the police investigative report. I turned to the reports of Luke and Hargrove and noted the serial numbers of the rifle, 1052682, and of the scope, 69431. I jotted the numbers down on a scrap of paper and stuck it in my pocket.

Before leaving the office to go to Carolyn's house, I called Dixie. I had to tell her that I would be late coming home, which necessitated my telling her that I was going by her mother's house and why.

Dixie thought that I had lost my mind and that I was going to needlessly upset her mother. Carolyn, I explained, seemed perfectly fine and calm to me. Dixie insisted that I come home and pick her up. The kids, she said, were at my mother's house.

The drive from home to Carolyn's house was silent. Carolyn greeted us at the door, as gracious as she had always been. She said that Rusty, Russel's oldest son by his first marriage, had wanted a few of Russel's guns, but they were handguns. The "long ones," she said, were upstairs. I followed her up the stairway to Matthew's old bedroom. Carolyn opened the closet. "I think there are two or three up there," she said, pointing to the shelf above the rack of clothes. I stood on tiptoes and removed several hatboxes, shoeboxes, and folded linens. Yep, there were several weapons.

I pulled the first one down and immediately saw that it was not the Beckwith gun. It looked nothing like it, no scope and too new. I laid it on the bed. It was the same with the second weapon. As the third one eased over the edge of the shelf and came into view, my heart quickened. It appeared to be an old gun with a scope and a short wooden stock. I pulled it down, held it directly under the light, and gazed. My hands were sweating so much it was a wonder I did not drop it.

I brought it closer and studied it from muzzle to butt, turning it at various angles. Several places on the stock, the barrel, and the scope had some etchings: "OML 6/12/63." OML, the initials for O. M. Luke, the detective who had found the murder weapon twenty-six years ago. I handed the gun to Carolyn and asked her to hold it to the light while I compared serial numbers.

My hands were shaking as I pulled the paper from my shirt pocket. I began ticking off the numbers, comparing them with those on the weapon that Carolyn held. "One, zero, five, two, six, eight, two!" The hair on the back of my neck stood on end and the adrenaline was pumping. I wanted to laugh and yell at the top of my lungs, but I had to remain calm. I wasn't sure how Carolyn would react. I should have known. Unlike Dixie, she was always cool and under control.

"Carolyn," I said in the most calm and matter-of-fact voice that I could muster, "this is it, and you know I've got to take it."

Without hesitation she said, "I know."

Dixie and I were barely out of the driveway, making the loop around the lake in front of Carolyn's house, when she asked, "What are you going to do with it?"

"Obviously, I can't do it tonight, but tomorrow morning I'll have to take it in and log it into evidence at the police department. I'll just have to take it home tonight."

"Well, I don't want the kids seeing it in here. Let's go home, and while you do whatever you're going to do with it, I'll go to your mother's house and pick them up." After a pause: "Will you have to tell where you found it?"

"Sooner or later," I said.

Things were coming together, slowly but surely, out of nothing, from nowhere, yet from everywhere: the crime-scene photos and fingerprint comparisons from an unmarked box in a little-used closet at police headquarters, and the murder weapon from my father-in-law's house.

It was a trumpet blast to me. It was skywriting penned by the Almighty, asking me what He had to do to get my attention, assuring me that His hand was truly guiding things along, and reminding me to have faith and keep working. Persistent prayers were paying off, not that God had finally heard me, but that I had finally heard God.

I felt a quickening in spirit, a sense that I was being led, even pushed, to see this mission through. I couldn't wait to get up each morning to see what new little nugget of information or evidence the Lord would have waiting for me to find. Something special was unfolding, and I was in awe to be a part of it.

Yet, I was concerned about causing any embarrassment to Carolyn and the family. There was never any question but that the gun would have to be a part of any reprosecution, but just having the gun, the fingerprints, and the crime-scene photos would not be sufficient. We had to have witnesses and something new, something that Waller didn't have. What if we never came up with anything new? Would the benefit of bringing the gun to light outweigh the attendant harm? At that juncture God was in control, and I knew that somehow things would work out.

Just before going to sleep that night, I read a short article in *Time* mag-

azine about Beckwith and the reinvestigation. The whole thing was a
joke to him. I could picture him on his mountaintop in Signal Mountain,
Tennessee, having a big laugh at our "investigation." He didn't realize the
miracle that was taking shape and the evidence we were amassing.

Then it hit me. Beckwith himself could be the answer to my
dilemma. Full of himself and sure that nothing would ever come of what
he called our "foolishness," he was talking to every reporter seeking an
interview with him. Strutting about like a bantam rooster, he would be
his own worst enemy and hang himself if given enough rope. Even if he
didn't say anything that could be useful in court (I never expected a confession from him, certainly, but something establishing motive was not
out of the question), he could convict himself in the court of public
opinion.

I made my decision. I would not log the gun into evidence. It would
stay hidden in my house. I would tell only a select few people within my
office: Ed, Crisco, Doc, Benny, and Cynthia. For now, nobody else would
know. In the meantime, Beckwith's mouth could only hurt himself. If he
knew we had the gun and other evidence, he would clam up, seeing how
serious our "foolishness" had gotten.

If, on the other hand, nothing ever came of the case, if we turned up no
further evidence or witnesses, then no one else would learn about the
gun and the circumstances of its discovery. I would give the gun back to
Carolyn to do with as she pleased, with nobody getting embarrassed.

After I filled Ed in, he shook his head in disbelief but agreed with my
plan and the reasons behind it. For it to work, though, we couldn't even
tell Myrlie Evers. I knew from my telephone conversations with her that
she frequently talked with reporter Jerry Mitchell. We did not yet know
Mrs. Evers as we would later come to know and appreciate her, and we
were afraid that the temptation to tell Jerry the good news would be too
strong to suppress. We couldn't take the risk.

Next, I called my brother-in-law, Matthew, and filled him in on my
discovery of the gun.

After briefing Cynthia, I walked around the corner to Doc's office to
tell him. As senior investigator, Doc had other responsibilities on his
shoulders. As important as the Beckwith case was, hundreds of other
pending cases needed his attention. With a new court term around the
corner, Doc would have to devote his energies to those cases.

Crisco, Benny, and I would have to work on the case as and when we
could, and Doc would not be able to work on it at all unless absolutely
necessary. But after his work locating and interviewing the jurors of the
1964 trials, he deserved to know about the gun. The news was absorbed

in true "Doc-like" fashion: emotionless, all business, and matter-of-fact.

"That's good, but they had that twenty-five years ago. Based on what the jurors told me, you better hope you get something else before getting serious about this."

It was true and I told him that I agreed. He wished me luck and let me know that I could depend on him later if needed, but that I was in good hands with Crisco and Benny.

I found the two in Benny's office. Both told me I was full of shit and kept waiting for the punch line of the joke they were certain I was playing at their expense until I finally convinced them that I was in earnest.

I packed up what then constituted the Beckwith file, a single expandable folder, and went home. I told Dixie that I was taking off the rest of the holidays and asked if she wanted to spend the balance of the season in Russel's cabin in Destin, Florida. She passed, so I hurriedly packed a few clothes for the kids and myself, loaded the van, and took off on the six-hour drive.

The quiet evenings in Florida that holiday week of 1989, after the kids went to sleep, afforded me the opportunity to spread out my file on the floor and plan the next several steps in our investigation.

After we returned on January 9, I received a telephone call from FBI agent Al Waites, the legal adviser for the Jackson field office. I assumed that he was going to tell me whether they had anything. Instead, he asked me what, exactly, were we looking for.

"I don't know, Al. We don't have a transcript to see what evidence was introduced. I want it all. Whatever the FBI has on this case, I want it."

"Bobby, I want you to understand that the FBI wants to cooperate in every way, but it has certain policies and procedures. There are very good reasons for them, don't take me wrong, but some, I know, don't seem to make a lot of sense."

"Like?"

"Like you will get more from the Bureau by being as specific as you can about what it is you want."

"Al, if I had a checklist, I'd tell you specifically, but I don't. I don't have a transcript. All I know to say is if the FBI has any evidence or information on this case, I would like to have it."

He laughed. "I understand what you're saying, believe me, I do. Mainly, I want you to know you have our cooperation and I'll be back in touch."

It had occurred to me in Florida that even though the transcripts were lost, newspaper accounts of the trials might indicate the identity of the witnesses, or at least some of them. The next step, I decided, was to visit the state archives and review those articles.

On Thursday, January 11, Crisco and I walked to the archives building. All of the newspapers, Crisco and I were told, had been put on microfilm. Each of us at a machine, Crisco and I wound our way through an era of Mississippi history one page at a time. Each reel contained about a month's worth of papers, so it was impossible to go directly to a particular date and stop it on a dime. It was slow and, for me, almost nauseating. Watching each page dart across the screen quickly gave me motion sickness. While my partner was scanning the reel that included coverage of the first trial in early 1964, I wanted to see what the papers had said about the murder itself, so I was reading the reel with the June 12, 1963, editions.

"Gov. Ross Barnett branded the ambush slaying of Negro leader Medgar Evers today 'a dastardly act' and pledged complete cooperation in seeking the killer," one article reported. "The ambush killing of Medgar Evers, a local colored citizen, last night is indeed regrettable," the governor was quoted as saying. "Apparently, it was a dastardly act, and as governor of the State of Mississippi, I shall cooperate in every way to apprehend the guilty party."

Another article contained a few quotes from Medgar Evers:

A muscular six-footer, Evers in a recent interview discussed threats on his life and said, "If I die, it will be in a good cause. I've been fighting for America just as much as the soldiers in Vietnam." Evers reportedly deplored violence. "I do not believe in violence either by whites or Negroes. That is why I am working tirelessly with the NAACP in a peaceful legal struggle for justice," he said. "I'm a native of Mississippi. I don't intend to live elsewhere. *But I'm determined we can gain some equality and be accepted as human beings with dignity.*"[Emphasis added.]

How cogent and powerful, I thought. I pressed the COPY button and circled the quote in red. I planned to use it later, maybe in a closing argument.

Interestingly, the *Greenwood Commonwealth,* Beckwith's hometown newspaper, in an editorial, condemned the murder, stating: "Murder from ambush is the vilest, most savage crime warped souls can sink to. Nothing justifies such an act." I hit the COPY button again. I would add that quote to my closing-argument notes, as well. I wondered about

Beckwith's reaction when he read his paper that day. The crazy bastard probably thought the whole state would shout in jubilation and hold him up as a hero. He was probably the most surprised (and disappointed) man in Mississippi when it didn't happen. I read article after article from most major newspapers across the Magnolia State condemning the murder, stating that even if one disagreed with what Evers had been doing, his murder could not be rationalized.

I thought it sadly ironic as I perused one article that gave some specifics of Governor Barnett's plan in seeking the killer: "Barnett said he had ordered the highway patrol to be on alert in identifying all nonresident vehicles that may be attempting to leave the state."

We ran out of time after getting the articles on the first trial, but the information we had was more than expected. Trial coverage, at least of this case, was much more thorough than any coverage of any trial I had read in contemporary times. There was a recap of every witness's testimony, not just a few highlighted by the reporter. I looked to see what reporters' names appeared on the bylines: Gavin Scott, Bill Simpson, W. C. Shoemaker, and Jerry DeLaughter.

DeLaughter? A DeLaughter was following this case twenty-six years earlier? It was yet another bizarre twist. I learned later from my father that Jerry is a distant cousin. After leaving the Jackson paper, he spent some time writing for the *Memphis Commercial Appeal.* Daddy lost track of him after Jerry retired.

We began reviewing the list of witnesses to see which ones were still living and could be located. Of course, Fred Sanders and John Chamblee testified, since they were the two detectives assigned to the case. Sanders was now head of security at a local hospital, and Chamblee was with the state fire marshal's office.

Capt. B. D. Harrell Jr., on duty in the homicide office when the call came in, was listed in the telephone book.

I knew Joe Alford, one of the first two uniformed officers to arrive at the Evers home. Joe was the captain in charge of the vice and narcotics squad when I first started practicing law. Although he did not testify in 1964, Alford's partner, Eddie Rosamond, did. Rosamond was now a local Realtor.

O. M. Luke, of course, testified. He had found the gun. Luke was now a probation officer with the State Department of Corrections.

Capt. Ralph Hargrove, Crisco knew, was retired, getting on up in years, but still alive and residing in Jackson.

All in all, we had 100 percent of the Jackson police officers who had testified. All were alive, all still lived in Jackson, and most were working other jobs. Crisco started making calls to them, asking them to drop by the office to pick up copies of their reports to read over. I asked him to arrange for either Sanders or Chamblee to meet us at the Evers house. I wanted a firsthand-guided tour. Crisco set it up with Fred Sanders for the following week.

Crisco, Benny, and I swung by the hospital to pick up Fred. He directed us first to the parking lot of what had been Joe's Drive-In and showed us where Beckwith's car had been seen parked in the far rear corner. The building that once housed Joe's was still a joint, but was now home to dopers and winos and was decorated with the latest gang graffiti.

We got out of the car and Fred commenced his tour, pointing a finger where the honeysuckle and hedgerow, among which the rifle had been found, once grew. The vacant lot that appeared in the 1963 photos, where Beckwith had hidden and fired the fatal blast, was no longer vacant. Several houses had been built on the site. The Evers house was totally obscured by these newer homes, fences, and trees. Fred pointed out the largest tree, a sweet gum, standing between two of the newer homes: "Of course, I can't be sure now, but I just believe that's the tree he hid behind and propped his rifle against. We found marks rubbed on the bark about the height the gun would've been. We figured he steadied his aim there."

"You found the bullet, didn't you?"

"Yes, sitting on the countertop right by a watermelon."

"You're kidding."

"No, sir."

We drove around the block, turning right off of Medgar Evers Boulevard (formerly Delta Drive) onto Ridgeway, taking an immediate right on Missouri Street, and then an immediate left on Margaret Walker Alexander Drive (formerly Guynes Street). I wondered who would have been more surprised by a major city thoroughfare being named in honor of Evers: Medgar or Beckwith? As we pulled in front of the third house on the left, I was startled by its deteriorated condition. A pall of gloom and shadows enveloped the place. Was it the giant oak by the driveway or something else? Intangible, but nevertheless felt.

I knew from conversations with Myrlie Evers that she still owned the house. Although she had left Mississippi for California soon after the 1964 trials, she simply could not part with it. Its only inhabitants for twenty-six years had been tenants, who obviously did not share Mrs. Evers's emotional attachment. The loose strips of dark green paint peeling from the walls and the tall grass evidenced years of neglect. The driveway and carport were empty. I assumed the place was vacant until I heard a door open and a woman came out of the house into the carport.

She said nothing, just looked at us, wondering, I'm sure, why four white guys were walking around her yard.

I stood transfixed in the driveway, trapped between the shadows of the towering live oak and the house that had known so much love, but also immeasurable sorrow. It was certainly not my first visit to a crime scene. I had been to countless ones, but never had my heart suffered such melancholy, nor my lungs felt smothered by such a sensation of foreboding, as they did at 2332 Guynes Street. Nobody was saying anything. Did they feel it, too? No traffic, no neighborhood kids playing. There was dead silence everywhere except for a slight wind rustling the leaves in the oak. The atmosphere of morbidity was as colossal as the tree.

"Was that tree here at the time, Fred?"

"Nah. In fact, it would've been directly in the line of fire if it had been there."

"That's what I was thinking. Tell me everything, Fred."

Fred began his narrative of Medgar pulling up in the driveway that spring night so long ago under a full moon and being shot in the back as he got out of his car. The bullet had ripped through his upper body as he stood just about where I was standing. Fred described the thick stream of blood the police had found across the hood of the powder blue Olds, like a long crimson finger pointing toward the front window of the house. I knew the pane had long since been replaced, but I found myself walking to the window, reaching out, and moving my fingers across the glass. I closed my eyes and the black-and-white image of the crime-scene photograph that zoomed in on the bullet hole flashed in my mind, as if the flashbulb were going off with the camera in my hand instead of that of a police photographer a quarter century earlier.

Fred pointed along the grassy edge of the driveway. "After he was shot and fell, he drug himself along here, all the way to the base of the steps in the carport. There was a steady trail of blood all along the way." We retraced the route to the carport. "This is where he collapsed. When we got here, he had already been transported to the hospital, but I tell you, there was so much blood here it looked like somebody had butchered a hog."

The scene described earlier to me by Myrlie Evers at our first meeting played out in my head—her bursting through the door, knowing in her gut what she would find outside; yet upon seeing her husband lying mortally wounded at her feet, blood everywhere, her screaming his name: "Medgar!"; their three young children following on her coattails: "Daddy!"; then their screams subsiding into pleas: "Daddy, please don't die, please get up"; tears mingling with blood. I felt another chill and damn near wept. Not now, I told myself, not in front of these cops. Then I noticed moisture in their eyes, too.

"What kind of man could do such a thing in front of his wife and kids?" I asked aloud but to nobody in particular. "It had to have been meant that way. The bastard could've just as easily shot him coming out of his office or on the road, and his office would have been a lot easier than the house. Extra efforts were made to make sure it was done at home."

"One sick son of a bitch," Benny replied.

"A dangerous, ruthless one, too," Crisco added.

My mind's eye divided into a split screen. On one side, I pictured Medgar getting out of his blue Olds carrying Christmas presents in his arms and trying to sneak them inside without the children seeing. On the other side, I pictured him getting out of the same car carrying JIM CROW MUST GO T-shirts, a bullet ripping through his body and tearing through the interior of the house where Myrlie and the children were.

On one mental screen I envisioned the laughter and smiles of the children meeting Daddy in the carport as he got home from work. A game of catch with Darrell, a ride for Reena on his shoulder, a toy truck for toddler Van. The image then distorted to the carnage they had witnessed when Daddy got home from work on June 12, 1963. They would never be the same, I suspected. Who would?

Myrlie had refused to succumb, though. She had taken the children to California, finished her education, and through hard work become a commissioner of the public works department of Los Angeles. She had raised all three children into fine adults. Darrell and Reena had families of their own. All outward appearances revealed survival turned to success. But what about inside? I had not yet talked to her children, but I sensed from my conversations with Myrlie that dark recesses of the heart and soul still looked much like the dilapidated house and would remain so unless and until justice was conclusively done.

I talked to Mrs. Evers a long time that night. I told her about the feelings that I had experienced at the house and asked her to send me copies of anything she did not mind sharing with me about Medgar. The starker the contrast between Beckwith and him the better, as far as a jury would be concerned.

Upon my mentioning the big live oak, Mrs. Evers asked, "Would you believe that it was Medgar who planted that tree not too many months before he was killed? It was such a little thing then; you could barely see it, but Medgar was so proud of it. He put his heart and soul into everything around that house. He took such pride in it."

I thought of how the tree had flourished over the past twenty-six years. It was massive now, standing like a towering sentinel watching over the household, protecting it from the malevolence that had lurked across the way.

Whenever I had doubts about the case or the wisdom of my involvement in it, I would drive out to the house at 2332 Margaret Walker Alexander. Sometimes I just sat in the car, gazing and reflecting. Reruns of the murder ran through my head—Myrlie, the children, their tears. I would snap back as I felt my own tears trickle down my cheeks. I always left refortified and determined.

One thing that I had to guard against—and it required a lot of self-discipline—was spending all of my time on the Evers case. Life went on over the next several months. Doc found time to locate some of the jurors from the first 1964 jury. Although there was never any indication of jury tampering in the first trial, I was still interested in their views of the case. Most of their opinions mirrored those of the jurors from the second trial.

One of the jurors from the first trial, though, described Beckwith as "an arrogant fool. He wore a Citizens' Council pin on his lapel and would make it a point to hold it so the jury could see it." The juror then revealed the initial split of that first jury: "When we first went out and voted, I think it was ten to two to convict him. As time went on, one or two more went over to acquit him. That was as close as he ever came to being convicted. I thought he was guilty and still believe it."

Doc had now run down all of the second jury and half of the first. I told him not to worry about the other six jurors on the first panel. We were well beyond that phase of this investigation.

Crisco and I continued in our attempt to locate witnesses and evidence. The FBI notified us that it had found a few items at its crime lab, such as a few photos of the gun, a fingerprint found on the scope, and Beckwith's known fingerprints.

We also continued our search at the state archives for the names of witnesses. FBI firearms instructor Joseph D. Peggs testified that he had observed a semicircular fresh scar above Beckwith's right eye following his arrest. It appeared to Peggs to be from being hit with a telescopic sight by the recoil of a high-powered rifle. Agent Peggs said he had asked Beckwith about it. "He said, 'No comment.'"

Dr. Forrest G. Bratley, a pathologist, established the cause of Evers's death and further testified that, at the DA's request, he had examined Beckwith in the jail on June 23, 1963. He described the same semicircular scar over Beckwith's right eye. When he asked Beckwith about it,

Beckwith responded, "It looks like a scar." Asked how he had gotten it and when, Beckwith snapped, "You, an expert, should be able to tell that."

Dr. Bratley said he measured the arc of the scar and found it comparable to the diameter of the telescopic sight. The scar, in the doctor's opinion, was ten to thirty days old when he examined it eleven days after the murder.

As much as I was interested in the state's case, I was more anxious to see what evidence the defense had put forth.

Mrs. Willie Mae Bishop Patterson lived in the house directly behind Pittman's Grocery. She had testified that she had heard the sound of a gun, looked out her front door, and seen Evers fall at his doorstep. Three men, she claimed, had run down the street a moment later. In his cross-examination, Waller presented Mrs. Patterson with photos and diagrams that showed a large tree and another house in the line of vision between her front door and the Evers driveway. When Waller asked her "to explain to the jury how you could see through a tree and a house," Mrs. Patterson then changed her vantage point, maintaining she had not been looking out her front door after all; she had moved, she said, from the door to a window.

According to one article, Lee Cockrell, owner of Joe's Drive-In, was called to dispute the testimony of the carhops. "He said he saw no car parked in the corner of his lot and heard no car drive away. But, he added, his attention had been distracted by two men in the front of his place who were about to fight. Neither, he said, had he heard the blast of a gun. 'Who was in a better position to see' the dark corner of the lot, Waller asked on cross-examination, 'the carhops or you?' 'The carhops,' Cockrell said."

Doris Sumrall, described as a brunette waitress at Joe's, testified that she had heard a shot, looked out a window, and gone outside through the kitchen door in the back of the building and never seen a car leave. On cross-examination, however, she said she heard "all three shots before going to the back of the building to look out." Thus, she didn't look in the back until after Houston Wells had fired his shot of alarm. Beckwith would've been long gone by then.

Ancie Lee Haven was described as the "young waitress in charge of the drive-in until 11 P.M., the night of the murder." She testified that the car was a Dodge rather than a Plymouth Valiant. She admitted under cross-examination that she had given detectives a signed statement that the vehicle was a light-colored Dodge or Plymouth and that she had gotten only a "fleeting glimpse" of it, whatever it was.

The defense put on three witnesses, Mrs. Audrey Branch, her son, Charles, and Fred Conner, to say that Beckwith couldn't have gotten the scar over his eye the Wednesday morning of the murder, since he had had it when they saw him at a bus station in Greenwood the Sunday evening before. Three other witnesses, John Book, James S. McCoy Sr., and McCoy Jr., all coworkers of Beckwith's, testified they had seen him with the cut on Monday.

The Greenwood police officers who provided Beckwith with his alibi were Lt. Hollis Creswell and Off. James Holley. As I would've expected, Waller grilled the cops as to why they had not said anything to the FBI or Jackson police rather than letting someone they "knew" was innocent languish in jail for over eight months. Holley explained, "If any authorized person asked me, I would've told them everything I knew."

I remembered seeing the names Holley and Creswell in the police report. Not once, but twice, Fred Sanders and John Chamblee talked to both of those law enforcement brethren in Greenwood. The first report read:

Officers Creswell and Holley (Greenwood Police) Date: 6-25-63, We talked to these officers while in Greenwood. (Not as an interview but as four policemen.) Both knew we were on the case and we talked some about it. Creswell made the statement, "I know he didn't do it," but did not give a reason. Officer Holley didn't say much.

The second report stated:

Lt. Creswell and Officer Holley (Date Jan. 25, 1964). Conversation took place in Crystal Grill. Creswell made the statement that Beckwith was not guilty and made it strong. We did not argue or discuss the guilt or innocence of Beckwith. Creswell did not give a reason for saying this but did say Beckwith might could [*sic*] tell who the guilty party was but would never do it. Officer Holley again didn't say much.

In two conversations with the detectives in charge of the case, these officers said nothing about an alibi.

Although he had refused to talk to the FBI, even before his arrest, and had declined to talk to the detectives about his gun, scope, car, or anything else connected with the murder, Beckwith took the witness stand in 1964. "Beckwith's surprise appearance as a witness highlighted the fifth and final day of testimony in the trial. He had not been expected to take the stand. His testimony—which lasted from 3:25 until 5:45—was his first public statement about the case since his arrest last June 22," one article read.

Beckwith denied ever seeing the two cabdrivers and told the jury, "I don't even know where the Continental Trailways bus station is in Jackson." One article observed, "He was asked about testimony of witnesses who said they had seen a white Valiant identified as his at the 'Handy Andy' Pittman Grocery near Evers' house before the shooting. He denied knowing where the grocery is, and that he had ever been there."

Beckwith admitted owning several Enfield .30-06 rifles similar to the murder weapon, yet not one cartridge of that caliber was found in his house. "Beckwith then examined the weapon in evidence, checking its bolt and sighting it over the heads of the jury. 'There's much similarity between this weapon and several weapons I possessed,' he said." Waller asked Beckwith if he was accurate with his Enfield at two hundred feet— the distance between Evers's driveway and the spot from which the shot was fired. "'Yes,' Beckwith said, 'more than that.'"

When asked about his refusal to talk with FBI agents about the scope he had purchased from John Goza, Beckwith said it was because he thought they were civil rights investigators. "The defense entered a newspaper clipping which quoted a Leflore County Bar Association resolution urging citizens not to talk to investigators about civil rights matters."

Waller established Beckwith's motive for the murder through various letters written by him: "I believe in segregation just like I believe in God," and he would "make every effort to rid the U.S.A. of the integrationists." Additionally: "When I go to Hades, I'm going to raise hell all over Hades till I get to the white section. For the next 15 years we here in Mississippi are going to have to do a lot of shooting to protect our wives and children from a lot of bad niggers."

Beckwith urged Waller to "see the humor in it," to "laugh at the humor and to see the serious side of it, too."

Waller asked Beckwith if he had expressed a belief that his imprisonment was a "sacrifice to the cause." Beckwith snapped, "Yes, sir! This is a cause." Beckwith told Waller—while Hardy Lott tried in vain to object and get his client to shut up—that he was compiling information for a book "about the subject matter of this trial." He said "one of the ten" proposed titles for the book was *My Ass, Your Goat and the Republic.*

The scar over his right eye, he explained, was indeed caused by the telescopic sight on a gun he had fired, but it was not on Wednesday, the morning of the murder, it was on the previous Sunday while target-practicing on a shooting range near Greenwood. What a gift! So what if it was then? His explanation fit perfectly within a scenario of planning, reconnaissance, and practice.

I reconstructed the scenario in my mind. Beckwith, the author of the letters Waller introduced, became livid at Evers's television appearance just weeks before the murder. Evers had to be eliminated "for the cause." For his own sick reasons, the assassin wanted the family to see his handiwork. Beckwith came to Jackson and unsuccessfully attempted to find Evers's home address in the telephone book. The number was unlisted. Who would know the streets of Jackson better than anyone else? Cabdrivers. He found two—Speight and Swilley—and questioned them, stating that he had to locate the address in a couple of days. Later that Saturday he found the house. He scouted the area, looking for a place from which to shoot and a place to park undetected. During this preparation, he was seen walking through the wooded lot by Mr. and Mrs. Pittman, and the Pittmans' teenage son and a friend noticed his car.

The next day, Sunday, Beckwith went to a firing range to practice and shot round after round with the Enfield .30-06, making sure its telescopic sight was set perfectly. In the process, as the gun recoiled, the rear edge of the scope cut him over his right eye. At work on Monday, he was preoccupied with his upcoming plans. All he talked about with John Book and his customers was segregation and guns. Then Tuesday came, and the rest is history.

I would have bet that the firing range was the one where the Greenwood Police Department practiced. It wouldn't have surprised me if Creswell or Holley had arranged access for him.

We were locating the bare bones of Waller's case, but we had still not turned up anything new. That changed on May 1, 1990, with a telephone call from a lawyer friend in town—Jack Ables. Jack had graduated from the Ole Miss Law School a few years ahead of me and was a partner in a large insurance-defense firm in Jackson.

After asking me if I was still looking into the Evers assassination, and after I confirmed that I was, Jack told me that he was representing Orion Pictures and film producer Fred Zollo in a defamation suit filed by former Neshoba County sheriff Lawrence Rainey and other alleged Klansmen, who were upset with their portrayal in Orion's *Mississippi Burning*. Since truth is a defense in such a lawsuit, Jack explained that he had been spending months reading everything he could get his hands on about the 1964 murders of the three civil rights workers in Neshoba County.

One of the books he was reading was a biography of a Methodist minister who was in the Klan, worked his way to a trusted position with Imperial Wizard Sam Bowers, and then turned informant for the FBI. Most of the book, titled *Klandestine,* was about Rev. Delmar Dennis's experiences as an informant and about his surprise testimony for the government in the federal prosecution against Rainey, Bowers, and others for the Neshoba County murders. "But," Jack explained, "there is one short paragraph on page thirty-eight that might interest you. I have it right here." Jack read:

Once at a training session, Dennis and other Klansmen allegedly heard Byron De La Beckwith speak. The accused killer of Jackson NAACP official Medgar Evers is reported to have fully admitted his guilt in that crime. "Killing that nigger gave me no more inner discomfort than our wives endure when they give birth to our children. We ask them to do that for us. We should do just as much. So, let's get in there and kill those enemies, including the President, from the top down!"

"Is this guy Delmar Dennis still alive? Where is he?"

"Things got so bad for him after the Neshoba trial that he left the state and went into seclusion somewhere in Tennessee. That's as much as I know. Maybe the guy who wrote this book knows where he is. You want the author's name?"

"I want more than that, Jack. I've got to get that book."

"It's out of print. You can have this one when I'm through with it, but I can have a runner bring you a copy of the part that I just read. I'll also send you the information on the jacket about the author. His name is William H. McIlhany the second."

"Thanks, Jack. I owe you."

"Just do me one favor."

"You name it."

"For the time being, anyway, keep me out of this. All this mess I've been reading has really got me spooked about these guys. They're crazy, dangerous, and for real. It's not Mickey Mouse bullshit to them, and they are very much still around. They just aren't as open about it as they were thirty years ago. You carry a gun?"

"I have some at the house, but I don't carry one."

"I would if I were you."

"Man, most people around here aren't like that. They're decent folks."

"No doubt, but I'm not talking about most people. How many does it take to pull a trigger?"

"I get your point, but nothing is going to happen."

"Okay, but until you check with me and I tell you otherwise, don't mention my name and we never talked. Deal?"

"Deal."

I had just hung up the phone when it rang again.

"Hey, Bobby, this is Jerry."

"What's going on, Jerry?"

"Well, it's now May and there are folks beginning to wonder how serious your office is in pursuing the Beckwith case."

I felt trapped. If I defended the office and myself and told him everything we had, it would be all over the papers and potential sources of information would dry up—including Beckwith. If I didn't report any progress, then unrest among some in the black community, goaded by Jerry Mitchell and the *Clarion-Ledger,* would continue.

"Jerry, since it's an open investigation, I really can't comment, but we are continuing to follow up on every lead. As to specifics, I'm not able to comment."

"Is that really all you want me to quote you as saying? You know, we're really trying to help you."

I lost it. In a way I am glad that I did, but it could have been disastrous. "Help me? Jerry, if you and your paper want to help me, stay out of it, back off, and let us do our job."

"You know I can't do that. Inquiring minds want to know."

"Okay. You want to help? You can help me find a guy named Delmar Dennis. Otherwise, we have nothing else to discuss." I was hanging up when Jerry said something that froze me.

"You want Delmar? Hang on, I've got his number right here."

I damn near dropped the receiver. I also dropped my voice a few hundred decibels to a conciliatory tone. "You know Delmar Dennis?"

"Yeah, we're good friends. I first met him-+ when I was doing those pieces about *Mississippi Burning* and the Neshoba County murders. He helped me out a lot with background information, but I didn't know he was involved in the Beckwith case. Why do you want him?" Jerry, unlike me, never lost his cool; or at least he didn't show it if he did.

I couldn't tell Jerry, but I couldn't afford to piss him off any more than I already had. I needed Dennis's number and getting it from Jerry would save time. "Same reason you needed him—just background information about the Klan, the civil rights days, and so on. Just looking for leads, Jerry."

"Yeah, right. Okay, here's his number. He's in Sevierville, Tennessee."

"Dollywood, USA."

"Yep. Well, let me know what he says, if it's anything useful." I didn't say anything. "Bye," he said.

As I was punching Delmar's number, Jeanie Stewart, our office receptionist, came in and handed me an envelope. It contained the copies Jack had sent over. I reached Delmar without any trouble. I explained who I was and the purpose of my call. I read him the pertinent paragraph and asked if it was true. He confirmed that it was, but he quickly let me know that he wanted no part of our case. He had tried to do the right thing from 1964 to 1966 and had been paying for it ever since. He said that he had just begun to get his life somewhat back in order, and while he wished us luck, he wanted us to leave him out of it.

One step at a time, I told myself. I begged him to talk with me, face-to-face, about everything he knew concerning Beckwith and the Klan—not just in reference to Evers's murder. I promised him we would only use it for background information, and unless he authorized it, his name would never be mentioned. He was scared to death of Beckwith and the Klan, but after some shameless begging on my part, he agreed to meet with me if I made the trip to Sevierville. I told him I would leave first thing the following morning. It was a long drive, so we agreed to meet the morning after that. He would not give me his address. I was to call him after I checked in a motel and he would then tell me where we would meet.

The adrenaline was flowing. This was the first chance to obtain something new that Waller did not have in 1964. In spite of what Delmar had told me about not wanting to get involved, I had a good feeling about Delmar Dennis. Maybe after a trip to the mountains of Tennessee, I would have that new evidence we had been hoping for. The mountains of east Tennessee? That's where Beckwith lived. I located an atlas and looked to see where Signal Mountain was situated in reference to Sevierville. I would have to go right by it.

I wondered if Beckwith himself would grant me an audience on his mountain. He was running his mouth to everyone else. He just might, I thought, talk with me, perhaps to pump me for information about the investigation. What did I have to lose? I picked up the phone and dialed Signal Mountain directory assistance.

I was in luck; the number was listed. He answered on the second ring. My stomach was doing flip-flops, but I put forth an air of confidence and explained who I was.

"Yes, suh, Mr. DeLaughter, I'm delighted to hear from you. Tell me what's going on down there with all this tomfoolery."

I patronized him. "Well, Mr. Beckwith, we've been backed into a corner on this thing and agreed to take a look at it. Of course, we've heard a lot of claims from some people pointing a finger at you, but substantiating those claims is a different ball game."

"I know what you mean, suh. I'm very familiar with the burdens with which public officials and lawyers such as you must bear. I come from a long line of lawyers—blue bloods. My muhthah was a Yerger [pronounced by him as "Yoi-guh"]. Her muhthah, Susie Yerger, was the best personal friend of Varina Howell Davis, the wife of President Jefferson Davis. That's of the CSA. After my muhthah died, I lived with my uncle Will Yerger, who was a lawyer. Where are you from, Mr. DeLaughter?"

"I grew up right here in Jackson."

"Wonderful."

"Anyway, Mr. Beckwith—"

"That's Byron De La Beckwith the sixth. My son is the seventh, and his son, already a fine hunter and marksman, is the eighth. Do you hunt, Mr. DeLaughter?"

"I used to, but I don't have time anymore."

"You need to, Mr. DeLaughter, you need to."

"Anyway, Mr. Beckwith, I don't want to just hear one side of the story. We certainly want to be fair and would like to come up and visit with you and hear anything that you can share with us."

"Oh, Miss Thelma and I would love to have you come up, but I was hoping you would be telling me some information."

It was Tuesday. Crisco and I would leave Wednesday morning and drive to Sevierville, stay overnight there, and meet with Delmar Dennis Thursday morning. We could drive back to Chattanooga Thursday afternoon, stay overnight there, and meet Beckwith Friday morning. I'd see if Benny wanted to go with us.

"Would Friday morning around ten be okay?"

"That would be wonderful, but first we need to clear up the preliminaries."

"Preliminaries?"

"Yes, suh. You know I don't allow riffraff up here. I don't let anyone on my property that isn't white right Caucasian Christians. Now, you sound white; are you?"

"Yes, sir."

"And are you a Christian?"

"Yes, sir. I'm a deacon in the Baptist Church."

"Mighty fine. I'm an Israelite, myself."

What the hell was I getting myself into?

Beckwith continued, "Miss Thelma and I look forward to you joining us in some Southern hospitality and genteel conversation and refreshments." An image of Beckwith and Miss Thelma lacing a mint julep with arsenic flashed through my mind. "Now, will you be bringing anyone with you?"

"Yes, sir. I have two investigators who will be coming along."

"I need those names, please, suh." I gave him Crisco's and Benny's names. "And do they meet my qualifications?"

I couldn't resist the temptation to play with him a little. "They're Baptists, too."

"And what is their race, creed, and color?"

"To be perfectly honest with you, Mr. Beckwith, they both have curly hair, but they're white."

"Now, when you say 'curly,' Mr. DeLaughter, do you mean 'nappy' like a pickaninny or 'wavy' like King David? He wasn't no Jew, you know, he was an Israelite like me."

"I would say they're more of the King David type." I swallowed hard.

"Very good."

I had enough and asked for directions to his house from Chattanooga. He described all the turns and gave me all the distances in between. His house was the one on the left with the owls on the mailbox and the large Confederate flag hanging across the porch.

Before I hung up, Jeanie was buzzing me to let me know I had another call. I hit the button. It was Jerry Mitchell again.

"Delmar told me he talked with you and what it was about."

I couldn't believe, as nervous as Delmar had sounded when I talked with him, that he would have confided our conversation with Jerry, unless it was in confidence. I said as much to Jerry.

"Oh, it was in confidence," Jerry explained. "Like I said, we've been friends for a while. He did seem nervous about meeting you, but I told him it was okay."

"Thanks. You told him your conversation was off-the-record?"

"Yeah."

"So nothing will be printed about it?"

"Not unless my editors pull rank on me. I have to tell them."

"Jerry, this guy is as nervous as a cat. If the paper runs with this, it could scare him off for good. He could run off and disappear again and it could be years before we found him."

"I have to tell my editors. I think they will go along with it."

"Well, when you talk with your editors, tell them that it's put-up-or-shut-up time for them. They've been stirring this thing up from the very beginning and talking about how justice needs to be finally obtained, how the sins of the state need to be cleansed, and how Ed Peters and I are stonewalling. Now that we may have the biggest break yet, if this information gets out, it could all be down the tubes. We could lose this break and it might even put this man's life at risk. Promise me it won't be published—at least until after I get back and know whether Delmar is hitched to the team."

"Bobby, I have to tell them, but it's just a formality. I'm sure they will understand and go along."

"Okay. Thanks again. And, Jerry, I'm sorry I snapped at you. Thanks for the help."

I got off the phone with Jerry and called Delmar back. He confirmed he had told Jerry all about our conversation but seemed satisfied that it was "off-the-record." They were friends, he said.

Crisco, Benny, and I left the office early to go home and pack. We agreed to meet in the courthouse parking lot early the next morning.

Tuesday, May 1, 1990, had truly been a day of shocks. It wasn't over, yet. As I walked into my house, Dixie was holding the kitchen phone in her hand, covering the mouthpiece, a horrified look on her face. "It's Byron De La Beckwith for you!"

I wasn't alarmed, but I didn't have time just then to explain everything to Dixie. "Hello."

"Mr. DeLaughter, this is Byron De La Beckwith, and I wanted to let you know that you and your investigators are no longer welcome here at my home." His entire demeanor, tone of voice, had changed. It couldn't have been more than an hour ago that I couldn't shut him up and he was welcoming us with open arms.

"Well, Mr. Beckwith, we don't have to meet you at your home. We will meet you anywhere you like."

"No, suh," he snapped, "my wife [he no longer referred to her with me as "Miss Thelma"] and I have talked with our lawyer and he advises against it. And I have always done what my lawyers have told me to do over the years. But I'll tell you what I would be willing to do. If you wish to come alone and meet me wherever I say, I'll be glad to do that." It was the only time in the conversation that he laughed. I felt a cold chill.

"I can't do that. I would be putting myself in the position of being a possible witness. I always have an investigator with me when I interview someone."

"Witness to what, Mr. DeLaughter?"

"To anything that is said."

"I thought you were coming up here to fill me in on what is going on in your little investigation. Now, you don't need a witness to that, do you?"

"Mr. Beckwith, I told you that as a matter of fairness I wanted to afford you the opportunity of telling your side of it. If you don't want to do that, fine. But my procedure for years is to always have an investigator with me, and I'm not breaking that habit for you or anyone else."

"Good day, suh," he said, "and good luck." Dial tone.

It was difficult going to sleep that night. I drifted off thinking that for once in his life, Beckwith's brain had overpowered his tongue and he had called a lawyer.

I got up Wednesday morning and walked outside to get the paper, unfolding it as I walked back inside. "Son of a damned bitch!" I yelled as I read the headline: "1975 Book Adds Impetus to Evers Case." The article named Delmar and quoted him extensively. That was bad enough, but I was livid as I read on. "Beckwith, contacted at his home in Signal Mountain, Tenn., said he knew Dennis but denied making the statement attributed to him in the book."

I knew then why the sudden change in Beckwith's attitude and the cancellation of our meeting. Jerry Mitchell had called him, told him about the conversation with Delmar, then asked Beckwith for a comment. Un-damn-believable. On top of that, Jerry had relayed the information to Myrlie Evers. I was looking forward to telling her, but only if we got a commitment from Delmar. There was no use in needlessly building up expectations. Mrs. Evers commented in the article, "I hope that the district attorney will continue to pursue this case with more vigor than what they've done in the past."

Well, thanks a lot. This case was practically all I was living and breathing. Wasn't anybody in our corner? I had no time to dwell on it; we needed to hit the road. I dropped the kids off at school and met Crisco and Benny in the parking lot.

The drive to Sevierville took most of the day. Although I volunteered several times to drive, I was relegated to the backseat. I napped some and talked a little, but mostly I just stared out the window, immersed in my thoughts rather than conversation. What talk there was centered mainly on the case and predictions of what we would find with Delmar Dennis. Would he even talk to us after the revelation to the world in the morning paper? Surely, by the time we arrived, he would have heard about it. Our collective mood was somber. The pieces were beginning to come together, but we were still a long way from going to a grand jury.

"Bobby, let me ask you something."

"Sure, Benny."

"Do you really think we will ever be able to do anything with this son of a bitch? I mean, even if Delmar Dennis helps us, will that be enough?"

"I just don't know. Six months ago I would never have dreamed we would have what we do right now. But if we can find at least one of the cabdrivers, the Pittman boy, and one or two other witnesses, we might have a chance *if*, and it's a big *if*, Delmar Dennis comes through and *if* what he says can be corroborated in some way."

"You mean," Crisco asked, "if the FBI has some report that backs him up?"

"Yeah. It wouldn't have to be verbatim to what he says. It wouldn't even have to say that Dennis reported to the agents that Beckwith bragged about the murder. Even if he told them, I have my doubts about that part being in any FBI report."

"After two hung juries and Beckwith's release, they wouldn't exactly want it known that they were told by one of their informants that Beckwith confessed, would they?" Benny observed.

"Probably not, for at least two reasons," Crisco offered. "They would have to give up their informant, and then there would be yet a third trial. Back then, who was to say the result still wouldn't have been the same? And, once it got to the point that a conviction would be a possibility, the damn Bureau would be too embarrassed for it to get out that they had been told about a confession way back and never said anything about it."

It was after dark when we pulled into the Comfort Inn in Sevierville. After checking in, I called Delmar. He wasn't in, according to his wife, but she said we were to meet Delmar at eight the next morning at the local Cracker Barrel Restaurant.

We arrived there at 7 A.M., Thursday, May 3, 1990. We picked out a table by the front window. None of us had a clue what Delmar Dennis looked like. I had given him descriptions of us when I talked to him on the phone from the office on Tuesday. We indulged in a big country breakfast of eggs, bacon, ham, sausage, hash browns, and biscuits dripping with thick gravy. By seven forty-five, we were through.

We paid our checks and went outside to sit in the rocking chairs on the front porch. It was a cool, crisp mountain morning in the Smokies.

My reverie was soon broken. "You Bobby DeLaughter?" I heard someone say. I matched the voice with the telephone conversations I had had with Delmar Dennis as I turned my head from the mountains in the south to the porch steps. I got up. "Mr. Dennis?"

"That's right."

I extended my hand. "I'm Bobby DeLaughter, and these are my investigators: Charlie Crisco and Benny Bennett."

After everyone exchanged greetings and shook hands, I asked Delmar if he would like some breakfast.

"No thanks. I've already eaten and I'd like to get this over with, if you don't mind."

At least he didn't tell us to take a hike. Evidently, he was still going to talk with us. "Fair enough," I said. "Where can we talk?"

"You got your car here?"

"Yes, sir. We're in that blue Chevy Caprice." I pointed to Benny's unmarked patrol unit. "You want to ride with us?"

"No. I'm in that pickup there." He nodded in its direction. "If you boys don't mind riding for about twenty or thirty minutes, I know a place that will be just right for what we need."

"We're all yours."

"Then y'all follow me."

As we headed toward the vehicles, I couldn't help watching Delmar. He was much larger than he was in the picture Jack Ables had included with the excerpt from *Klandestine.* It did not surprise me that Delmar had put on some weight over the last twenty years—which was about how long it had been since the book was published—but he was also a lot taller than I'd expected. He appeared to be at least six feet two, in the three-hundred-pound range, and balding. In sum, he was an imposing figure.

We got in our car and followed him south out of town and past the tourist attractions. Crisco drove. Soon a large brown sign greeted us: "Welcome to the Great Smoky Mountains National Park." We started going up, winding our way up one of the mountains and breaking through a mantle of mist that had gathered in the valley. It was beautiful.

Delmar turned, leaving the main road. We followed, taking each turn behind him, going higher and encountering less and less traffic, until we were on a road with nobody but Delmar in sight and the only sound that of the gears in Delmar's truck shifting, then downshifting.

"Where do you think he's taking us?" Crisco asked between gulps of Pepto-Bismol. His ulcers were flaring up again.

"Your guess is as good as mine," I said.

"I got a guess for you," Benny said. Not waiting for a response, he continued, "You know he could be so scared of Beckwith and the Klan that, if he knows Jerry Mitchell told all, he's leading us into a trap. What better way to get the heat off him than to deliver us to the Klan? Hell, the sons of bitches could be hiding anywhere along here for a perfect ambush. Don't you think it's funny old Delmar wouldn't ride with us?"

The road was bordered by the forest and abandoned campsites. Delmar turned onto a graveled road. I was getting a little uneasy myself. My concern momentarily waned as we wound our way through a sea of crimson, purple, and yellow blossoms. The rhododendrons and yellow clintonia were flowering. The beauty of the world that God has created, and with which He has entrusted us, never ceases to amaze me.

The brake lights on Delmar's truck flashed. He killed his engine and got out.

"Crisco, pull in close directly behind him. We'll never find our way out of here. He isn't leaving until we do."

We parked and got out. I heard the sound of running water. Delmar turned to walk down a path. "Walk this way." We followed as I thought of the same line in Mel Brooks's *Young Frankenstein*. Benny and Crisco, I could tell, were steadily scanning the landscape—for snipers, I supposed. We soon came to a clearing among the trees with huge boulders strewn here and there, together with a felled tree or two. It was flanked by a clear mountain stream. The water's steady flow over the rocks was the sound I had heard. We found a place to sit.

Delmar hadn't mentioned Jerry Mitchell's article. I decided I wouldn't either unless Delmar brought it up.

"Mr. Dennis," I began, "you know why we're here. Do you mind if we use a tape recorder instead of trying to write it all down?"

"Not at all."

I nodded to Crisco, who pushed the RECORD button on a handheld recorder.

"I know generally that you spent some time with the Klan back in the sixties. Would you tell us a little bit about yourself, what your role was within the Klan, and how you came about providing information to the FBI?"

"Well, for three years, from '64 through '67, I worked undercover in the White Knights of the Ku Klux Klan of Mississippi for the FBI, and it was almost a daily job where I was in contact with Klan people for almost exactly three years. I was primarily gathering information that was later used in the trial of Klansmen who were accused of killing the three civil rights workers in Neshoba County. I was the one who broke that. You see, I was an officer in the Klan for a ten-county district, which was basically east-central Mississippi. I testified in that case in '67, first before the grand jury, then again in the jury trial. Since then, I've had various jobs and lived in different parts of the country."

"You mentioned that you held a position within the Klan. What was that position?"

"I was a Province Titan, which was an administrative job that gave me contact between Sam Bowers and local groups in that ten-county district. So, I got information going both ways."

"Who was Sam Bowers?"

"Sam was the founder and head of the White Knights of the Ku Klux Klan of Mississippi. He lived in Laurel and actually ran the Klan more like a military group than anything else, even though ostensibly it was a democratic type of organization. He really was the one who gave the orders for the Klan."

"You started with the Klan about what year?"

"'Sixty-four."

"And how soon after that did you start being an informant with the FBI?"

"I joined the Klan in the spring. I think it was March of '64, and by June, I had become inactive in the Klan. I went back in September for the FBI, so it was from September of '64 through September of '67 that I worked for the FBI."

"If you can say, how was it that you came about doing that?"

"They knew that I had dropped out of the Klan because on the sixteenth of June of '64 something took place in Neshoba County that caused me to drop out. A church was burned. I think it was five days later, the twenty-first, that the boys were killed."

"Weren't you a minister?"

"I was pastor of the First Southern Methodist Church in Meridian."

"What agents did you normally deal with?"

"John L. Martin and Tom Van Riper."

"Tell me about any encounters you've had with Byron De La Beckwith."

"Well, there's only two that I remember. There may be other times we were at meetings together, but I remember two because, one, he came to my home. He said that Sam Bowers had asked him to come by and ask me to do what I could to help him. He was running for lieutenant governor and was thinking the notoriety he'd gained from the trials might get him elected."

"What was the second encounter?"

"When he made the speech to a state Klan rally somewhere near Byron, Mississippi."

"Could it be 'Byram'?"

"Could be, if it is south of Jackson a little ways."

"It is."

"Okay. I remember crossing over this old rickety bridge."

"Swinging bridge?"

"Yeah. Anyway, he gave a motivational talk to inspire Klansmen to be more active and violent. He referred to the killing of Medgar Evers by saying, 'When I killed that nigger, I didn't go through any more trouble than your wives go through to have babies. You're free to go out and do it. We're gonna have to go out and kill them from the top down, from the President on down.' I remember how shocked I was and how stupid I thought he was for saying to some hundred men, you know, 'I did it. You can do it, too.'"

For years, I had heard that the land across the Pearl River from Byram and south of the swinging bridge was owned by L. E. Matthews, whom the FBI believed to be the Klansman who made the bomb found in Beckwith's car trunk on the Lake Pontchartrain bridge near New Orleans in the early 1970s. "Was the meeting close to the bridge you mentioned?"

"It might have been. I remember that the outstanding thing about the meeting was that Beckwith was there and that security was real high. There were a lot of people there with hunting rifles, high-powered rifles. People were being searched."

"What kind of meeting was it?"

"It was just a general 'get the troops together and get 'em fired up' meeting. It was not a recruiting meeting. Nobody was there except people who were already members. Beckwith spoke, and somebody gave a talk on how to make explosives and how to burn a building."

"Crisco, you have anything you want to ask?"

"Yeah. When Beckwith made that statement, Mr. Dennis, did he make it clear he was talking about Medgar Evers?"

"Yes. There was no doubt that he was talking about Medgar Evers. It was specific. We all knew who he was talking about because that's why he was invited to speak. He was a Klan hero. The Klan looked up to him because he had done something. He was there to motivate other Klansmen to be willing to go out and do likewise."

"You say 'other Klansmen.' Was he in the Klan?"

"He had to be or he couldn't have come to that meeting."

"What about as a guest speaker?"

"Naw. We didn't have anything like that. The Klan was no civic club." Delmar laughed.

"I understand," I said, feeling foolish.

"Was there a good turnout for this particular rally?" Crisco asked.

"Yeah."

Crisco continued, "Probably because he was the featured attraction."

"Right, right. He was a draw."

Crisco was through.

"Did you report this to the FBI?" I asked.

"I'm sure that I did. Somewhere in the FBI's files should be what I reported that night because I would be briefed every night after a meeting like that."

"Do you have any idea why the Bureau never came forward with your information, knowing the State of Mississippi was interested in Beckwith's role in the Evers case?"

"Well, there wasn't any cooperation between them. There was more or less a state of hostility between the state authorities and the Bureau. There were a lot of state and local officials that wouldn't cooperate with the FBI. They said, 'You guys get out of here and go back to New York and Washington, and we'll take care of it.' But the attitude of the federal government at that time was 'That's not true. They're not gonna take care of it. They're gonna let it go.'"

"I guess what I'm wondering is, since it was evident the state was trying to do something with Beckwith—"

"They should have helped them," Delmar interrupted. "But they wouldn't have let me do it because they wouldn't have wanted me to surface until I could testify in the Neshoba case."

"When did you surface?"

"At the trial—October '67."

"I asked you if you had any idea why the FBI didn't ever come forward with your information about Beckwith. Why didn't you after you testified in the Neshoba case?"

"I volunteered to help the state in another Klan murder—the Vernon Dahmer murder case in Hattiesburg. I was the first one Sam ever talked to about it. It was within hours after that firebombing death, and the DA in Hattiesburg said, 'I don't want anything to do with him because he's a paid informer and I cannot get a conviction using a paid informer in Mississippi,' and that was his attitude. So I got the impression that nobody in state government or any of the courts in Mississippi wanted me to testify. Remember that the Neshoba case was not a murder trial. It was in federal court for civil rights violations. It was clear to me that Mississippi authorities didn't want anything to do with me."

"Which meant," Crisco interjected, "they didn't want anything to do with the FBI."

"That's true," Delmar agreed.

"Mr. Dennis," I said, "I'd like to know everything you know about Beckwith."

"Well, he believes in the destiny of the white race as reflected in what is known as the Identity Movement in America today, which teaches that the white Anglo-Saxons, and not the Jews, are the real Israelites."

I remembered Beckwith's comment to me during our first phone conversation that he was an Israelite.

Delmar continued, "He believes that people of other races will not be saved eternally because it's only for white people. He's now an ordained minister in that group."

"And how do you know this?"

"Well, I just—I just know it," Delmar said, chuckling.

It was time to learn where we stood with Delmar. "Mr. Dennis, I'm not going to mention your name to anybody, but as you know, Jerry Mitchell knows about our meeting."

"He calls often." Delmar chuckled.

"I can't tell you not to talk to him. I can tell you that whatever you say to him will be printed. Like I was saying, I'm not going to mention your name, but if we rounded up enough evidence and I came to you and said, 'Mr. Dennis, will you testify?' would you?"

Delmar paused, taking a deep breath. I held mine. Only the rustling leaves and the babbling brook could be heard. "I don't know. All I could say today is that I would think it would be right for me to testify, if there was something I thought I could do to help. On the other hand, I did that twenty-five years ago and I have suffered for it ever since; and here I am, fifty years old next week, fixing to ruin the rest of my life. So I'd be very reluctant to do it. I just don't see how I could afford to do it if I had a choice."

"He's just an old man," Benny said.

"That old man is probably the most dangerous of anybody I ever knew in the Klan. I told Jerry Mitchell the other day, 'I'd just rather not get involved in this,' and he said, 'Well, they're thinking about reopening that case.' I said, 'Yeah, and you're gonna mess around down there and get me shot before they even have a trial.' He said, 'Naw, I'm not gonna even use your name.' Then he called back right after I talked to you and he said, 'Well, my editor said it's in the book, so we're gonna use your name.' I said, 'Well, thanks a lot.'"

My mind raced. He didn't say no. In fact, he said it would be the right thing to do and had qualified his reluctance or refusal on if he had a choice. Was he telling me he would testify if subpoenaed? Now was not the time to push it. It would have to wait until all other necessary pieces were gathered, but I had the impression that when it came down to it, Delmar Dennis would be in our corner.

"Mr. Dennis," I said, "I can't ask for more. We're going to keep working and you keep thinking about it."

"You can do one thing for me. Since Brother Mitchell has really fixed me up down there, if you're asked if I am cooperating and will testify, will you say, 'No. He's been scared off'?"

"Sure, no problem." Yep, I really had a positive feeling about Delmar.

I was refortified in that feeling when we got back in the car and Crisco started to turn it around, allowing Delmar to lead us back to civilization. "You know you've got him, don't you?"

"You really think so? What about you, Benny?"

"Hook, line, and damn sinker."

"I hope y'all are right," I said. "I hope y'all are right."

"You can mark it down, man. He won't be able to resist," Crisco assured me.

The ride back to Jackson was much different from the trip up there. The three of us rarely stopped talking. We discussed what we had thus far, including Delmar, and what we needed to do next. Finding witnesses would be difficult, but my investigators were now genuinely excited and downright fired up. The mood had shifted from "what if" to "when" we get this bastard.

Our enthusiasm dampened momentarily as we went through Chattanooga and passed the sign reading, "Signal Mountain Next Exit." What else would we have garnered on our trip if Jerry Mitchell and the *Clarion-Ledger* had kept their word with Delmar?

I never could stay angry with Jerry for long for the simple reason that he would usually follow up on whatever he had done to irk me with some useful information. The episode with Delmar Dennis was no different.

Monday, May 7, was spent, for the most part, returning phone calls and answering letters. Around 4:45 P.M., Jerry called. What balls, I thought. He sounded subdued and asked if I could wait in my office for him. He wanted to see me before I left for home. I was still fuming, but I agreed. Jerry was there at straight-up 5 P.M.. Everyone in the DA's office was leaving for the day. As Doc passed by my office, he stuck his head in the doorway. "Mitchell is out here to see you. What do you want me to tell him?"

"Tell him I'll be there in a minute." I buzzed Crisco on the intercom and asked him to stick around for a few minutes.

I met Jerry in the lobby. He had a large briefcase with him. Once in my office, I shut the door.

"I'm sorry about Delmar—my editors."

"I've already told you what you can tell your editors."

"I know, but I've got to talk to you."

"I'm listening."

"They've taken me off the case." *What a shame.* "I won't go into all of that, but now that I'm off the case, I don't consider some things that I know or have in my possession to be privileged." *Yeah, and some things you know while on the case were evidently not considered privileged either.* I didn't say anything, though, and allowed him to go on. "Anyway, I have something here I think you would be interested in, but I need your word you won't tell where you got it—at least for now."

I promised and he opened his briefcase, revealing three large binders. "What is it?"

He pulled out one of the binders and handed it to me. I flipped it open and read, *"State of Mississippi v. Byron De La Beckwith,* Reporter's Transcript of First Trial, Volume 1 of 3 Volumes—Pages 1–307."

I found my chair, slowly stumbling backward into it, and sat down. "Where in the world did you get this? I've been looking everywhere for this."

"As you can see, it's just a copy, but I thought it would still help you."

"No question, but where did you find it?"

"Myrlie Evers."

"What!" Ed and I had talked about the need for a transcript with her during our first meeting back in December. What was going on here?

"Look, I've got to go, but I'll leave these with you and let you borrow them to make your own copy, if you like. But I need them back tomorrow."

"Sure."

"I've also got some tapes here of an interview I did with Beckwith. There's not really anything on there, just Beckwith and Thelma rambling on about a conspiracy to poison the white race through fluoridation of the public water system."

"Conspiracy of whom?"

"The Jews, of course."

"You gotta be kidding me."

"That's what he says. Anyway, those are just copies, so I don't need them back. Call me tomorrow around noon and I'll come over and pick up the transcript."

Crisco agreed to stay late and make the copies. When I arrived at the office the next day, he had our copy divided into six volumes instead of three—less bulky, he explained.

We had our transcript—another piece of the puzzle, and Myrlie Evers had indirectly provided it. But why send it to Jerry Mitchell and not to us? It was evident she did not entirely trust us. I'm sure she'd had suspicions to begin with. That's the reason I'd unilaterally resolved to phone her every Friday evening, regardless of any progress in the case. If we were going to get anywhere, we had to trust and depend upon each other. But I had to admit, in spite of these weekly calls, it had been Jerry who first broke the news to her about Delmar Dennis. While she clearly trusted Jerry, she did not entirely trust me.

My hunch was later proven correct when she admitted to a reporter for the *Los Angeles Times* that she had waited until she was satisfied with our efforts to reconstruct the case. It was not a situation of "Oh, you need a transcript? I've got one." I understood her misgivings, yet the situation necessitated that I still keep the discovery of the murder weapon from her. The risk was greater than ever that she would confide in Jerry. Once that was done, one need only ask Delmar Dennis what would happen to confidential information.

Crisco and I spent the next couple of days poring over the transcript, listing the witnesses and noting the substance of their testimony. We already knew most of the names from the newspaper articles. The subpoenas in the court file provided some addresses, but not all of the witnesses had been formally subpoenaed. With the transcript, we had the names of all the witnesses, including some we didn't already know about, and addresses for all. Granted, the addresses were twenty-six years old, but it was a start.

Crisco took the list and renewed his efforts at locating everyone, including James Holley and Hollis Creswell, Beckwith's alibi witnesses. He succeeded on Tuesday, May 15. Holley still lived in Greenwood. He was a city alderman, no less. Holley agreed to talk with us in Greenwood the next week. It wouldn't be at his home or city hall. Crisco and I were to call him when we got to town, and he would then tell us where to meet him. His ward had a high percentage of blacks and he did not want it known that he was one of the witnesses who had provided an alibi for the infamous Byron De La Beckwith. According to Holley, his partner, Hollis Creswell, had moved to Maben, a small town east of Greenwood.

Creswell told Crisco he would not meet with us, talk to us, or give us the time of day. He said we were just wasting taxpayer money. Jerry Mitchell had quoted him in an earlier article as saying, "If I see you, Byron De La Beckwith, or the blackest nigger in the country putting gas in his car around the time of a murder, then that's what I'm gonna say."

I sent a letter to the FBI asking for all reports and information the Bureau had on Delmar Dennis. I wanted to see if any of his reports mentioned the Klan meeting near Byram and Beckwith's talk there.

Crisco contacted Richard Barnes, an officer with the Police Mobile Crime Lab Unit, about taking the rough crime-scene sketches of Sanders and Chamblee and enlarging them "to scale" for courtroom use. He also called United Binocular, the distributor of the scope on the murder weapon, to see if it still had the invoice from the sale to John Goza, who had, in turn, traded it to Beckwith. The owner, Mr. L. J. Thomas, told Crisco that he personally gave the invoice to the FBI in 1963 and had not kept a copy.

While Crisco was busy in these endeavors, I focused on absorbing every word of the transcript. Our work was briefly interrupted by national media attention. Ed and I were contacted by ABC's *Primetime Live.* The show was doing a segment on the case and wanted to interview us. We agreed, so it was set up for Wednesday, May 16, in the courthouse. I asked for some parameters, if not the actual questions, of our interview. The producer would not provide the questions, but he did furnish a list of topics the show wished to discuss: the case against Beckwith in 1964, the atmosphere of the trials, new revelations about the Sovereignty Commission, what would be needed to have a third trial, the status of our investigation, Beckwith's record, missing evidence, and transcripts.

The interview was conducted in the law library on the third floor of the courthouse. The questions were rather accusatory. The DA's office, I felt, was being put on trial: "Why aren't you reprosecuting Beckwith?" We gave general assurances that we were working hard, but, as yet, simply did not have enough evidence to go to a grand jury. That much was true, but still not wanting Beckwith to know just how tightly the rope was slowly wrapping around his neck, we gave no specific information.

Ed fielded most of the questions, one of which was "Do you have the gun?"

"No," Ed responded.

Until then, we had only kept silent about the murder weapon's discovery. Now, though, our denial was an asserted lie on national television. I felt a quickening in the pit of my stomach. Like Ed, I still felt it was a necessary, but uncomfortable, strategy.

We were asked about Delmar Dennis. Wouldn't his testimony about

Beckwith's confession be enough? Honoring Delmar's request if I was asked such a question, I said that Jerry's article had scared him off and that he would have nothing to do with us.

We were quizzed about Rev. R. L. T. Smith and Willie Osborne, who, according to the *Primetime* people, claimed to have seen Beckwith at a mass meeting in a local church earlier on the evening of the murder. If true, it would have shot down Beckwith's alibi. I had grave doubts about these claims, though.

The Reverend Mr. Smith had met with Detectives Sanders and Chamblee as early as June 19, 1963. Although it was before Beckwith's arrest, he had assured them that he would do anything that he could to help them in the investigation. He even volunteered to "go out and try to find any loose talk that is going around" and report anything that he heard. If he truly saw Beckwith, as the TV folks told Ed and me, why didn't he tell that to the detectives? It would certainly have been more substantial than "loose talk." Yet, the police report was silent concerning any information that the Reverend Mr. Smith might have had.

I was also hesitant about using these new claims because they were not "new" at all. Doris Allison and Alphanette Bracey had made the same claims in 1963, yet Allison picked out the wrong photo from a police photo spread. Bracey said that the man she'd seen at the mass meeting was the same one she'd seen at Evers's office on June 11, the man police had identified as being from Flint, Michigan. Another reason for my skepticism was that neither the Reverend Mr. Smith nor Willie Osborne had contacted our office. It was certainly no secret by then that we had reopened the case and were attempting to see if it was reprosecutable.

I didn't automatically discount these claims, but relying on them would put our case on shaky ground. The inconsistencies would be ammunition the defense could use to shoot down the testimony of these witnesses. Nevertheless, we would check into it some more.

Immediately following the interview, I asked Crisco to contact the Reverend Mr. Smith and Willie Osborne. Osborne agreed to talk with us at ten-thirty the next morning at his house. The Reverend Mr. Smith said that he needed a letter outlining what we needed to discuss with him. That, in itself, was strange, but we sent him a letter that day.

Crisco and I met Willie Osborne as scheduled. He stated that, when he arrived at the mass meeting, "this man that they say was Beckwith was standing in the back of the church with his foot propped against the wall," and he left out of the back door prior to Osborne's leaving. He couldn't remember if other white males were there as well, but he said that it was not unusual for whites to attend such meetings.

"Why didn't you ever go to the police and tell them—especially after the first trial and it came out in the paper that Beckwith was saying he was in Greenwood all night—'He's lying. I saw him in Jackson at my church that night'?"

"I couldn't say why, but I wasn't called as a witness."

"Well, how would the DA know to call you as a witness if you didn't let somebody know what you saw?"

"I just didn't bother about it."

Osborne told us about another man, Frank Conic, who also saw Beckwith that night at the church. He gave us Conic's address and phone number. We told Osborne we would like to go by his church and just look around. He telephoned his pastor and arranged it for the next morning.

When we arrived at New Jerusalem Church, Crisco and I were greeted by Osborne, his pastor, the Reverend Mr. Lofton, and last, but not least, a camera crew from *Primetime Live*. We kept the visit short.

Crisco contacted Frank Conic, who agreed to talk with us in our office on Monday morning. He was seventy-nine years old, and although he had never been a member of New Jerusalem Church, he was there for the meeting the night of June 11, 1963. According to Conic, a man he believed to be Beckwith stood on the east side of the church; not the back, as Willie Osborne had recalled. Already the two witnesses were in conflict. If I put on one man to testify, the defense would put on the other and eat our lunch.

When pressed if the man might have stood at the back of the church, Conic was firm that it was the east side. He knew because the man left through the entrance on that side after Medgar Evers issued an invitation to him: "Won't you come sit down, brother, down here in the front? There's room here for you." Asked why he had not shared this information with the police or the FBI in 1963, Conic stated that "the climate of the situation" caused him and a lot of people to remain silent. "Really," he explained, "I thought it was a helpless cause. It didn't matter what evidence or how much evidence they had; no jury in Mississippi at that time was gonna convict him, anyway."

Included in the morning mail was a letter from the Reverend Mr. Smith, agreeing to meet with us on "Monday, May 28, 1990, at 9:00 A.M., at 403 South State Street, in the office of Attorney Isaac Byrd, Jr. I am willing to cooperate with you fully. God Bless America," signed "Robert

L. T. Smith." Since that date fell on Memorial Day, we agreed to meet the day after.

Crisco and I went to the movies Tuesday morning, May 22, but not at a theater. We were back at the archives building watching newsreel after newsreel of anything that pertained to civil rights in Mississippi from June 12, 1963, to mid-April of 1964. The news-film collection was indexed generally by subject matter, but not specifically enough to afford us the luxury of fast-forwarding to only what we wanted. We found some footage of the Evers house, yard, and carport taken the night of the murder. Nothing was shown that was not in Captain Hargrove's photographs, but we isolated the segment anyway.

We also viewed a segment showing Beckwith arriving back at the Hinds County jail from his stay in Rankin County during the litigation concerning his mental examination. Clad in a dapper-looking dark suit, white, French-cuffed shirt, and cuff links, instead of prison stripes, he smiled and joked with reporters and deputies between puffs on a big cigar. He looked more like a movie star strolling down the red carpet at a premiere than an inmate at a booking desk. I've never seen a more sinister-looking grin. The other shots were of brief interviews with the lawyers for both sides coming and going on the courthouse steps. We gave the curator a list of the segments we wanted, and he agreed to have them copied on standard VHS tape for us.

I took a copy of James Holley's 1964 testimony home that night to study. Crisco and I were to meet him the following morning, and I wanted to be able to compare his comments to us with his sworn testimony twenty-six years earlier. I did not plan on confronting him with his prior testimony just yet, though. I didn't want to give him an opportunity to explain away any conflicts. The confrontation would come later. For now, I would not even let him know we had a copy of his testimony. I'd play dumb and let him believe that I was merely looking for long-lost information. In truth, I would be making mental notes of conflicts in his story, to be exposed in a more crucial setting.

The most damaging thing for us would be if Holley simply said "I don't remember" to every question we asked. It was vital, in overcoming a speedy-trial challenge later, that Beckwith be able to present the same defense as he did in 1964: an alibi. The prosecution would be derailed if that defense was no longer available because all of his witnesses claimed they could not remember the events to which they had testified earlier. The significance would not be lost on Beckwith's lawyers. Once he was reindicted and lawyers talked to Holley and Creswell, I feared, the ex-cops would suffer memory loss, whether or not they truly remembered. It would be the easy out for them and would help Beckwith.

Even if there were no conflicts in their stories, just capturing a story, whatever it was, on tape now was important. If they subsequently claimed a total lapse of memory, we could show that the lapse did not occur over the past quarter century, but rather since Beckwith's lawyers had talked with them.

Crisco put his Blazer on cruise control and could very well have set it on automatic pilot, if it were equipped with such, for Highway 49 extended straight in a single direction. We zipped past the fields of cotton and soybeans, as well as the growing number of commercial catfish ponds. Humphreys County, Mississippi, is the Catfish Capital of the World.

We crossed numerous muddy creeks and rivers, meandering slowly but surely on their journey toward Ole Man River—the Mississippi. As we approached one river bridge in Holmes County, I recognized it as the one pictured in an old article of Hazel Brannon Smith's paper, the *Lexington Advertiser*. Following Beckwith's release in 1964, some supporters had strung a banner across the top of the span proclaiming: "Welcome Home DeLay." The photo accompanied a scathing editorial by Mrs. Smith denouncing the gesture.

Around 10:45 A.M., we pulled into a Charter convenience store just inside the southern city limits of Greenwood, on Martin Luther King Drive. Crisco went to a pay phone outside to call Holley. I went inside the store to get a couple of cans of Dr Pepper.

Before long, a truck, driven by a heavyset guy with a crew cut, pulled alongside us. Crisco and I got out and approached it. Holley stayed seated. After brief introductions, I asked him where we could talk.

"Right here will be fine," he replied as he got out of his truck and started walking to the Blazer. He climbed into the front passenger seat and shut the door. Crisco and I exchanged bewildered looks, then got in, too—Crisco at the wheel and me on the backseat.

Before we could say anything else, Holley instructed Crisco to back up farther on the parking lot. Our position by the pay phone, he said, was too visible. Crisco eased the Blazer as far back as we could go, right next to a big Dumpster, flies buzzing, with the rancid odor of its contents wreaking havoc on our collective olfactory nerves.

Yet, I was less offended by the stench of our environs than I was by the presence of our company. I wanted to get our business done and be on our way home. I nodded to Crisco to turn on the tape recorder.

James Holley was now sixty-one and had retired from the Greenwood Police Department, as a captain, in 1981. He had put in twenty years before calling it quits. Thus, I calculated, as of the original investigation and trials, he had only been on the force for a couple of years. According to Holley, he and his partner, Hollis Creswell, normally went on duty at 11 P.M. The night or morning of the murder, he told us, they were on routine patrol in the south part of town. Creswell was driving and "one of us needed cigarettes." He couldn't remember if it was Creswell or himself—both men were smokers. I recalled that he had testified that he had wanted the cigarettes. They went south, "right by here on Main Street," he indicated to us, "down to the Billups service station."

"I'm turned around. I thought that was Martin Luther King," I said.

"Back then it was Main Street. It's the same street. The name has just been changed. If you keep going south, it changes to Highway 49, and then when you get to Jackson, it changes to—well, it was Delta Drive years ago. I don't recall what it is now."

He looked flustered. I thought I'd help him out. "Medgar Evers."

"What?"

"The street. It's Medgar Evers Boulevard now."

"Oh."

The irony escaped him that the route connecting Beckwith's hometown with Medgar Evers's home was named after Evers on one end and Martin Luther King on the other.

Holley continued. Creswell and he went to the Billups station because it never closed. As they were pulling out to leave, he noticed "DeLay's car and DeLay standing by it, while the attendant pumped gas in it at the Shell station, which was just north of the Billups." He was not sure how late the Shell stayed open.

Holley couldn't remember the name of the attendant who he claimed gassed up Beckwith's car, but he said he was a white guy who had worked there for a long time. I was curious why the attendant had not been called as an alibi witness, too, unless he had either moved away before the trials in 1964 or was otherwise hard to locate. Neither was the case. Holley said it would not have been hard at all to talk to him and have him subpoenaed to testify back then. Yet, he had not been called, nor, as far as Holley knew, had the defense even talked with him. The guy who allegedly waited on Beckwith and pumped gas in his car at the time of the murder was ignored? If there were an ounce of truth in Beckwith's alibi, the defense wouldn't have passed up the chance to put on the attendant standing next to Beckwith instead of two witnesses who saw him from the next parking lot.

Holley couldn't remember if Beckwith had seen them and waved, and with no prompting from me, he volunteered that he had had no reason to have really paid any attention to Beckwith. Holley could not recall anything else that had occurred that night: no particular calls while on duty nor anyone they saw. The passing years did not account for this inability. On cross-examination in 1964, he had given Waller the same answers, in addition to testifying that he could not remember whether he saw Beckwith on June eighth, June ninth, or any other particular night. Waller asked him, "When do you recall having seen Mr. Beckwith at any specified time and place," other than June 12, 1963? "I don't," Holley answered.

The only time he remembered seeing Beckwith was at 1:05 A.M., June 12, 1963. The only person he remembered seeing on patrol on June 12, 1963, was Beckwith. Yet, the only thing Beckwith did to leave such an indelible mark on Holley's memory was to have gas put in his car. Why would that stand out in Holley's mind and immediately be recalled ten days later? After all, Holley acknowledged in his 1964 testimony that he had not seen anything different than he had "with a thousand other people that I know and run into quite often in the line of duty." Creswell's story was the same. Although he refused to talk with us, he testified in 1964 that he never had any contact with Beckwith—"never anything other than just passing."

Holley told Crisco and me that he and Creswell had left the Billups while Beckwith was still getting gas next door at the Shell. They went north on Main Street a short distance to Bracci Dantone's Grocery and got a sandwich. Holley explained that he knew it was about five minutes after 1 A.M. because he asked Creswell what time it was. Dantone usually closed between 1:15 and 2 A.M., and they wanted to get a sandwich before he closed. Since it was so close to one-fifteen, they "hustled" from the Billups and went "straight" to Dantone's. That version differed from his trial testimony, in which he swore that they left the Billups, going north, and "made a round uptown and came back to the store and ate supper."

Creswell had testified that after leaving the Billups "we drove uptown, and as we went by Bracci's—he was out front—I hollered and told Bracci, 'Don't close up. We will be back in a few minutes.'" I asked Holley if they went anywhere else on patrol before going to Dantone's.

"No," he said, they were in a hurry to get to the grocery store before it closed, and no, they did not see Bracci Dantone that night until they actually went inside to eat.

The cops first heard of Evers's murder sometime later that same

123

morning on the car radio before they went off duty at 7 A.M. They didn't
know Beckwith was a suspect until his arrest ten days later and immediately knew, according to Holley, that DeLay couldn't have done it.

"With that in mind, did you report what you knew to anyone?"

"We didn't contact anyone. DeLay's lawyer contacted us. He told us
not to discuss it until it came trial time." Holley explained that Hardy
Lott, Beckwith's chief lawyer, just meant not to discuss it with anyone
outside of law enforcement circles, and in fact, Holley claimed that he
had told Fred Sanders exactly what he had told us. In his 1964 testimony,
Holley swore he did *not* tell anyone with law enforcement because they
did not ask, and that he had never met, much less talked to, Fred Sanders
or any other Jackson police officer.

Creswell, in his testimony, admitted knowing Sanders and Chamblee.
Holley's current statements were in conflict with his prior testimony and
with that of his partner, Creswell. We were on a roll.

I moved on to another topic with Holley. "Do you know anything
about Beckwith being in the Klan?"

"He could have been; he could *not* have been."

"What about you?"

"What about me?"

"You ever been in the Klan?"

"No, sir."

"Was Beckwith in the Citizens' Council?"

"I really wouldn't know about that."

"Hardy Lott?"

"I really wouldn't know about that."

I remembered reading in the police report that the Citizens' Council
had a legal defense fund for Beckwith and had placed a big jar labeled for
that purpose in various establishments in town, including the Crystal
Grill, a popular local restaurant.

"Citizens' Council Legal Defense Fund?"

"I really wouldn't know about that."

"I read that Beckwith caused some trouble here, handing out literature
at his Episcopal church, condemning the church's stand against segregation. Did you ever hear anything about that?"

"I'm a Baptist. I don't mingle in their affairs."

"I also read that he stood guard, armed, at the Greyhound bus station
here to make sure it stayed segregated, and the police had to ask him to
leave."

"I really wouldn't know about that."

"Is Thorn McIntyre still around?" Crisco asked.

"I think. He's a farmer over around Itta Bena," Holley replied, referring to one of the many Delta communities with Indian names. "I can't tell you much more than that. I really"—Crisco and I joined in finishing his singsong answer—"wouldn't know about that."

"Well," Crisco said, "tell us where a good place to eat would be."

"The Crystal Grill is your best bet. I've eaten there for years and it's always good."

Right, I thought, *and not once did you ever see that jar for old DeLay's defense fund sitting by the cash register there.*

"Great," I said.

Holley gave us directions, then volunteered to take us by the old Billups and Shell stations. That took only a few minutes, and then we dropped him back off at his truck at the Charter. With a wave, Crisco and I bid him adieu.

At the Crystal Grill, I made another decision over an excellent selection of fish. When we went to a grand jury, Holley and Creswell would be there. I'd subpoena both of them. Each occasion they talked, some points in their versions differed, conflicting with each other and, in Holley's case, with his own previous testimony. A grand jury presentation would give us a third opportunity to catch Holley in some discrepancy and a second shot for Creswell. Besides, I wasn't going to let Creswell get by with refusing to talk to us. He would have his discussion with Ed, the Silver Fox, in front of eighteen grand jurors.

Crisco and I returned to Jackson that afternoon pleased with the interview with Holley. Upon our return to the office, Crisco called directory assistance to see if Thorn McIntyre was listed in Itta Bena. There was a McIntyre listing, but not for Thorn. Crisco tried it anyway, and it turned out to be a relative who was cooperative. According to the relative, things had gotten difficult for Thorn following the 1964 trials, when it became known that he had provided the police with the first information linking Beckwith to the murder. Finally, in 1972, he left his farm in Itta Bena and moved to Alabama. Crisco contacted him on Friday. He had stuck his neck out before, at great sacrifice, and he was willing to do it again. Needless to say, I had a good progress report to give to Mrs. Evers that week.

Monday, May 28, was Memorial Day, and all government offices were closed. The next morning, at nine-fifteen, Benny accompanied Crisco and me to meet with Rev. R. L. T. Smith at Isaac Byrd's law office.

The Reverend Mr. Smith was eighty-seven years old and had a difficult time hearing us during much of the interview. He stated that he was at the mass meeting at the New Jerusalem Church the night of Evers's murder, along with well over a hundred other people. Medgar, according to Smith, came in late looking terribly worried, stayed only for a few minutes, then left. Smith saw the man he later recognized as Beckwith on the east side of the church. That point differed from Willie Osborne's account, which placed Beckwith along the rear or south wall. Smith's fit with Conic's recollection, but Smith said Beckwith "was sitting." According to Conic, Beckwith was standing and left when Evers offered him a seat in the front row. Smith told us Evers said nothing to Beckwith.

When Beckwith's picture appeared in the paper following his arrest, Smith immediately recognized him as the man he had seen at the mass meeting.

"Did you tell anybody with the FBI or the police department about that?"

"Well, no. I didn't because I didn't trust the police department or the FBI."

Crisco had obtained a mug shot taken of Beckwith following his arrest, along with black-and-white mug shots of four other inmates from the same time, all with similar physical characteristics. He showed the photo spread to the Reverend Mr. Smith, who identified an inmate in one of the filler photos as the man most resembling the individual he had seen at the meeting.

I'm convinced that the Reverend Mr. Smith, Osborne, and Conic meant well and truly believed they had seen Byron De La Beckwith at that meeting. Maybe they did, and maybe if some of our jurors were black or liberal-minded whites, they would appreciate the mistrust of the three of the investigating authorities and their silence in the 1960s. The jury, though, would not include solely that genre.

A seasoned defense attorney could attack this testimony on several fronts. Ed and I decided we couldn't risk putting them on the stand if we wanted to win.

Wednesday morning, June 6, Ed asked what I thought about appointing Patricia Bennett as a special prosecutor in the Beckwith case to work in conjunction with our office. Pat, a former ADA and federal prosecutor, now a law school professor, is African-American. My facial expression must have reflected my thoughts. "It's just an idea," he said. "Think about it."

I did. In fact, I thought about little else the rest of the day. I liked Pat okay and her ability was no issue. I kept asking myself, though: *Why a special prosecutor?* Nobody in the office had a conflict, and I felt that Crisco, Benny, Doc, and I had made tremendous progress. I couldn't see any practical advantage in having a special prosecutor.

Was there a political advantage? Not that I could see. The case needed to be prosecuted by whites for at least two reasons: (1) just because it was the right thing to do—to set matters straight, so to speak; and (2) if a black special prosecutor, Pat Bennett or anyone else, came in at that juncture, the black community would claim that nothing had been done with the case until one of their own got involved, which simply was not true.

The only political advantage would have been if we were *not* going to reopen the case. If a well-respected black prosecutor decided that the case was going nowhere, how could the black community complain? But we *were* making progress, and I expected to present the case to a grand jury for a new indictment by the fall. The investigators and I had put in too much work to do otherwise.

It occurred to me that Ed might have been trying to protect me from the political fallout that would come with the case, regardless of the outcome. After all, Ed knew I hoped to be a judge someday. If that was his motivation, I appreciated the concern, but I couldn't shelve my beliefs for political expediency. I strongly believed that, to win, the case had to be prosecuted as any other murder case, which meant that the prosecutors who would normally tackle a murder case needed to be the ones to take on Beckwith. I concluded my journal that night with this resolution: "I'm going to ride this one out for better or worse. It's just the right thing to do."

Thursday morning, I had barely got seated at my desk, sipping on the ever-present cup of coffee, when Jeanie buzzed me and said that I had a call. *Great, it's started already,* I thought. It's always the days when you have the most to do that the interrupting phone calls never end. I couldn't even finish my first cup of coffee. I needed to start preparing for a capital-murder case coming up soon. A young girl's stepfather, C. W. Taylor, who was separated from the girl's mother, had lured her out of the house one summer day in 1989, killed her, and left her body in a bean field.

I snatched up the phone. "Hello," I gruffly said.

"Is this Assistant District Attorney Bobby DeLaughter?"

"Yes, it is." Which would it be? A caller wanting to know why I was wasting taxpayer money by prosecuting "that old man," or one wanting to know what we were waiting on to retry him? I braced myself, but it did little good. I still almost flipped over in my chair when she identified herself.

"This is Thelma Beckwith."

I wished that one of my investigators was there as a witness to what was said, but they were out serving subpoenas for my capital-murder trial. They also had the tape recorders.

"Mrs. Beckwith, I'm glad to listen to anything you say, but I hope you understand that I have a job to do, so I won't be doing much talking."

"You're not doing your job. If you were, you wouldn't be putting DeLay through all of this. You're just trying to satisfy the niggers. DeLay is a fine man, a good man. He's well respected up here."

If that was the case, Signal Mountain had to be a hotbed of the Klan or the Identity Movement. She continued, "He gives talks all over the state." Spreading his poison, no doubt. "He's having his book published in thirty days, and then you and everyone will know who is behind all of this."

"Behind all of what?"

"Of killing that nigger Evers."

"And who is really behind it, Mrs. Beckwith?"

"The Jews."

"The Jews killed Medgar Evers?"

"They didn't pull the trigger, but they're behind it."

"Well, who pulled the trigger?"

"DeLay's book will be out in thirty days. Read it yourself."

"I'd love to."

"I will tell you DeLay didn't do it."

"How do you know that?"

"I asked him."

"How long have you known him?"

"I met DeLay seven years ago, and there isn't a finer man alive, but all of this is just about to get him. He's been in good health, enjoying his visits with all the reporters who came up here to see him, and he was even looking forward so much to talk with you when you called, but that crew from ABC that was up here yesterday really upset him—so much so that he's at Vanderbilt Medical Center now. He'd have a fit if he knew I called you. A lawyer friend warned us about talking to you, but I just want you to know some things about DeLay."

"I'd love to know all about him, Mrs. Beckwith."

"You would?"

"Absolutely."

"Well, I've got copies of a lot of things he's written and things that have been written about him. If I send them to you, will you read them?"

"Oh, yes, ma'am. I assure you that I will carefully read every word."

"You'd really be interested in that?"

"I would be most interested in reading everything you can put your hands on about your husband and the kind of person he is." I gave her the office address and assured her that I looked forward to receiving her

Aerial view of the scene, June 12, 1963. The Evers home is at the top of the photo. The dots denote the locations of Evers and Beckwith at the time the shot was fired. *X* marks the spot where Beckwith's car was seen earlier by witnesses at Joe's Drive-In (the building in the foreground on the left) and Pittman's Grocery (the building in the foreground on the right). *(Photo by Jackson Police Department)*

Beckwith's view of the Evers home from the spot where the shot was fired. *(Photo by Jackson Police Department, June 12, 1963)*

The Evers home, Medgar's Oldsmobile, and Myrlie's station wagon,
at 2332 Guynes Street, taken shortly after the murder.
(Photo by Jackson Police Department, June 12, 1963)

Trail of blood and T-shirts indicating the path
and distance Medgar crawled after being
gunned down. "Jim Crow Must Go" was
printed on the shirts, referring to the segregation laws that formed the racial barriers Evers
and others were attempting to tear down.
*(Photo by Jackson Police Department, June 12,
1963)*

Pool of blood in the Evers's carport, at the
base of the steps to the doorway, indicating
where Medgar collapsed and was found by
his wife, Myrlie, and his children, Darrell,
Reena, and Van. *(Photo by Jackson Police
Department, June 12, 1963)*

Bullet hole in the lower left pane of the front window at the Evers house. After passing through Medgar, the .30-06 bullet tore through the house, entering at this point. *(Photo by Jackson Police Department, June 12, 1963)*

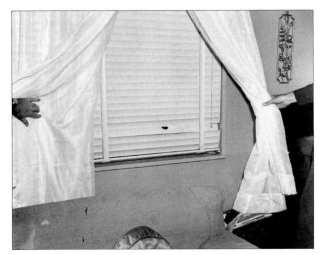

Interior view of the front window. The bullet hole is in the fourth slat from the bottom of the venetian blinds. *(Photo by Jackson Police Department, June 12, 1963)*

After passing through the front window, the bullet crossed the living room and entered this interior wall, which separates the living room from the kitchen. The hole is in the center of the wall, below the plaque and to the right of the electrical switch. *(Photo by Jackson Police Department, June 12, 1963)*

The bullet blew out this ceramic tile above the toaster upon entering the kitchen and then crossed the kitchen. *(Photo by Jackson Police Department, June 12, 1963)*

The bullet next struck the center of the refrigerator and ricocheted to the right at a forty-five-degree angle. *(Photo by Jackson Police Department, June 12, 1963)*

The pen on the countertop indicates where the bullet came to rest and was recovered by Jackson detectives. *(Photo by Jackson Police Department, June 12, 1963)*

Ground view of Joe's Drive-In (or Lee's). Witnesses had seen Beckwith's car earlier in the far right corner of the parking lot. *(Photo by Jackson Police Department, June 12, 1963)*

Det. L. C. Bennett Sr. (the father of one of DeLaughter's investigators, Benny Bennett) points to the location in the honeysuckle vines where Beckwith's rifle was found later in the morning of the murder. The opening in the trees and brush to the left leads to the corner of the parking lot of Joe's Drive-In, where Beckwith's car had been seen earlier. *(Photo by Jackson Police Department, June 12, 1963)*

Capt. Ralph Hargrove took this photo of Det. O. M. Luke as Luke retrieved the Enfield .30-06 from the honeysuckle vines. *(Photo by Jackson Police Department, June 12, 1963)*

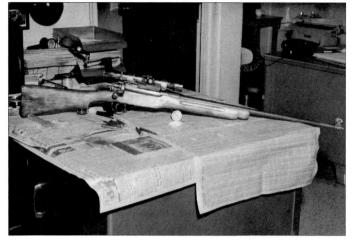

Beckwith's Enfield .30-06 rifle on the desk of Capt. Ralph Hargrove, who found and lifted a fingerprint from the front area of the scope. *(Photo by Jackson Police Department, June 12, 1963)*

This photo, taken by Hargrove, shows the actual fingerprint on the scope prior to his lifting it for evidence and comparison. The print was subsequently identified as that of the right index finger of Byron De La Beckwith VI. *(Photo by Jackson Police Department, June 12, 1963)*

Front view of Beckwith's 1962 white Plymouth Valiant on the police impound lot following his arrest. DeLaughter had crime lab technicians focus on the rearview mirror area in this photo to ascertain if an emblem, described by two witnesses as a Shriners' emblem, could be seen. *(Photo by Jackson Police Department, June 12, 1963)*

Rear and side views of
Beckwith's Valiant. The "whiplike" antenna described by witnesses is on the rear passenger
side, folded down. *(Photo by
Jackson Police Department,
June 12, 1963)*

Computer-enhanced photo of the rearview mirror in
Beckwith's Valiant showing the sword, crescent moon,
and star of what witnesses referred to as a "Shriners'
emblem." This emblem is what was best remembered
about the car by two teenage boys. *(Photo by Jackson Police
Department, June 12, 1963)*

Beckwith, shortly after his 1963
arrest. *(Photo by Jackson Police
Department, June 12, 1963)*

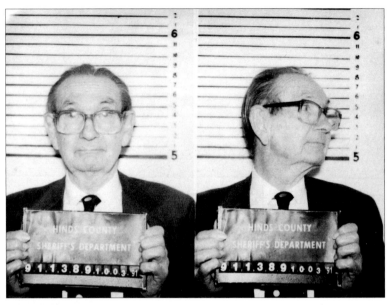

Beckwith's mug shot, taken when he was booked in the Hinds County Sheriff's Office following his extradition on October 3, 1991. *(Photo by Hinds County Sheriff's Office)*

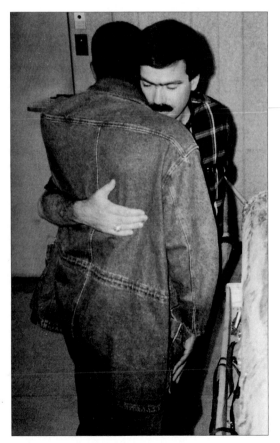

Bobby DeLaughter and Van Evers, following a private moment gladly given for Van to be with his father at the Albany Medical Center in June 1991, shortly before a second autopsy was performed by noted forensic pathologist Michael Baden. *(Photo by New York State Police)*

package and reading his book when it came out. I wondered if it might still be named *My Goat, Your Ass and the Republic.*

"Oh," she kept on, "I almost forgot to tell you. DeLay didn't even know that informant. DeLay said he only saw him once at some kind of meeting."

Bingo, Mrs. Beckwith! And I bet it was a Klan meeting near the Byram swinging bridge, just as Delmar Dennis said.

"Where was that meeting?"

"He didn't say." The conversation quickly ended.

The rest of the day was spent working on the Taylor case. At the close of the day, I had a talk with Ed, explaining my feelings about a special prosecutor. He understood and said that it was just a possibility that he had wanted me to consider; if I didn't think it was a good idea, that was fine. The subject never came up again.

By this time, my calls to Myrlie Evers were more frequent—no longer just every Friday evening. That Thursday night I called her to bring her up-to-date and to check on her emotional well-being. The twenty-seventh anniversary of the murder was coming up the next Tuesday, and Father's Day commercials were running on television. It would be a tough time for her. I was sorry to learn that she was down with a back injury. We talked for about forty-five minutes. She found my conversation with Thelma Beckwith the most interesting development. We both expressed the hope that Miz Thelma continued to stand by her man and come to his defense with the utmost zeal, bombarding me with every piece of paper and other information concerning him that she could find.

On Monday, June 11, I thought about how twenty-seven years ago, to the day, was the last day Medgar Evers saw his family and they him. And the guy responsible had eluded conviction by the criminal justice system for twenty-seven years, continuing to spew his venom in a most arrogant manner. It wasn't right. Somebody had to knock him off that mountain and have him pay the price. He had enjoyed himself too long at the expense of the Evers family and Mississippi, and he had spit in the eye of the criminal justice system, to which I had devoted so much of myself.

When I got to the office, I found that Thelma Beckwith's package had arrived. It contained a résumé of sorts, dated January 25, 1987, and addressed "To Whom It May Concern, Ref: Currently seeking full and complete citizenship in TN & U.S.A." Beckwith, it said, was born on November 9, 1920, in Colusa, California, so he was sixty-nine years old. He had married Mary Louise Williams of Knoxville, Tennessee, in 1945, but the marriage ended in 1965, a year after his trials for murdering Medgar Evers. Concerning those trials, the résumé stated: "Twice tried for the murder of a Negra, Medgar Evers, Executive Secretary of Mississippi NAACP, with two hung juries to my favor, 1963, 1964—the case later passed to the files."

The following year, in addition to what was apparently the final dissolution of his marriage to Mary Louise Williams (I recalled the subpoenas that I had found in the court file for what appeared to be documents indicating a tumultuous relationship between Beckwith and "Willie," as he called her), Beckwith was subpoenaed to appear before the House Un-American Activities Committee (HUAC). "In 1965, 25 business and professional men, planters and retired veterans were ordered before the HCUA [sic], in Washington, D.C., as accused White Knights of the KKK of Mississippi leaders. . . . We returned to Mississippi in several days—all at government expense—with honor and dignity—no charges pending, of course." They all claimed "the Fifth," refusing to answer any questions.

The résumé said that Beckwith "served on the membership committee for years of the Greenwood Citizens' Council" and further claimed that he had "come from a long line of old Southern aristocracy and of nobility." In fact, Miz Thelma's package included an old postcard from Greenwood. It had a drawing of the Confederate monument that Crisco and I had seen there. The shrine had the figure of a lady tending a wounded soldier, and someone (probably Mrs. Beckwith) had written on the card that the lady was Beckwith's grandmother—the one who was a friend of Jefferson Davis's wife, Varina.

Beckwith's résumé stated that he was "constantly polically [sic] active" and "ran a good first time race for Lt. Governor of Mississippi in 1967—did not come in last of 6 all white and Christian candidates." It would have been during that campaign that Imperial Wizard Sam Bowers sent Beckwith to seek help from Delmar Dennis. A copy of a speech Beckwith must have made along the campaign trail offered some insight into the man:

> Everybody knows what my platform is. It's absolute white supremacy under Protestant Christian rule. . . . I'm not trying to please everybody; I don't want the "Nigger" vote. . . . Nothing, absolutely nothing, is more important to me than your race and your color and your creed, and I want to help you preserve these things. . . . As one of our past presidents said, "We need to do something constructive for this country." This is the sort of construction I'd like to see going on in Mississippi. We ought to erect a gallows here and there on which to hang a half dozen of those grizzly anti-

white, treasoning [*sic*] renegades, parading about our state. It won't take many public executions of these criminals before we will have completely flushed the commode on the entire black power in Mississippi. . . . Ladies and gentlemen, this grand and glorious republic, the United States of America, was founded for the white man, by the white man, and was meant to be preserved for the white man's prosperity. Our forefathers did not intend to smear this country with the Japanese, with the Negro or with the Eskimo. Furthermore, it was our Anglo-Saxon race who understands our constitution and it is only you and I who qualify to live under it or to rule by its authority.

Beckwith, according to his résumé, was an active Episcopalian until 1967, when he joined the First Independent Methodist Church of Greenwood, Mississippi. Since 1975, though, he had become "increasingly active in the Identity branch of Christian service as it is more in accord with my background and my motto, 'on the white right Christian side of every issue.' No exceptions." Among the papers with the résumé was a copy of an award or certificate, evidently from one of these Identity groups, as it spoke of the "Nation of Yahveh." The certificate of award, dated January 25, 1990 (less than six months earlier), read:

For and in consideration and recognition of uncommon valor and bravery, in the face of innumerable enemies, the recipient hereof has consistently and valiantly acted in defense of the true cause of Christ. For these and other honorable considerations, Byron De La Beckwith, VI, is hereby awarded "The Southern Cross of Valor" . . . by the grateful Nation of Yahveh, our Father, on behalf of our Chief Captain of our salvation, in the brotherhood of the White Stone.

In June 1983, Beckwith married Thelma Lindsay Neff, a nurse. The couple served "on the Board of Policy of 'The Spotlight,' a rightest [*sic*], Washington, DC publication." Mrs. Beckwith enclosed a 1987 edition of that publication, obviously a white supremacy newspaper. One article, which she had circled, condemned Beckwith's firearms or explosives conviction in Louisiana in the early 1970s. He had been arrested while transporting a live bomb in the trunk of his car from Jackson to New Orleans. His target was the home of Adolph Botnick, head of the Anti-Defamation League. He was first tried in federal court for crossing state lines with a bomb and was acquitted. The State of Louisiana then brought him to trial on charges of possessing an explosive device without a permit: two different sovereigns, two different charges, therefore no double jeopardy. He was convicted and served time in Angola Penitentiary. The résumé spoke of this chapter in Beckwith's life:

In 1973–74, I was tried in federal court in New Orleans, LA by a [sic] 11 member white, Christian jury having one old darkie on it and a darkie as an alternate for 5 days, by 2 Federal prosecuters [sic] who heaped enough charges on me to choke the mouth of the Mississippi River. After much deliberation, the jury returned a unanimous, polled verdict of not guilty of any charge whatsoever—to return home with dignity and honor. One year later was caused to return to Orleans Parish, New Orleans to be retried on the same charges by a jury of only 5 Negra women and a Jewish prosecutor who in less than 2 days, gave me 5 years plus $1,000 fine—the fine was suspended and after the Louisiana Supreme Court ruled against me 5 to one—then I was caused to serve my time in Louisiana Penitentiary at Angola, LA. . . . A jury of my peers—ha! Finally, I was expelled January 13, 1980 on good behavior!!

Miz Thelma's enclosures were intended to convince me that the grandson of a Confederate heroine, convicted for attempting to bomb a prominent Jewish leader's house, and author of racist statements, could not possibly kill a black civil rights activist. Was I missing something?

Crisco decided to take the rest of the week off and go with his family to Tampa. He could stay at his in-laws' place and play golf. He also planned to visit with Richard Poppleton, the former ballistics expert for the FBI who testified in the 1964 trials.

When I got home Tuesday evening, there was a message on the answering machine from reporter Ed Bryson. The first segment of a special would be on Channel 3's six-o'clock news. For the first time, I heard someone from the media say that the prosecutors were serious about gathering enough evidence to reprosecute the case. The segment that night dealt mainly with Evers's work leading up to his murder.

On Wednesday, the second segment of Channel 3's special included an interview I had given to Bryson and one that Bryson had had with Beckwith. It was tough keeping quiet about the gun and the crime-scene photos, but the chances of winning the war later were better if we stuck to the game plan. Beckwith was still running his mouth to reporters. He would definitely remain loose-lipped as long as he thought that he was home free and that we were just making fools of ourselves.

The next morning I sent a letter to Frank Melton, Channel 3's CEO, asking for a complete, unedited copy of Beckwith's interview with Ed Bryson. The local stations normally do not voluntarily (or even with a subpoena) provide portions of tapes that are not actually aired. I wanted to see what they would do in this case. The title of the special was "Can Justice Be Done?" We would see how much they wanted to see justice done.

Thursday morning's paper carried an article regarding the *Primetime Live* story that would air that night. I phoned my mother to make sure she knew about it and silently hoped that she would not witness her first-born being roasted on national television.

Within thirty minutes of receiving my letter, Frank Melton called and readily agreed to provide us with copies of Beckwith's entire interview after the final segment aired that night.

Jerry Mitchell dropped by. I hadn't seen him in a while. He gave me a copy of a letter-to-the-editor page from *Attack!* magazine, the periodical Jerry had described as a neo-Nazi magazine in his October 3, 1989, article. The page contained a letter from Beckwith, penned in his jail cell at Angola Penitentiary:

As you must remember, I was twice tried for my life back in 1963, accused of killing Mississippi's mightiest nigger. I suppose he was, but, sir, we have had no trouble with that nigger since they buried him—none! I hear that his brother Charles, the nigger mayor of Fayette, Mississippi, is still hanging on by a thread. . . . I also enjoyed reading Mr. Camerotta's fine article on Jimmy Carter's favorite darkie, Andy. It's about time Andy and Charles, just like old Medgar, saw the sign of the times. Indeed!

Just before *Primetime Live* was to air, Myrlie Evers called, sounding a little upset. She had received a call from the same producer who had phoned me, telling her that Diane Sawyer had spoken with Ed Peters, and reportedly, Ed had told her that the case would go to the grand jury in August, just months away. The producer told Mrs. Evers that Ed made the comment "off the record," but that Sawyer was going to work it into her closing comments. Mrs. Evers was concerned about two things. First, while she wanted the case reprosecuted, she knew, from our frequent conversations, that we were not going to be ready by August. She didn't want anything left out or rushed to the extent the case would be jeopardized.

I debated whether to tell her then about the gun. Something told me that if she was concerned about going to a grand jury too quickly, the secret would be safe with her. I held back, though. She was still close to Jerry, and while I trusted her, I knew she trusted Jerry and I didn't. The story was about to unfold on national television and I chose not to take that chance. I will always second-guess that decision.

The other thing that troubled her was that if Ed had made the remark "off the record," Diane Sawyer had no business working it into anything she said on the air. Mrs. Evers worried that would somehow jeopardize the case. I assured her that the case would not be going to a grand jury in August and that I seriously doubted that Ed had said it would. I had not talked with Ed about the case since the previous week when I'd conveyed my feelings about a special prosecutor. Even then, I told him that my best estimate for going to a grand jury would be in the fall or possibly the first of the year, and that was barring any unforeseen problems.

I explained to Mrs. Evers that Ed was probably asked the earliest date a grand jury could hear the case. I was quite certain that Ed had simply responded that our next grand jury would meet in August. I assured her that when we decided to go to a grand jury, she would hear it from me and not from some newsperson. She, in fact, would be a witness.

Sawyer did not mention any quote from Ed or say anything about the grand jury's considering the case in August. I was astonished, though, to see an interview with Delmar Dennis, the guy who had made me promise, if asked about his cooperation, to say that he had told us to get lost! Yet, on national television he was telling all and saying that he would cooperate and testify.

I was certainly glad that he would help us, but his proclamation, coming on the heels of my saying that he wouldn't, sure made me look inept. The show even took credit for producing Delmar. They didn't mention that we had talked with him weeks before they did.

Friday's paper had an article about the show. I especially liked Ed's quote: "I hope someday this crime can be solved and some form of trust level can be developed with the people who distrust the court system because of this case." What were our plans? "If and when," Ed continued, "we have enough evidence to present to a grand jury, then we will do that. Then it will be a question of law whether we can go to trial and a question of fact whether we get a conviction." That pretty well summed up the situation.

I hoped that the telecast would prompt other people with information about the case to contact us. The broadcast provoked contact, all right, and not all positive. A woman in Mesquite, Texas, for example, wrote a letter to Ed the night of the show: "Dear Mr. Peters, I don't normally write letters of this nature, but I just watched *Primetime* television show and I have never seen a more blatent [*sic*] frame of anyone in my life. . . . The same people that killed Kennedy killed Evers; not Beckwith."

Jeanie informed me the phone lines were buzzing with calls of a similar nature. There were so many, she said, she didn't bother transferring them to me but assured the callers that I would get their messages.

A more substantive call came from former chief of police Jim Black. Jim was part of the undercover police detail in 1963 that was assigned to attend mass meetings and keep tabs on "the movement," paying particular attention to all whites who showed up. The police were not only interested in leaders, such as Evers, but also the "outside agitators." Jim had no doubt that Beckwith had killed Evers, but Jim was absolutely certain that Beckwith was not at the mass meeting Evers had attended the night of the murder. Jim was positive because he was there, closely scrutinizing the handful of whites present. If Beckwith had been there, Jim said, he would have seen him and then recognized him following his arrest.

Jim hoped that we had other evidence to convict Beckwith, but thought if we were relying on witnesses putting him in the church at that mass meeting, we would get our legs cut out from under us. Jim was right, but I didn't tell him. Jim did private investigative work, and I suspected he would be in touch with whatever defense lawyer ended up representing Beckwith. Although I didn't intend putting on any of those mass-meeting witnesses, I wanted the defense to think I was relying heavily on them. My thinking was that by staying quiet on the matter, the defense would expend preparation time and energy getting ready to negate those witnesses, and not as much on the real witnesses.

One call, also evidently sparked by the program, was to Jerry Mitchell. He told me that someone had telephoned the *Clarion-Ledger* claiming to have some information on the whereabouts of the murder weapon. Jerry asked if we had received similar calls. I told him that we had not. I pressed Jerry for details, knowing that if I did not, he would suspect something. He told me that he was back in good graces with the paper and, therefore, could not give me any information.

Sunday, June 17, was Father's Day. As I got ready for church, random thoughts went through my mind, first about how blessed I am to be the father of my children. I'd heard them whispering behind my back the day before, debating various ideas for a present. Of course, I was thankful that my father was alive and, for the most part, healthy.

I couldn't help, however, having less pleasant thoughts. It was the first Father's Day that Dixie's family had without Russel.

Working on the Evers case now permeated my entire life. It was impossible on Father's Day not to think how Father's Day was for Medgar Evers's children; what all he had missed; how their lives were different in his absence; and the turmoil and frustration Mrs. Evers must have endured in rearing them.

The sermon that Sunday dealt with prayer, hopes, and dreams. A dream delayed is not necessarily a dream denied. God has his own timetable. It's been said that justice delayed is justice denied.

Perhaps, I thought in church that Father's Day, if the case had been forced on a third jury any sooner, an acquittal would have resulted, forever barring further prosecution and forever freeing the assassin. I hoped that we had become a more enlightened society, more accepting of the differences in our fellow men, and that a jury in the 1990s, with as much or more evidence, would return the verdict that had so long eluded justice.

My principal concern for a third trial was a change of venue. Our chances would be better right here in Hinds County or in any county with enough of a black population to ensure a racially mixed jury. I worried about getting tossed into "Klan territory" or into a heavily white-populated county where apathy, if not racism, would produce feelings of "Why prosecute this old man now? Who cares?"

Everything else had fallen into place thus far. I got goose bumps at times when I put it together in my mind. I just had to have faith that the Lord would take care of the venue, as well as everything else. In the words of Ralph Waldo Emerson, "All I have seen teaches me to trust the Creator for all I have not seen."

Monday's mail included a letter from Billups Allen, supervisory agent of the FBI's Jackson office, acknowledging receipt of Delmar's sworn authorization to release the Bureau's information and documents concerning him. My request and Delmar's authorization were being forwarded to FBI headquarters for consideration. Other than to read that brief letter, I spent no time on the case. I had the Taylor capital-murder trial coming up soon. Yet, June 18 was the day all hell broke loose.

Toward the end of my son Burt's baseball practice that evening, I noticed two guys sitting in the bleachers, one wearing an orange tie matching his hair—Jerry Mitchell. His companion was Michael Rejebian, another *Clarion-Ledger* reporter.

My truck was parked behind the bleachers, so there was no avoiding them. As they descended from their seats, I sent Burt on to the truck. "Bobby," Jerry began, "we've got it from a very reliable source that the

DA's office already has the gun; that it was kept by Judge Russel Moore for many years and that you got it from his family."

"You know I can't comment on what evidence we have." I walked on to my truck, making no further reply, and drove home.

Jerry phoned: "I think you should know that your brother-in-law, Matthew, confirmed everything to us, and a story will be coming out in the morning paper."

Matthew? Damn. He was a lawyer. What was he thinking? He was aware of my promise to his mother that, for the time being, I was not going to reveal that I even had the gun and would return it if we weren't able to proceed with the case; that I would never say where I found it unless absolutely necessary. I had called Matthew and told him so the day after I found it. I was trying to spare Russel's family unnecessary embarrassment, yet Russel and Carolyn's son had confirmed it to the paper.

Jerry was waiting for a response. The story was coming out. The discovery of the gun would no longer be a secret kept from Beckwith. Nothing would be gained by further denial. The time had come to confirm our possession of the evidence and explain our reason for keeping it under wraps.

After giving Jerry my confirmation and explanation, I called Myrlie Evers. I knew that instead of rejoicing that the gun was available for evidence, the vultures would start circling, screaming "cover-up." I wanted Mrs. Evers to hear from me that I had been in possession of the gun and that the press now knew it. I wanted to explain my reasons for releasing the false information. We talked for almost an hour. Obviously she was surprised by the news and disappointed that I had not confided in her. She was also hurt, which, in turn, made me feel even smaller. Yet, she was understanding and even elated that we had the murder weapon.

Next, I phoned Ed, Benny, and Crisco, in that order, advising them of the developments. Crisco had just returned from his vacation and briefed me on his meeting with Richard Poppleton, who was now in his late sixties but in good health and willing to help. He told Crisco that along with his original work notes at the FBI Crime Lab should be some spent hulls that he had test-fired from the gun. If the question was ever raised as to whether the gun we had was the same as the one he examined in 1963, considering the obvious break in the chain of custody, he could test-fire some more from the weapon we had and compare the markings on those spent hulls with the ones test-fired by him in 1963.

The final call that night was to Matthew. "I didn't realize it was a secret," he said.

"Damn, Matthew, I told you."

"I mean that I didn't know you still didn't want anybody to know."

"Didn't you see the *Primetime* piece?"

"Yeah. Why?"

"Didn't Ed's response on national television that we didn't have the gun give you a clue that nothing had changed?"

"Look, Bobby, I'm sorry. I just didn't realize it was so important to be such a big secret. Besides, it was evident when Jerry talked to me that he already knew you had it. I just confirmed it."

"Thanks, Matthew, you might have picked up a phone and warned me."

Tuesday's paper was full of the news: "Gun Used in Evers Slaying in DA's Hands: Prosecutors Had Maintained Since November They Didn't Know Where the Weapon Was." At least Jerry included my explanation: " 'Part of building a prosecution and conducting an investigation is strategic,' " read my quote, " 'and for strategic reasons, we felt that the prosecution would be more successful if the target of the investigation knew as little as possible about what was being accumulated.' "

Matthew's words stunned me. "Somewhere along the way," he said he had asked his father, " 'Where'd that gun come from?' He said, 'That is the gun that was allegedly used to kill Medgar Evers.' "

What in the world was going on! When I had first called Matthew to ask point-blank if the rifle that Russel had told me had been used in a civil rights case was the one used in the Evers murder, Matthew told me that he had no idea.

I was so angry with Matthew and so baffled by his statements and actions that I never mentioned anything about the case to him again. (God rest his soul; he was killed a few years later outside his office.)

Ed was just as miffed, but felt that Matthew honestly didn't realize the situation in which he had placed us with that single comment. If Matthew knew from the very beginning that the murder weapon was in his parents' house, then surely, the public would assume, he would have told me, his brother-in-law and the prosecutor spearheading the investigation. I spent all day talking to reporters trying to explain.

Jerry Mitchell came by and conveyed some of what had led them to their discovery. Someone in law enforcement in Tennessee had called him, claiming he was close to Beckwith and knew where the gun was. Jerry and Rejebian had driven to Tennessee to meet this person, who informed them that Beckwith said that "Ed Pete" had it on a mantel at his house. Jerry wouldn't say who told him that Judge Moore had it, but from what I pieced together from Matthew's various statements, once

Rejebian (who covered the city hall beat where Matthew worked as an assistant city attorney) learned that, he went to Matthew.

Naturally, the news was all over the television that evening, and just as I expected, the media was relishing more in calling me a liar than celebrating our discovery of the gun. The significance of the find, however, was not lost on Medgar's brother, Charles. Toward the end of Jerry Mitchell's article in the paper was this quote: "Evers' brother, Charles Evers of Jackson, said he was pleased the gun is in the prosecutors' hands. 'If they have the same evidence and it came before a jury now, they would convict him [Beckwith],' he said. 'I believe that's how far we've come in Mississippi—equality and justice for all.' "

Myrlie Evers was quoted as saying, "I certainly hope that more 'missing' information will surface." How about the transcript? She had yet to mention to me that she had it. We were still working from the copy Jerry had provided. I didn't know what to think anymore.

It was tough emotionally to keep going. I was totally demoralized. Headlines in the paper the following day said that city councilman Louis Armstrong was requesting "federal intervention" to see if the DA's office had anything else we were not disclosing to the public. *What a nut,* I thought. *He might as well ask the city to fly Beckwith to Jackson so we could go through the investigative file and evidence with him. We could even have it televised.* Primetime *might even come back for that.*

Again, though, I was grateful to Jerry for including my response in the article, which was twofold: that if I was part of a cover-up, I would have destroyed the gun, rather than save it for prosecution; and that the long-term goal of a successful prosecution was more important than the glory of the moment that would have come from being the media's pal by disclosing that I had found the gun.

Ti Hua Chang, the producer of the *Primetime* segment, called and asked why Ed and I had lied; why didn't we just say "no comment"? Ironically, I told him, it was because we had been too honest and open with the media from the beginning of our investigation. In the early stages, when we told the media that we didn't have the gun, it was the truth. To say "no comment" after I'd found it would have signaled a change in circumstances.

Thus, we had remained consistent in our responses, giving a complete denial, so as not to spook the suspect. In retrospect, I should have just said "no comment" from the very beginning. It was a mistake I won't repeat.

That afternoon I had a message that Morris Dees had called. I hadn't heard from him since our meeting in December when Ed and I had first met Myrlie Evers. I assumed he wanted to join the media feeding frenzy and take a bite out of my butt, too. I put his message on my desk. I'd call him tomorrow.

Crisco got a call from Nancy Binder, the wife and secretary of my first boss and mentor, Al. A woman named Peggy Morgan had called Dr. Aaron Henry, a civil rights figure and personal friend of Medgar Evers's, and told him that she and her ex-husband had lived next door to Beckwith in the early 1970s. Beckwith, she said, bragged to them about killing Evers and getting away with it. She had given Henry her phone number (she had moved to Mobile, Alabama), and he, in turn, had telephoned his friend Al and asked that he pass the information on to us. At first, I wondered why Peggy Morgan had called Aaron Henry and why neither one of them had called the DA's office.

Then it hit me. With all of the allegations in the news claiming a cover-up on the part of our office, she had probably called the most prominent civil rights activist she knew about in Mississippi, and Dr. Henry, in turn, wanted to make sure that his trusted friend Al Binder knew. That way, there could be no cover-up of Peggy Morgan's information. The adverse publicity was having a negative effect on my previous plea for information.

Crisco talked to Morgan and got directions to her house. Her information warranted a visit to Mobile, but it would have to wait. We had the Taylor capital-murder trial coming up in Bay St. Louis, and another death-penalty case was set for trial right on the heels of the Taylor case. The latter one, the Davis case, involved the murder of an off-duty police officer.

I phoned Myrlie Evers after I got home and told her about Crisco's visit with Richard Poppleton. I also wanted to make sure she still wasn't upset with me. She still seemed to understand, and I felt a lot better. In fact, she commented on what she called my "positiveness." I told her it was because we were talking "when" we went to a grand jury for an indictment, and no longer "if."

Mrs. Evers wanted to know if the media was bombarding me. I assured her that they were, but that I was more determined than ever to see this thing through.

"You remind me a lot of Medgar."

"Ma'am?"

"I said that you remind me of Medgar. He was so determined to do a good job, especially when things got tough. He was quiet, he was dignified, but he was strong. It was an inner strength. And, Mr. DeLaughter, I sense that in you."

"Mrs. Evers, that's one of the nicest things anyone has ever said to me, and it couldn't have come at a better time. Thank you."

"If we're going to get through this, we have to lean on each other, but it's true. I try so hard not to get my hopes up. It's been so, so long. I know that but for you, this case would have been deep-sixed, and I thank God for placing you in this position at this time. But I know all too well what that responsibility involves, and while I don't want to add to that pressure, my family and I are really depending on you. So, Mr. DeLaughter, I want you to know that you are in our prayers. We pray that God will give you strength to continue on and to protect and bless you and your family."

"Thank you, ma'am, and my prayers will be with you."

"Besides, in the long run, I think we will be better off for you handling this gun issue just the way you handled it."

If we were talking face-to-face, I would've given her a great big bear hug. She requested copies of the newspaper clippings, and I asked her for any letters or speeches that Medgar had written that might help me get a feel for him as a person and his aspirations. I wanted them, I told her, to see what portions I could weave into a closing argument. I wanted them for other reasons, too. I needed to see if there was any room for the defense to put the victim on trial, which is not an unusual desperation tactic when the defense has little else. Also, if I really did remind Mrs. Evers of Medgar in some way, by learning more about him, I might just learn something about myself.

Channel 16's news that night ran a story that Councilman Armstrong had called a meeting at city hall for the next day of disgruntled officials who were displeased with our investigation. An editorial in Thursday's paper entitled "Lying" said Ed and I should be ashamed. I had learned my lesson, but considering the lies the paper had made to Delmar Dennis, the waxing indignant seemed a bit hypocritical.

When I got to the office, I had a message that Morris Dees had telephoned again, so I returned his call. It was a pleasant surprise. Dees was friendly and encouraged by the progress of the investigation. He even offered to write letters to some federal officials with whom he was friends, to see if they could help speed up getting Delmar Dennis's files to us and to ward off Councilman Armstrong's call for federal intervention.

More encouragement came on the evening news. Following coverage of Armstrong's news conference, Charles Evers jumped all over him, saying that he (Charles) was sick and tired of ten-cent politicians prostituting the name of his brother. If any federal investigation needed to be done, he would be the one calling for it. He had all the confidence in the world in the district attorney's investigation and thought that our office and the *Clarion-Ledger* had done a "jam-up" job.

A similar quote from Charles appeared in the morning paper: "I'm sick and tired of these politicians politicizing off my brother's name. . . . With the evidence the *Clarion-Ledger* has brought and with the evidence the district attorney has uncovered, he [Beckwith] is going to be indicted."

Charles had that right. I felt it in my bones. One of the things we still needed, though, before going to a grand jury was Mrs. Evers's transcript. We had come a long way together, but I was unsure how to broach the subject with her. The last thing I wanted, on the heels of the gun fiasco, was to do anything that might strain our relationship. Yet, I feared, if I told her that I knew she had it, that I had been working from a copy provided by Jerry, but that the time had come for me to get whatever she had, such a strain might well be the result. I simply wasn't sure that I could refrain from an intemperate response if she claimed that she didn't realize we needed a transcript. The lack of one was discussed during our first meeting in December 1989.

I wanted the transcript, not an argument. I had to make a tactful request, certainly not a demand. I sent her a letter asking for the transcript. I explained about our being out of town for quite some time and left the numbers where we could be reached, fully expecting to hear from her.

CHAPTER FIVE

"AGAINST THE PEACE AND DIGNITY"

I
t was September before I was able to return full-throttle on the Beckwith case, as Ed and I had two capital-murder trials out of town on
changes of venue. During this time, I heard nothing from Mrs. Evers.

The FBI's contribution to the 1963 investigation and to our reinvestigation was invaluable. The resources available to the agency, which it can
pass on to local law enforcement, are amazing. But anyone who doesn't
believe the Bureau is bureaucratic is in for a rude awakening. I certainly
was. Shortly after returning to work in Jackson in early September 1990,
Al Waites of the local FBI office invited Benny, Crisco, and me to his
office. After exchanging greetings, Al gestured with a sweep of his hand
to the mountains of reports, stacked waist-high along two walls.

"I've received clearance, oral and written, to give you all of this—sort
of," he started. My eyebrows shot up. "But, we have to go through everything first and remove any information regarding any federal grand jury
or information concerning informants."

"Informants! Al, that's *especially* what I asked for—anything regarding
Delmar Dennis. He's already signed two releases for you guys. What's
going on?"

"Bureau procedure. You don't realize how rare it is for the Bureau to
release this much to you. Besides, they haven't received Dennis's second
release. But, be that as it may, I've gone through this once and I can safely
tell you that what you wanted concerning Delmar Dennis is not in there,
but there is something else regarding another informant that would be of
great interest and benefit to you. But I can't let you have that."

"Al," I said, "please tell me what I need to do to get clearance for the information that will help me."

"You write a letter asking for it."

"I did that almost a year ago."

"You didn't ask specifically for this."

"I asked for *everything* concerning Beckwith and Medgar Evers."

"You can't ask for it generally like that. It has to be a specific request."

"Okay, tell me what it is. You don't have to show me anything now or let me copy anything."

"I can't; you don't have clearance for me to tell you."

"How can I possibly be expected to ask for something with specificity if you don't tell me what I need to specifically ask for?"

"I can see the bind you're in, but it's Bureau policy."

Arriving back at the office, I phoned Delmar Dennis. He assured me that he had mailed his second release to the FBI.

"Delmar, is your number still listed?"

"Yeah, why?"

"I was just wondering why, if the finest law enforcement agency in the world, with almost endless resources, was expecting to receive a document from you, but didn't receive it after two or three months, they didn't pick up a phone and call you to follow up on it."

"No reason in the world, as far as I can see. But I know what they'd say if you asked."

"What's that, Delmar?"

"Two words—'Bureau policy.' "

Early Thursday morning, September 6, 1990, Benny, Crisco, and I piled into Crisco's Blazer and headed south to Mobile to interview Peggy Morgan.

She appeared to be in her late fifties, so I was shocked when she said she was born in 1947. Peggy Morgan was only forty-three years old, but a hard life had aged her far beyond her years.

Born and raised in the Mississippi Delta, she had lived on the Gulf coast since the late 1970s—first in Pascagoula, Mississippi, then in Mobile.

"How did you end up on the coast?" I asked.

"My work."

"What was that?"

"Welder, shipbuilder."

"I'm sorry?" I wasn't sure I'd heard correctly. I couldn't imagine the lady I was looking at being a welder or a shipbuilder. She repeated herself.

She hadn't worked in several years. Like so many other employees at the shipbuilding yard in Pascagoula, she was disabled from asbestosis.

Peggy and Lloyd Morgan were divorced. They had married in 1964 when she was seventeen. They had moved from place to place around the Delta, and at one point in the marriage they had lived in an apartment on Dewey Street in Greenwood. A man, whom she came to find strange and dangerous, moved into an apartment across the street: Byron De La Beckwith.

Jimmy Dale Morgan, Lloyd's brother, was serving time at Parchman Penitentiary. Some Sundays Peggy and Lloyd traveled to the prison to visit Jimmy Dale. A few days before one such trip, Beckwith expressed a mysterious interest in joining them. Crisco turned the tape recorder on.

"I can't remember how it came about," she began, "but he came over to our apartment. We didn't really know him, but he worked at Barren-tine Manufacturing Company where Lloyd and I worked at the time, and we had seen him around there. He said that he had heard we were going to Parchman and that he had to go, too. He asked my husband if he [Beckwith] bought the gas and supplied the food and stuff, could he go with us. He said it was real important for him to see a guy up there. My husband said, 'Sure.'

"Well, on the way he told us that the guy he was going to see had helped him destroy something. I don't remember what he said the guy up there had gotten rid of for him, but he said he had to get to this man, who-ever he was. He said that we may run into a problem because he wasn't related to the guy and because he had been locked up hisself. He said that he could get into trouble if they found out who he was, so he said for us to keep cool."

"How did you react to that?"

"I knew something was up and I guess he saw the look on my face, 'cause he then said that he had killed a nigger but nobody was ever able to prove it, so we'd better keep our mouth shut after this visit to Parchman."

"Or the same thing would happen to you?"

"He didn't say it, but that was the implication."

"What did Lloyd say?"

"They laughed and made a joke out of it. My husband even said, 'I think all niggers ought to die,' or something like that. Beckwith said, 'I think so, too.' This man is, you know, real prejudiced. I mean he defi-nitely hates niggers. He said, 'I'll tell you what, I could kill a million of them and never blink an eye.'"

"What happened after you got to the prison?"

"Pulling into the gate, he said, 'Now, remember what I said, don't y'all ever let anyone know y'all brought me in here.'"

"So, he wasn't just catching a ride with you, but sneaking in there with you."

"Yes, sir. He told us he had to sneak in there. He said, 'Look, I can't let these people know who I am.'"

"What happened then?"

"We got in and the man he was going to see was in the same area as Lloyd's brother. We had stopped along the way and picked up some Kentucky Fried Chicken. We got in and set it down and he [Beckwith] walked over to the guy and said, 'Man, have I gotta talk to you.' The other guy said, 'Let's go,' so they walked off by theirself in the far corner."

"Tell me about the guy Beckwith was visiting."

"If I seen a picture of that man, I'd know him. I was paying close attention, believe you me, 'cause things wasn't just right and I knew it. I was scared, you know?"

"Did Jimmy Dale see him?"

"Yes, sir."

"Could you hear Beckwith call him by name?"

"I'm not sure. For some reason, the name Tommy sticks out."

"Where do Lloyd and Jimmy Dale live now?"

"Greenwood."

"Okay, go on."

"Well, on the way back home he mentioned to us several times not to ever say anything about us taking him in there. He said we could all get in trouble and he assured us we better not talk."

"Did you ever see him after the trip?"

"Oh, yes, sir. A few days later he come back over to the house and asked, 'Why don't y'all come over to my place and visit a minute?' So, my husband and I went over there and he [Beckwith] made it a point to show us all his guns. I mean it was an apartmentful, too. Then he brought up the Parchman trip again."

"What did he say?"

"As he was showing us his guns, he told us again that we better not ever mention it. I—I was scared. . . ." Her voice trailed off to silence and she wiped a tear with the back of a hand. I paused before continuing.

"When did you move from Dewey Street?"

"It wasn't long after that."

"I bet," Crisco muttered.

"Did Lloyd know you were upset and scared?"

"Yes, sir, but all he said was 'Don't you breathe a word about any of this.'"

Poor thing, I thought. At eighteen or so, she must have been scared out of her wits and nobody to turn to for comfort. Her fear, she said, quite understandably, was the reason that she had never told any of this to the authorities. "I'm still scared, 'cause I'm gonna tell you, this is dangerous stuff.

"In 1986, I kinda made a turnaround in my life and I don't like wrong-doing. I detest it. I've been done wrong in the past myself. To see some-body mistreated and run over, I don't like that. I felt like it was part of my responsibility to bring it out, you know. Hey, people are human beings, you know. I mean my daddy was a Klansman at one time."

As many times as she had dropped the N-word, it didn't surprise me to hear that about her father. "What happened in 1986? You said you made a turnaround in your life then."

"I lost my mother. She froze to death and my father was killed." Crisco, Benny, and I exchanged quick glances. "I mean, you picture your mother laying in a ditch there with ice in her hair and mud in her nose." At once, Crisco and Benny jumped up, Crisco asking where the bathroom was located and Benny announcing he was going outside for a smoke.

Mrs. Morgan continued, "I come from an abusive situation all my life. My mother and father were alcoholics. One day, I just kneeled down in this chair and I said, 'Lord, you know I want you to put my mother's death out of my mind.' I thought I was going to have a nervous break-down."

"Why wait three or four years after your turnaround to say anything?"

"I didn't know the law was doing anything until I saw what you were trying to do on television. That's when I called. You see, although I'm still scared, because I turned everything over to the Lord, I had to tell you what I know."

I told Mrs. Morgan how appreciative we were and assured her that her information would be strictly confidential until an indictment was returned. We would then have to furnish Beckwith's lawyers a copy of her statement, but we would not provide them with her address or phone number.

I believed Peggy Morgan, but as with Delmar Dennis, it was important to find everything that we could to corroborate her information. We would start with the Morgan brothers.

"You know they won't talk to us," Crisco said.

"Probably, but we lay a grand jury subpoena on them, and then if they don't talk, the sheriff will find a cozy spot for them. Also, we get the prison records for Jimmy Dale, Beckwith, and Tommy Tarrants."

Tarrants was one of the more militant terrorists for the Klan, with connections to Imperial Wizard Sam Bowers. Tarrants did time in Parchman for the 1968 attempted bombing of a Jewish businessman's house in Meridian, Mississippi. He "found the Lord" in prison and following his release was involved in the ministry.

"You think that he might be the mysterious 'Tommy' that Beckwith was seeing?" Benny asked.

"Maybe. It would certainly fit. Once we get their records, we should be able to narrow the time frame when the Morgans' trip to Parchman occurred. It had to be during a time when Jimmy Dale and Tarrants—or whoever the mystery man is—were both in prison. And it had to be between Beckwith's release in the Evers case in April 1964 and his incarceration in Angola for that Louisiana bombing charge. The prison records usually include personal histories, previous employment, addresses, and that sort of thing. If one of Beckwith's previous addresses is on Dewey Street in Greenwood and one of his places of employment is Barrentine Manufacturing, then Peggy Morgan is definitely telling the truth."

Frances Harrison, a local woman, telephoned me to say that she had some information she wanted to pass on about Beckwith. It may or may not help, she said, but she promised I would find it interesting. So, on Tuesday, September 11, Crisco and I met with her.

Mrs. Harrison, a widow, appeared to be approximately the same age as Beckwith. She had lived in Greenwood for many years before moving to Jackson in 1961 and referred to Beckwith as "DeLay."

One afternoon in the 1963 late spring, on her way home from the downtown real estate office where she worked at the time, Mrs. Harrison saw Beckwith at the Gulf gas station (seems he was always seen at gas stations) located at the corner of Woodrow Wilson and North West Streets in Jackson. She didn't notice him until she was going by and only had time for a quick wave. She wasn't even sure at the time if he had seen her. She gave it no other thought at the time.

"Well, it wasn't that long—maybe a week or so after I saw him in Jackson—that he was arrested. By the time of the trial, I moved back to Greenwood. One day, DeLay's lawyer, Hardy Lott, called me up out of the clear blue sky. 'Can I come by and have a cup of coffee with you?' he asked me. 'Suits me,' I said."

Lott had coffee with Mrs. Harrison and, according to her, talked "about everything in the world except what he wanted" and was recalling "how nice it was when my son and his kids were little."

Finally, she told him, "Now, Hardy, you're the busiest lawyer in town. Don't kid me. You're not over here to talk about what happened whenever these kids were little."

"Well," he said, "I heard you saw DeLay in Jackson."

"Yes, I did."

"Well, do you remember when you saw him?"

"No, I do not."

"Well, if Bill Waller or the FBI come to see you, will you let me know?"

Since she had not mentioned seeing Beckwith to anyone, Mrs. Harrison knew only Beckwith could have been aware of the brief chance encounter. Whether she remembered the date was crucial to him. In fact, his lawyer was picking her for details that very moment. It was probably fortunate for her that she couldn't recall the date, but the spunky lady's answer to Hardy Lott's last question about letting him know if the DA or the FBI contacted her was "Naw, Hardy, I don't think I will."

Years later, Mrs. Harrison was at a party in Greenwood when a local politician there came up, put his arm around her, and said, "Frances, I wanna tell you something. You know, ol' DeLay sho was relieved when you couldn't remember what day you saw him down there. That was the day that two policemen swore he was in Greenwood."

"Well," Mrs. Harrison told us, "I couldn't remember what date or I'd of flat come forward. See, I'm not a member of the good ol' boy system. If I could've remembered the date, I would've volunteered to testify. I just sorta forgot about that until [he] mentioned that. I guess I'd got run out of town, too."

Then Crisco asked if she knew Beckwith's first wife.

"I knew Willie," Mrs. Harrison replied.

"Where is she now?"

"I don't know."

"Did she ever remarry?"

"I don't know. Willie was a good ol' hill girl from Tennessee, and bless her heart, she had a drinking problem. DeLay was mean to her. I know drunks can worry the fire out of you, but he was brutal. She stuck by him, though. They were characters in town, that's for sure."

"I'll bet she would be interesting to talk to," Crisco said.

"Willie Beckwith may be dead."

Al Waites called the next day. The Bureau was ready for us to review whatever it was going to let us see. Two reports contained hearsay information from confidential informants about an alleged conspiracy in the planning and execution of Medgar Evers's assassination. All names, except that of Beckwith, were deleted.

According to the reports, the murder was a Klan hit, with the Citizens' Council implicated as well. Subsequent reports showed that the FBI attempted to follow up on this hearsay tip but was unsuccessful in securing any corroboration.

The most intriguing piece of information was the report of one informant (not Delmar Dennis) that while at a Klan defense fund-raiser in Laurel, Mississippi (hometown of Imperial Wizard Sam Bowers), Beckwith confided to the informant that he had killed Medgar Evers and had taken a Shriner's oath to kill Charles Evers, too.★ This was the report Al had referred to in our earlier meeting but couldn't tell me about. He still wouldn't let me have a copy of it or provide me with the informant's name.

Furthermore, notwithstanding a signed release from Delmar, we were still denied access to his files. Al did, however, read aloud a few things from an outline his analyst had prepared from a review of those reports. Delmar told the FBI back in the 1960s that the assassination of Evers was a planned Klan hit. Although the report didn't set out exactly what was said by Beckwith, Delmar did report that Beckwith had spoken at a Klan meeting near the swinging bridge in Byram and was made State Kleagle of the Klan at the same meeting. According to the Constitution of the White Knights of the Ku Klux Klan of Mississippi, a copy of which was given to me by Delmar Dennis, the State Kleagle was the Klan's top recruiter, appointed by Imperial Wizard Bowers.

The FBI had also found the original invoice from International Firearms to Thorn McIntyre for the murder weapon. The serial number on the document matched that on the rifle. There were also some photographs of Beckwith's house, which we did not have. A close look at the ones showing the front door revealed two organizational insignia affixed to the doorpost: the Masonic Lodge (Shriners) and the Citizens' Council.

I expressed my thanks to Al, who promised to press further to get clearance for me to get Delmar's reports and the name of the other informant.

★The Shrine (full name is Ancient Arabic Order of Nobles of the Mystic Shrine) is a fraternal organization that admits only men of high rank in the rites of Masonry. Although, according to Delmar Dennis, many Klansmen, such as Dennis and Beckwith, were also Shriners, there is no intent here to malign all Shriners. The fraternal order supports numerous hospitals throughout the United States and is active in many other community services.

Having done all that we could at the moment to corroborate Delmar Dennis, we began a similar endeavor regarding Peggy Morgan. On Thursday, September 13, Crisco and I drove to Parchman Penitentiary to pick up a copy of Jimmy Dale Morgan's records, commonly referred to as a pen-pak. It would tell us the dates of each hitch Jimmy Dale had served there and possibly some information that would help locate him and his brother, Lloyd.

Christine Houston, the records supervisor, had the pen-pak ready for us. Jimmy Dale Morgan was in Parchman on three occasions: from May 30, 1966, to March 25, 1967, for auto theft; from December 2, 1970, to July 30, 1973, for burglarizing a hardware store and stealing twenty-eight rifles and shotguns; and from May 25, 1977, to March 6, 1978, for burglarizing a lumber-and-building-supply store. Once we'd received Beckwith's pen-pak from Angola and compared it to Morgan's records, we ought to be able to narrow the time frame of Peggy and Lloyd's trip with Beckwith to Parchman.

Former Klan terrorist Tommy Tarrants was in Parchman much of the time that Morgan was an inmate. Finding him would give Benny something to do. Even if Tarrants wasn't the man whom Beckwith visited, because of his previous Klan connections, I thought that he could possibly corroborate what the FBI was unable to do in 1963: that Evers's murder was a Klan hit involving other conspirators. If Tarrants had truly changed his ways and was seeking redemption, maybe he would help us.

After two days in the Delta looking for the Morgan brothers, we came up empty and returned home. Over the weekend, I read Tarrants's book, *Conversion of a Klansman.*

Benny told me that he had tracked down Tarrants in a Virginia town and had sought the assistance of the local police department. A detective agreed to contact Tarrants and see if he would call us. Benny had the detective on the line when I walked in his office.

Tarrants, according to the detective, said that he didn't know Beckwith personally, and no, he would not even speak to us. He had put all of this in his past.

That same week, Beckwith's pen-pak arrived from Angola. He was arrested, on the bomb charge, September 27, 1973, and began serving his five-year sentence in 1975. Thus, only the last prison term of Morgan, from 1977 to 1978, could be eliminated as the time when Beckwith hitched his ride with Peggy and Lloyd Morgan to the Mississippi prison. That left from May 1966 to March 1967 and from December 1970 to July 1973, just before Beckwith's Louisiana arrest.

Also during that week, Crisco located two of the last three living prosecution witnesses from the 1964 trials. Barbara Holder was one of the carhops at Joe's Drive-In who identified Beckwith's car. She told Crisco, who found her in Texas, that she and coworker Martha Jean O'Brien had received many threats after the earlier trials, and she wished us luck in coaxing Martha Jean back into a courtroom to testify. Ronald Mark Acy was one of the teenage companions of Robert Don Pittman's who had also identified Beckwith's car near the scene.

It was no easy chore, but Crisco had made contact with all of the 1964 prosecution witnesses who were still living, other than Martha Jean O'Brien. They were scattered from Maryland to Florida to Texas to California. The interesting thing to me was that not a single one of them—not even the local ones—had picked up a phone and contacted us.

Encouraged by our good fortune, Ed, I learned, had told Charles Evers that we were going to a grand jury by late September or early October. As far as we had come, we still weren't ready for that. We had no word yet from the FBI regarding informant records and no response from Myrlie Evers about her transcript. We were at a standstill, and I had no choice but to inform Ed so he could explain the situation to Charles.

The following Monday Mrs. Evers called. Charles had phoned her over the weekend, and she understood from her brother-in-law that we were ready to go to a grand jury but that she was the sole reason for the delay. I informed her that was not what was said. Charles had been told of my June letter to her and that I had not heard from her. I also explained, however, that the lack of her transcript was but one of several delays.

She had indeed called, Mrs. Evers said, after receiving my June letter, but Ed and I were out of town. Of course we were, I thought. I had mentioned that in the letter and even provided her with the numbers where we could be reached.

The truth of it, I reasoned after rereading my letter to her, was that we had both assumed that the other would call and resume contact. She thought, and was thereby offended, that we were using her brother-in-law as a go-between. Of course that wasn't the case; we both knew how to contact each other and needed no intermediary. We had simply been waiting on the other to call. It was good to clear the air and move forward.

We needed the transcript within the next few weeks if we were going to shoot for the December grand jury. I had to figure out a way to get an advance ruling on our ability to use it in providing the testimony of dead or infirm witnesses. A hearing would be required, and Beckwith would have to be given at least a thirty-day notice to afford him an opportunity to contest the move.

★   ★   ★

The transcript not only provided testimony from the graves of deceased witnesses, but it was also instrumental in placing Beckwith's car on the far corner of Joe's Drive-In the night of the murder and several nights earlier.

Robert Pittman, the teenage boy whose parents operated the grocery by Joe's, had told police that the car he had seen on those evenings was a white '62 Valiant with a long antenna. Beckwith's car was such a vehicle, but the defense argued in 1964 that any number of similar vehicles existed. Neither Pittman nor any other witness noted the license number, as the car was backed into the corner.

Working in the office one night, I made a key discovery hidden for nearly three decades in the two-hundred-thousand-word transcript. Young Pittman recounted, in his testimony, the description of the car, but he went further on the stand and explained to Waller that the thing that had stuck out most in his mind about the car was "the Shriner's emblem." Waller asked him to describe it. "It's one of these sword-looking things with a crescent that goes up in this point, and had some kind of hook on it, a semicircle thing. It was hanging from the mirror."

I retrieved the photographs David Adams had reproduced from the negatives he had found abandoned in the police department closet. I found one showing the front of Beckwith's car taken on the police impound lot. With the aid of a magnifying glass, I examined the rearview mirror. Something circular dangled from it, but I couldn't make out what it was.

David made an enlarged print the next morning. There was the Shriner's emblem, just as Pittman had described it twenty-six years earlier! Although we were without a license number, the noose around Beckwith's neck had just tightened yet a little more. How many white 1962 Valiants with a long, whiplike antenna and a Shriner's emblem could there have been? Plus the fingerprint on the murder weapon was that of the man who had such a car, and the cabdrivers had identified him as searching for Evers's house only days before the murder. Adding Beckwith's bragging statements to the equation, we had more evidence in the case than in many contemporary homicides.

Since our transcript had not been kept on file for a quarter century, I had to establish to the court's satisfaction that it was, in fact, *the* transcript of the first 1964 trial. I needed a ruling authenticating it before I hauled off and got an indictment. I couldn't afford to assume that I could use it and find out otherwise at trial.

I filed a formal motion for the court to authenticate it and set the matter for a hearing on November 19, 1990. A copy of the transcript, as well as a copy of my motion, was sent to Beckwith at his Tennessee home, to give him a chance to get a lawyer and oppose it.

Myrlie Evers was my first witness. She explained to Judge L. Breland Hilburn that she had testified at both 1964 trials and that subsequent to the second mistrial, DA Waller had provided her with a three-volume transcript of the first trial. After reviewing it, she had placed it in a trunk along with other papers of Medgar's. Some years later, she had realized its value and transferred it to her bank safe-deposit box. It had remained there until she hand-delivered it to me on Friday, October 12, 1990.

Bill Waller testified that he did, in fact, request Homerita Welborn, the court reporter in both 1964 trials, to transcribe the testimony of witnesses in the first trial for use in the second. Following the second mistrial, he gave the transcript to Myrlie Evers.

Waller reviewed the transcript prior to the hearing and testified that he was satisfied that it was the complete and authentic transcript that he had given to Mrs. Evers. John Fox III, who was Waller's assistant in 1964, echoed that opinion.

Court reporter Homerita Welborn was dead. So I had sent Crisco to the state supreme court to obtain several trial transcripts in other cases that were prepared and signed by her. Handwriting expert Tom Packer compared the signatures on those transcripts with that of ours. Packer testified that the signature was genuine.

Judge Hilburn ruled, "It will be the order of the court that the Circuit Clerk be authorized and directed to docket the three-volume transcript as the official transcript of the trial in Cause No. 17,824, styled, *The State of Mississippi versus Byron De La Beckwith,* and that those three volumes be entered as part of the official record of that cause number for all purposes consistent with the Mississippi Rules of Criminal Procedure and the Rules of Evidence of this court."

Outside the courthouse I exchanged hugs with Mrs. Evers. My excitement at being in court was matched only by the hope of Myrlie Evers of being *back* in court after twenty-six years.

"When do we go to the grand jury?" she wanted to know.

"Mrs. Evers, unless we get derailed in the meantime, it will be in December." I then explained that Crisco and I needed to hurry to catch our flight to Washington, D.C. We were going to meet with personnel at the FBI Crime Lab and, we hoped, prompt some action on getting Delmar Dennis's records. After one last hug, she handed me a brown envelope.

"Maybe you can read this on the plane. Now go, shoo!"

Once airborne, I retrieved the envelope Mrs. Evers had given me. It was the information I'd requested concerning Medgar. I wanted to learn something of this man whose death had reached out over the decades and rocked my previously sedate life.

Medgar grew up in Newton County, Mississippi, one of six children of James and Jesse Evers. His father worked in a sawmill and his mother did laundry for white families. Both parents were God-fearing people. James was a deacon and Jesse used what little savings she had to buy the land for her church. Although Medgar had five siblings, he was especially close to Charles, who was three years older. Charles gave Medgar the nickname Lope because of the way he walked. The two brothers were so close, after only one year of high school, Medgar followed Charles into the army during World War II and was assigned to service in England and France.

Having had a taste of freedom in Europe, Medgar vowed to make positive changes upon his return home. During the 1946 summer, Medgar, Charles, and four friends went to register to vote, but after they entered the clerk's office, a group of whites rushed in and ran them off. Medgar was quoted later as saying, "In a way we were whipped, I guess, but I made up my mind then that it would not be like that again—at least not for me."

Assisted by the GI Bill, Medgar completed high school and, in 1948, entered college at Alcorn, majoring in business administration, hoping one day to have his own business. On the Alcorn campus he met a young coed named Myrlie Beasley of Vicksburg. They married on Christmas Eve, 1951. The following year Medgar graduated and took a job in the Delta as an insurance agent.

During his travels on the dusty Delta back roads, he had a close, first-hand look at the desperate living conditions of the region's black populace. He could never shake that from his mind or heart. He had to get involved in trying to make a better chance at life for them.

And so it was that Medgar Evers became the first field secretary for the NAACP in Mississippi. Although the role was one of a general, Medgar's close friend Sam Bailey described Medgar as the organization's "mailman" because "he was always there." The rest is history and beautifully chronicled by Myrlie in her memoir, *For Us, the Living*.

The packet also contained a speech by Medgar:

I think it appropriate . . . that I make a confession to you . . . : I LOVE THE LAND OF MY BIRTH. I do not mean just America . . . , but

Mississippi. . . . The things I say . . . will be said to you in hopes of the future when it will not be the case in Mississippi and America, when we will not have to hang our heads in shame or hold our breath when the name Mississippi is mentioned. . . . But instead, we will be anticipating the best. . . .

We realize that Negroes and most whites are not really FREE in Mississippi. But it is our goal to work for the day when Negroes in Mississippi will be FREE as any American citizen. . . . When that day comes, the white man in Mississippi will be free. . . . And we can all work together to build a more prosperous State and Nation.

It reminded me of Abraham Lincoln's words over a century earlier: "In giving freedom to the slave, we assure freedom to the free—honorable alike in what we give and what we preserve." Lincoln and Evers correctly recognized the dehumanizing effects of racism on whites, too. White guilt for sins of the past? No. Just simply recognition that when we treat our fellow man inhumanely, it robs us of our own humanity.

Our visit in D.C. was brief. We met with Russell Davey, a FBI fingerprint examiner. George Goodreau, the examiner who had testified in 1964, had become seriously ill since Crisco had spoken with him. Davey would take his place. The FBI retained custody of the necessary fingerprint evidence, but Davey advised that once Beckwith was rearrested, he would need a new set of prints to compare with those held by the FBI to testify that this was the same individual whose print was on the rifle's scope.

We also met Richard Crum of the firearms and ballistics section, which still possessed the notes, photographs, and test specimens of Richard Poppleton. The former examiner was healthy, ready to testify, and would be given access to everything.

Actually everything we learned could have been relayed by phone, but the FBI requested that we make the visit. The Bureau wanted us to see exactly what it possessed so there would be no misunderstanding about it later. I also took advantage of the trip to hand-deliver the negative of Beckwith's car and put in a request for the lab to enlarge the area of the rearview mirror. It was a precautionary measure in anticipation that the defense lawyers might later try to attack my "Shriner's emblem" evidence by questioning the competence of an ID man from a local police department. The results were, as I expected, the same.

Lastly, but importantly, I spoke with Kevin Stafford at the Justice Department in an attempt to hasten the release of Delmar Dennis's informant reports to us. The authorization, he said, had to come "from the top," but he assured me that everything was being done that could be done.

Our return flight arrived in Jackson late that night. On my way home, I stopped by the office to check my mail and messages. The unedited videotaped interview of Beckwith by Channel 3 reporter Ed Bryson was on my desk. I took it home to watch.

In stark contrast with the words of Medgar Evers that I had read on the flight to D.C., those of Beckwith sickened me. Yet, they also encouraged me. Although denying his guilt, he laid out his motive in chilling, blunt terms. They provided a glimpse of how his evil, twisted mind worked.

Beneath the mask of an ordinary sexagenarian lay a smoldering rage, a pure malevolent darkness. He is not just a racist. Byron De La Beckwith is the quintessence of evil.

Above all else, Beckwith is a talker, and he felt a need to tell Bryson a little about himself before getting to a discussion of the case.

"I like people, all kinds of people, more especially those who like guns. I'm a gun crank. I think everybody should have guns. I don't care who it is."

"Do you own guns today?" Bryson asked.

"I cannot have any guns today and I am sorely vexed that I cannot."

"Why is that?"

"Well, you see, a convicted felon cannot possess firearms."

"Tell me about your conviction in Louisiana."

"Now, Orleans Parish, as all of Louisiana, is governed by Napoleonic law. I've got a lot of French blood in me, but that Napoleonic law worked against me. I asked my lawyer, 'Where's the jury?' And he said, 'Don't you see those five nigger women sitting up there on that bench?' I said, 'Five—*uno, dos, tres, cuatro*—is that all?' He said, 'Yep, that's the Napoleonic law.' So, you see, it worked against me."

"How's that?"

"Well, in about a day and a half or two days, that little ol' Jew prosecutor had gone through everything and so the judge said, 'Well, will you jurors go out and render your verdict?' But they weren't paying any attention. They were pulling their hose and picking their nose. They came back in about thirty or forty minutes and said, 'Guilty, lock him up.'

"So, then they gave me five years in Angola. And it worked out just like the Jews wanted it to, and the niggers were delighted, and they're still happy. Now, evidently, they want me to come back and be tried a third time about the Evers case down there in Jackson."

"What do you think of that?"

"I think it's a damn fool thing to do. I'm writing a book and I've been working on that doggone book since I was locked up down there in 1963, accused of killing that nigger."

"What do you think about talk that they will try you again?"

"Well, I say it's gonna make me sell a lot of my books. You see, all this publicity that you all are enthusiastically running up to give me nationally—I'm gonna cash in on it."

"I'm just wondering," Bryson asked, "what your reaction is gonna be."

"I'm gonna tend to my business like I always have. I've always tended to my business and looked after my God, Dixie, my family, friends, and the whole state of Christ's church. Now, that don't encompass anybody but white Christians. I don't consider any other race, color, or creed as Christians except white Caucasians who profess Christianity. All these other races, colors, and creeds—the people who worship Kali, Vishnu, Brahman, and all those idols—they're Antichrists. They believe in human sacrifice and they still do it and all this voodoo nonsense. You gonna call those folks Christians, eating each other?"

"You're serious?"

"Of course I am. There's niggers over there in Africa still eating each other, and several other races take the blood of their enemies and make food out of it—mix it with bread or make little wafers and serve it. Take Purim for example."

"What?"

"P–U–R–I–M. It's a feast that the Jews have every year, and those little wafers they serve are supposed to have the blood of nice little white Christian children mixed in it."

The camera was not on Bryson, but he must have given Beckwith the same incredulous look I would've given at this point.

"Don't tell me it ain't so! And the Jews know it because I find out all this information reading Jewish books in English. The libraries are full of them, but people just don't care much to go and read about it, 'cause they don't pay any attention to Jews."

"You don't seem to care much for Jews. Where does that hate come from?"

"I'm an Israelite. Jews are not Israelites. Jews are not Hebrews. Jews are what God made them: children of the devil. Anybody who calls Jesus a Jew is a damn fool. They're gonna suffer in hell or else they're ignorant. God put us here to rule over the dusky races."

"Concerning Mr. Evers, though," Bryson began.

"*Mister* Evers?"

"Yes. What do you think happened?"

"I think what happened, happened. The nigger got shot, and when they recovered the bullet, they found out it came from a particular rifle."

"Okay."

"You know, the reason people like that rifle so much is it has such a heavy action that you can unscrew the barrel and throw it away and put an entirely different caliber in there to increase the velocity and increase the pounds per square inch."

"Speaking of the action, there was talk about a cut over your eye. How did you get it? I understand it matched the scope."

"Well, hell, from shooting from a prone position!"

"Okay."

"I shoot all the time. I'd go to the police range in Greenwood."

The police range in Greenwood! I was right. I wouldn't doubt if Holley and Creswell were with him, getting their stories down.

"You know," Beckwith continued, "there were a couple of taxi drivers down there and they testified against me, and it seems like somebody just beat the hell out of them for lying. One of them died and the other one left the state, I think."

"Mr. Beckwith, do you think it's okay for white people to kill black people?"

"Depends on the reason."

"What would be a reason that would justify, in your mind, killing Medgar Evers?"

"I know what you're gonna say," Beckwith snapped. "Why would *I* kill Medgar Evers? I didn't kill Medgar Evers, but he's sho dead and he ain't coming back." A malevolent laugh followed.

"Under what circumstances do you think that was okay?"

"We have laws in the Bible that govern that. My Bible says, 'Thou shalt do no murder.' It doesn't say, 'Thou shalt not kill.' 'Thou shalt not kill' is a lot of baloney."

"What's the difference?"

"There's a big difference. I was trained from my youth to make war against the enemies of this white Christian republic and do it enthusiastically and with a great fever of spirit."

"So, fit that with Medgar Evers."

"A great enemy was slain."

"Go on," Bryson prodded.

"What reason do you think a nigger ought to be killed? Or a Christian, Filipino, Mexican, or a Jew?"

"You answer it."

"Naw, I don't have to answer it. Everybody knows. You don't kill people unless it is for your self-preservation, the preservation of your race, color, or creed. That covers it, yeah."

"Based on your philosophy and all the things you've told me, how can justice be done in this case?"

"You first gotta find out who killed the nigger and then for what reason. You've got to go into every facet of the nigger's past, present, and future, as well as his family."

"Do you, though, think that whoever killed Medgar Evers should be punished?"

"Like I said, it depends on why he was killed. If he was killed in defense of the preservation of this white Christian republic, that's not murder, that's self-defense."

"And you said that you considered Medgar Evers to be an enemy in that respect?"

"He was. When he was slain, a severe blow was struck against the NAACP."

"Go on."

"And in addition, you've got suicide."

"How's that?"

"When you keep on aggravating a certain race, color, or creed, you're gonna commit suicide. You're gonna bring it on yourself. Have you ever thought of that?"

"I can't say that I have. What do you recall about his activities?"

"He was a normal nigger in Mississippi doing what is normal for niggers to do. Evidently, he displeased someone and they smote him."

"If they find out who did it, then what?"

"Well, just do whatever the law says that you can do," Beckwith stated as he leaned toward the camera, "*if* you're big enough to do it."

Son of a bitch! The last remark wasn't directed at Bryson. It was directed at me. It was nothing short of a challenge, a throwing down of the gauntlet. I replayed it again and froze his challenging image with the PAUSE button. "You're going down, you SOB, you're going down."

Within a week of returning from Washington, we received copies of Delmar Dennis's informant reports from the FBI, at least as they pertained to Beckwith.

The Klan constitution states that the legislative branch is the Klongress, which was naturally divided into two houses: the lower house being the Klanburgesses and the upper house the Klonvocation. Klansmen in each of the eighty-two counties elected a senator. According to a report filed by Delmar, at a meeting of the Klonvocation held on August 8, 1965, on the banks of the Pearl River near Byram, Mississippi, Beckwith spoke.

The meeting was attended by senators from forty counties, as well as thirty-five "persons of state rank," for a total of seventy-five Klansmen. According to the report, Beckwith was made the State Kleagle, or top recruiter, for the Klan, appointed by Imperial Wizard Sam Bowers. The report verified Delmar's statement to us, but it did not go into details of Beckwith's talk.

In another report, dated May 27, 1966, Delmar stated that he was told by a Klansman that Beckwith was in Neshoba County to "check with Rainey, Price and Co.," referring to the sheriff, deputy, and others, including the Imperial Wizard, arrested for killing the three civil rights workers there. "Beckwith wants people to know he is a member of the Klan and furthermore he wants people to know that he got away with murder."

Bowers and other Klansmen were also arrested for the 1966 firebombing death of civil rights leader Vernon Dahmer in Hattiesburg, Mississippi. One of Delmar's reports said that the Klan had held a legal-defense fund-raiser for them at the fairgrounds in Laurel on July 11, 1966. "About 200 or 250 people were present. Klansmen were expecting about 3,000. Rain and wind completely destroyed the decorations on the truck which served as the speaker's platform. Overall, the meeting was a complete flop."

Once again, Kleagle "Beckwith was the featured speaker. His speech was one of violence throughout. Beckwith called for killing communists and urged the small but cheering crowd to start at the top and work down killing them. He said, 'The only time to be calm is when you pull the trigger. I am ready to do more than I have done.' He referred to himself as a soldier and that Charles Evers has overdrawn his account in this world. He has bounced his check but it ain't caught up with him yet."

Delmar noted that he had had a conversation with Beckwith following the speech. Beckwith remarked to Delmar "that things were going well with him and that he is selling fertilizer and making plans to be an even better worker in the Klan than he has in the past."

Local groups or chapters of Klansmen were known as Klaverns, headed by the Exalted Cyclops. In a report dated December 6, 1964, Delmar mentioned one such reputed Klan officer who spoke of the Evers murder. "Edgar Ray Killen is still very much in charge of the Neshoba

County Klavern, and Killen has been, and still is, the top Klansman in Neshoba County. Killen boasted at previous Klan meetings that any attempts to convict a Klansman for violent acts in the cause of segregation would be futile. He boasted that the Klan could infiltrate every jury selected in Mississippi. As an example, he cited the slaying of Medgar Evers. He said that this murder was a Klan project and that the Klan protected Beckwith by arranging to have Klansmen on the jury." Killen, if alive, had just earned himself a trip to the grand jury.

Crisco copied the reports and set up a second meeting with Delmar Dennis. We flew to Knoxville and met him in our motel room by the airport. Overall he was pleased and relieved with the details of his reports. Naturally, he was disappointed that the one regarding the Byram meeting didn't detail the talk Beckwith had delivered about the Evers murder and getting away with it.

"I know good and well I told Tom Van Riper," Dennis insisted.

"Did you type these reports?"

"Most of the time I met with the agents soon after the meetings and gave them a verbal report. They typed the reports on file."

"Then don't worry about it. You can't control what they type."

"What about some other documentation that he was there?"

"Every little bit helps. Why?"

"I thought he was so stupid for bragging about everything that night, and I wanted something to prove that he was there."

"Yeah, so what?" Crisco asked.

"So, I got his autograph and dated it."

"I'll be damned," I said.

"I know I've still got it somewhere. I'll find it and get it to you."

"No. Whenever you find it, just call me. I'll probably get you to call Sam Allen for him to hook up with you to get it. He can send it on to D.C. from the Knoxville office. I want the crime lab to compare the signature with Beckwith's known handwriting. Just send me a copy."

While attending our state prosecutors' fall conference in north Mississippi, I received some good news. Tommy Mayfield, who didn't attend, faxed a letter to me that came to the office. A woman had written, "During the summer of 1967, Byron De La Beckwith was introduced to me in a Greenwood restaurant as the man who killed Medgar Evers. He openly bragged that he had killed Medgar Evers. . . . I hate the thought of a murderer going free, regardless of his age. If my testimony will be helpful at this late date, I will gladly offer it. . . . Whether or not I can be of any use to you, you have my best wishes for a successful trial and conviction of

Byron De La Beckwith. He has been free for too long and it is time he paid for his crime."

Crisco and I arranged to take a statement from the woman as soon as we returned from the conference on November 26.

Mary Ann Adams, a white, forty-seven-year-old IRS employee, related that she and a coworker had arrived at the restaurant about dusk. Once seated, the coworker excused himself and walked to a table where Beckwith and several other men were seated. "He walked to the table, spoke to Beckwith, laughed, joked, and patted him on the shoulder, came back to our table, and said, 'That's Byron De La Beckwith, the man who killed Medgar Evers.'

"My friend asked me if I would like to meet Beckwith, and I said that I wasn't interested. As Beckwith and his group were leaving, they stopped at our table. A gentleman with him said something to the effect, 'Do you know who this is? He's the man who killed that animal Evers.' Beckwith was agreeing, you know, nodding his head, laughing, smiling, and saying, 'That's right.' I don't remember the exact exchange, but he was not shy about admitting that he killed Evers.

"He stuck his hand out for me to shake, but I refused. I told him I wouldn't shake the hand of a murderer. He got angry and we got into a heated exchange. He was just so bold and brazen about it."

"Were any of the other men with him saying anything?" I asked.

"I remember one of them said, 'He got away with murder.'"

"Was that in Beckwith's presence?"

"Oh, yes. He was laughing, smiling, and agreeing. He was, you know, 'Mr. Royalty,' a little man with a big ego."

"What prompted you to send the letter to us?"

"I saw in the paper that you were trying to reopen the case. I wasn't aware until then that you could do that. Someone told me there was nothing I could do because he had been tried and acquitted twice, so he couldn't be tried again because it would mean double jeopardy.

"Like I said in my letter, I'll gladly testify if it will help; but, please, don't use my name until you have to."

I promised that we would respect her wishes and thanked her once again.

Part of the files provided by the FBI included newspaper articles published around the time of the murder and subsequent trials. Crisco and I had previously read the ones from the Mississippi papers. One article, from the *New Orleans Times-Picayune,* dated the day of the assassination, mentioned "Dr. A. B. Britton, Jr., a Negro physician who attended

Evers." Since we had not yet found any medical witness concerning the fatal wound, the reference to Dr. Britton caught my eye.

According to the article, Britton said Evers "was shot through the right side of the back with the bullet passing out the upper right chest. 'It left a big gaping hole.' Dr. Britton further said that Evers had a premonition Sunday that someone would make an attempt on his life. 'Medgar knew it would happen, and I guess all of us are to blame that he was not protected.'"

I recalled Myrlie Evers telling me how she had begged the NAACP national office to arrange protection for her husband. All they would do, according to her, was offer to relocate them to another state, and Medgar was not about to leave the state he loved and the work that drove him.

Still practicing in a Jackson clinic, sixty-eight-year-old Dr. Britton was happy to visit with us on November 28. He had been the family physician for Medgar's family and had delivered the three children, he said. He and Medgar had developed such a close relationship, they talked practically every day. Had he seen Medgar after the shooting?

"Of course. I did not attend the meeting that night. I was delivering a baby. But later, after I got home, Myrlie called me while Medgar was still lying in the carport after he'd been shot, and her words were 'Oh, Lordy, Dr. Britton, they have shot Medgar.' I immediately handed the phone to my wife and left."

"To the house or hospital?"

"Directly to the house at first, but someone had picked him up and headed to the University Hospital. I drove up at the hospital as they were taking him into the emergency room."

"So, you got there pretty much when he did?"

"I was right behind them, and that's when I began to assist and appraise his condition."

"Which was what?"

"I found everybody frantically trying to gather things together to help this man who had a gush of blood rushing out of his chest. When I first came in, some of them spent a little time trying to prevent me from getting in to where Mr. Evers was on the table. This was 1963 and all of the hospital doctors were white males. So, naturally it was a common, normal reaction to want to know what in the world I, a black man, was doing in there. One of the doctors looked up and recognized me and said, 'Come on, Doctor, we're trying to get a drip started.' They were unsuccessful, so I volunteered, 'Let me see what I can do.' And so we probed there awhile while other doctors were trying to stop the bleeding. We finally got a drip started, and the next step was to try to get some blood in him.

"I pushed down on the dressing on his chest to try to stop the flow and talk with him. I said, 'This is Dr. Britton, Medgar.' He looked up and opened his eyes. I asked him, 'Do you know who shot you?' But all he said, was 'Oh, Doc, Doc, oh . . .' Then he expired."

Mrs. Evers remarked to me several times how much she had resented well-meaning neighbors restraining her from going with her dying husband to the hospital. I doubt she'll ever get over it. During at least one of these discussions, she asked a question that had haunted her: Was his death due in part to substandard treatment by uncaring white doctors in a segregated Mississippi hospital?

I broached the subject with Dr. Britton. "I know what has been said," he began, "that he was neglected medically and all that, but that's a lot of baloney. I was there, and everybody did all that they could. I don't care if we had ten gallons of blood hanging up there, it would not have saved him. He didn't have a chance, even if he had been at the Mayo Clinic."

Speaking to Mrs. Evers that night, I informed her of Mary Ann Adams's chance encounter with Beckwith, and added that although Dr. Britton's account provided no evidence, I hoped that it would bring her some serenity to know from her family's physician that no effort was spared in the futile attempt to save Medgar's life.

After fourteen months, we were ready to take the case to the grand jury. I was anxious to see what eighteen citizens from various walks of life thought about it. If eighteen grand jurors didn't think much of our case, why should we believe that the twelve people on the trial jury would view it differently?

Grand juries are greatly swayed by prosecutors. In fact, nobody on behalf of the defendant is there. But the last thing we wanted was an indictment if there was no real chance at a conviction. Thus, Ed and I took some measures on Beckwith's behalf that we were under no obligation to do.

Most grand jury presentations consist only of the prosecution's evidence. Rarely are prosecutors aware of an accused person's defense at that early stage. We had the luxury, however, of knowing that Beckwith's defense was an alibi. To ensure an accurate gauge of our chances, we decided to produce that alibi for the grand jury's consideration. Also, even though the grand jury votes solely on the issue of probable cause rather than guilt beyond a reasonable doubt, we asked these grand jurors, ten blacks and eight whites, to put themselves in the place of trial jurors and indict only if they would vote guilty.

Finally, I asked Special Assistant Attorney General John Henry to be on hand to answer any questions the panel might have concerning the much publicized speedy-trial issue.

We were set to go on Thursday, December 13, 1990, and Myrlie Evers was the first witness. It wasn't legally necessary that she testify, but since Beckwith's alibi witnesses would do so, I didn't want any appearance of an unbalanced presentation. Also, seeing how the panel received Mrs. Evers was as important as gauging their reaction to Holley and Creswell. She did a superb job. The vivid, heart-wrenching account was not lost on anyone, black or white. Her testimony would weigh strongly in our favor at trial.

Next up were John Chamblee and Fred Sanders, the two detectives who had spearheaded the police department's 1963 investigation. We finished the day with Crisco providing the details of our work over the past year, including the statements of Delmar Dennis, Peggy Morgan, and Mary Ann Adams. Media people were encamped in the halls outside the grand jury room observing who went in and out. I didn't want these new witnesses subjected to media exposure, and so far, the cooperation of the two ladies wasn't publicly known. I wanted to keep it that way.

We began Friday, December 14, with Edgar Ray Killen, the reputed head of the Neshoba County Klan.

When the small-framed man entered the room, I wasn't sure if it was Killen from Neshoba County or a Snopes right out of Faulkner's Yoknapatawpha County. He was short, wiry, and dressed in jeans and boots. Even in December, his hands were brown and crusted. The Stetson he held in his callonsed hand had pressed his thinning salt-and-pepper hair in a band around his head. As the foreman swore him in, Killen spoke with a distinct backwoods nasal twang.

"What do you do for a living, Mr. Killen?"

"I run a dairy farm ten miles south of Philadelphia, and I cut pulpwood from time to time to buy a few groceries."

I recalled Tommy Mayfield's telling me that Killen was known in the Klan as Preacher. "Are you not a preacher, too?"

"Yes, sir, part-time."

"What about in 1964?"

"I was a full-time preacher back then—a Baptist. Look here, can I ask why I'm here? I'm really mystified by being here."

"This grand jury is investigating the shooting death of Medgar Evers on June twelfth, 1963," I explained.

"But, you see, I'm really mystified because I didn't even know Mr. . . . whatever his name is—Beckwith."

"That's interesting, Mr. Killen, because I didn't mention the name of Beckwith in connection with the murder; you did."

"Well, I ain't never heard of him except in the news."

"Have you ever been a member of the White Knights of the Ku Klux Klan of Mississippi?"

"Many people testified that I was."

"You were one of several defendants, including Sam Bowers, who were tried for the deaths of the three civil rights workers: Schwerner, Goodman, and Chaney, correct?"

"Yes, sir, but I was acquitted."

"Actually, the jury hung up on your case, right? They couldn't reach a verdict."

"That's right."

"I ask you again, Mr. Killen, were you a member of the Klan?"

"Many people said I was."

"Do you deny saying in 1964, following the arrest of you, Sam Bowers, and the other Klansmen for the three murders in Neshoba County, that there was no reason to worry, that the Evers murder was a Klan project and the killer is free today because of Klan contacts with some of the jurors and that the same thing was going to happen in your cases?"

"Well, first, I didn't know Sam Bowers was in the Klan."

"You're telling us that you did not know that the Imperial Wizard himself was in the Klan?" I asked incredulously, drawing open laughter from the grand jurors.

"Sam was the Imperial Wizard, you say?"

More laughter.

"Are you telling us that you didn't know that, Mr. Killen?"

"I heard that, but as far as, you know, Sam coming up to me and saying, 'I'm the Imperial Wizard,' no, he didn't do that."

"Of course he wouldn't. As a matter of fact, when you join the Klan, you take a solemn blood oath of secrecy, don't you?"

"You know, I don't remember what words they said, but, yes, sir, I deny ever saying the murder of what's his name, Evers, was a Klan project."

"Okay, we'll come back to that in a minute. What's a klavern, Mr. Killen?"

"I don't know how to give you a legal definition."

"How about an illegal one, then?"

More laughter.

"I reckon I don't know that either."

"Try."

"I suppose it would be a group of men working together."

"Klansmen?"

"I suppose."

"A local chapter?"

"I'd say that."

"What's a kleagle?"

"I don't know. You'd have to help me on that one."

"Forget it. I want to get back to the Evers murder."

"The only time I ever seen Beckwith was when he come by the court-room when we were on trial and shook hands with us."

"I thought you said earlier that you never heard of him."

"I hadn't until then."

"And that was after his 1964 trials, right?"

"Right."

"And you never heard of him until your trial?"

"None other than the news."

"So, he was a Klansman, too, and came by to shake hands and support you, right?"

"I didn't know he was Klan. I had no way."

"You had no way of knowing, and therefore never knew, that anyone else was in the Klan but you?"

"That's partially true." The laughter turned to a collective groan. "You see, I wasn't out checking and I wasn't as active as your file there evidently has me."

I picked up the file and let the edges of the pages run down my thumb. "I'm glad you realize the extent of our information, Mr. Killen, and I want you to keep that in mind when I ask you again, do you deny under oath making the statement that the assassination of Medgar Evers was a Klan project and that the killer went free because of Klan connections with the jury?"

"Just so's to avoid a perjury charge, I'll say no, I don't deny it. I don't remember it, but I don't deny it either."

I was through and asked the panel members if they had any questions. One asked Killen if he had ever been to Greenwood. His answer was interesting: "I'm not dropping names or anything, but I used to drive very, very often to visit with Senator James O. Eastland at his house in Doddsville, and I'd stop in Greenwood and eat at a truck stop there." Eastland was a U.S. senator for many years, serving as the powerful chairman of the Judiciary Committee and later as the president pro tem of the Senate.

Exiting the grand jury room, Preacher Killen told awaiting reporters, "I'm a Klan sympathizer, and I've been grilled a good bit lately about that."

Committing perjury in a capital case can land the liar in Parchman for life. For three-time losers like Jimmy Dale Morgan, whom Crisco had found and subpoenaed to the proceedings, that life sentence means just that; the only way out is in a pine box. This was the first thing I covered with him.

"How long have you lived in Greenwood?"

"Practically all my life. I been out of town a few times."

"Not to embarrass you, but a few of those out-of-town trips were to Parchman, weren't they?"

"That's right."

I was in a somewhat difficult situation regarding Morgan. While I had to see if he would verify the trip that his sister-in-law, Peggy, had related to us, I didn't feel comfortable letting him know that she was the source of our information. I tried a bluff and held my breath.

"Mr. Morgan, the grand jury is investigating the murder of Medgar Evers. During the course of our investigation, we obtained records from every federal and state agency, every page that has the name of Byron De La Beckwith on it."

I started walking to a table where I had stacks of reports. I grabbed one and started flipping pages. I had no idea which one I'd picked up.

"And we came across one particular record that we need to ask you about." I was scared that he would ask to look at it. Instead, Morgan ducked his head and started nodding. I had him. "We want to know why Beckwith would be visiting you at Parchman."

"Some guy asked me to get him up there to see him."

"What guy?"

"Cecil Sessums."

It wasn't Tommy Tarrants, but it was another Klan terrorist. Sessums was the Exalted Cyclops in charge of the 1966 Klan firebombing murder of civil rights leader Vernon Dahmer in Hattiesburg. Imperial Wizard Sam Bowers issued the order, but it was carried out under Sessums's supervision.

"Did you know Sessums was heavily involved in the Klan?"

"I heard that."

"Were you in the Klan?"

"No, sir."

Sessums wasn't convicted until 1968, thus the visit had to have occurred during Morgan's second period of incarceration, between December 1970 and July 1973. We had already discovered that when

Beckwith was arrested in New Orleans in September 1973, he listed his address as Dewey Street in Greenwood, the same street on which Peggy Morgan had said he lived.

"How did this come about?"

"Cecil just asked me to do him a favor and get word to Beckwith to get up there to see him. So I wrote my mother a letter—she lived in Greenwood, too—and asked her to contact him and tell him that Cecil Sessums wanted to see him. He came with my brother, Lloyd, and my sister-in-law, Peggy."

"Your brother is here today?"

"Right."

"Where is your sister-in-law?" I didn't want to give him the first clue that I knew anything about her.

"Mobile, I think."

"What happened after they got there?"

"Me and my visitors went one way. Cecil and him went another."

I had gotten what I needed from Jimmy Dale Morgan. His sister-in-law was telling the truth.

Lloyd was a piece of work. The forty-five-year-old roofer with a third-grade education stated at first that he never knew Beckwith personally: "I ain't never met him."

"Are you denying, then, on your oath and recognizing the penalty for lying, that you and your ex-wife gave him a ride to Parchman to visit another inmate while you visited your brother?"

"I might have did, but I don't remember back that far. If I give him a ride there, I reckon I did. He lived right across the street from us."

"On Dewey Street?"

"Yes, sir."

I tried the same bluff that had worked with Jimmy Dale. "Mr. Morgan, with these penitentiary records I'm holding in my hands, are you saying that you did or did not make such a trip?"

"Seemed like I did give him a ride up there, but I don't know who he was going to see."

"What kind of car did you go in?"

"Red and white '64 Ford."

"You remember that?"

"Yes, sir."

"What kind of vehicle did Beckwith have?"

"A Barrentine Manufacturing Company pickup truck."

"And you remember that? What all did Beckwith talk about on the way up there or back home?"

"I don't remember."

"Don't remember that."

"No, sir."

"Mr. Morgan, every time you say you don't remember something, I remind you of your oath, and then your memory clears up some. This will go a lot faster if you're just honest with us the first time a question is asked. Understand?"

"Yes, sir."

"Do you deny that Beckwith talked about having killed someone and gotten away with it?"

"I ain't saying it wasn't said. I just don't remember."

"If someone talked about committing murder, that would be something you'd remember, wouldn't it?"

"Not really."

"Why is that?"

"I been prosecuted for murder a time or two myself."

After exploring that revelation, I asked, "And, of course, when you gave Beckwith the ride to Parchman, you knew he had been tried for murdering Medgar Evers?"

"No, sir; not till the other day."

"How long have you lived in Greenwood?"

"Practically all my life."

"And you never knew until the other day that he had been tried for that murder?"

"That's right. I ain't an educated man. The news is not something I've ever watched."

"And you've never heard anyone in Greenwood talk about Beckwith's trials?"

"Not till the other day." Laughter erupted throughout the room.

"What happened the other day for you to learn that?"

"When Jimmy and me got them papers to be here, I asked him what he thought it was for, and he told me y'all was looking into this and probably wanted to know about me giving him that ride to Parchman."

"So, you did give Beckwith a ride and recalled that the other day?"

"Right."

"I want to know about the statements Beckwith made, Mr. Morgan."

"You really need to talk to my wife."

"Why is that?"

"'Cause Peggy would remember everything that was said. She remembers that kind of thing." Most people would, I thought, and turned the questioning over to the grand jurors.

One panelist asked Morgan, "Who made the arrangements for Beckwith to go with you?"

"I think my mama did it. He told me that Jimmy wrote her a letter that somebody up there wanted to see him."

"You remember that, but you don't remember anything Beckwith said on the way?" another grand juror asked.

"He didn't talk much." Everyone in the room laughed.

"Are you saying that Byron De La Beckwith was a quiet, reserved man with nothing to say?" I asked.

"Seemed to me he was." Some jurors openly laughed, some had doubtful smirks, and others just shook their heads in disbelief.

The real test of our case followed: Holley and Creswell. The knots in my stomach relaxed as their testimony progressed. The more they talked, the more preposterous their claims appeared. Unlike in a trial setting, questioning of a grand jury witness is not limited to one lawyer. Ed and I took full advantage of the opportunity. I began the questions, and just as I started to tire out, Ed jumped in; then I'd get my second wind. And the jurors themselves couldn't resist joining the feeding frenzy, as if the cops were some game fish hooked by the absurdity of their tale.

Afterward, I turned the proceedings over to John Henry of the attorney general's office. He explained that while an argument could be made that an indictment would not be barred by time, there was also one to the contrary. Such a gray area of the law had no guarantees, and if the grand jury did not feel that another indictment was warranted in view of such uncertainty or for any other reason, it would be their prerogative to end the matter then and there.

As with a trial jury, nobody is allowed in the room while a grand jury deliberates and votes with respect to indictments. Peculiar to grand jury proceedings, an indictment is kept secret until the defendant is taken into custody. The purpose, of course, is to prevent the defendant from fleeing once learning of his or her fate.

I explained all of this to Mrs. Evers in my office as the grand jury deliberated that Friday evening. It would've been unthinkable for her to leave without knowing, but I wasn't going to jail for telling her the vote.

"You mean you will know today?"

"Yes, ma'am. It has to be signed by the foreman and me if one is returned."

"But you can't tell me?"

"No, but you'll know."

"How many votes do we need?"

"Twelve or more of the eighteen."

"So, a majority is not enough?"

"No, ma'am. Twelve is the magic number."

"Oh, Bobby, we have never been able to get that number before."

I nodded. "This vote will tell us a lot about how our case is perceived."

"How did it go?"

"It went fine, Mrs. Evers. It's just out of our hands now."

"And Mr. Peters?"

"Totally committed."

Soon after I left Mrs. Evers and returned to the waiting room adjacent to the grand jury's quarters, the door opened, and jurors started turning in their name tags to the bailiff and leaving. Their work was finished. Was mine finished, too?

Making my way into the room, I spotted the foreman, who was heading my way.

"Seventeen to one."

"Sir?"

"That was the vote, seventeen to one."

"Yes, sir, but which way?"

"Which way? Didn't anybody believe those clowns. You got your indictment. The only holdout was a lady who just didn't think it should be reprosecuted because of the time. It wouldn't have mattered to her how much evidence you had."

I excused myself and returned to my office to retrieve the indictment I had earlier prepared. I found Mrs. Evers visiting with the office manager, Clara Mayfield; Nancy Lee, our victim assistance coordinator; and Glenda Haynes and Linda Anderson, two of the office's black prosecutors, in Linda's office. I shut the door after entering.

All eyes were focused on the seriousness on my face, but those of Mrs. Evers were penetrating. I slowly broke into a big grin and opened my arms wide.

"Yes!" Mrs. Evers exclaimed as she jumped out of her chair. As we embraced, I felt the rise and fall of her breathing, followed by the quick staccato spasm of weeping.

"Oh, Bobby," she said, wiping away tears of joy with the back of her hand. I handed her my handkerchief. "I can't believe it. We've come such a long, long way."

"Yes, we have, Mrs. Evers, but we've got a long way yet to go."

"Well, then, let's get the son of a bitch."

"My pleasure, ma'am."

I returned to the grand jury room with the indictment. The foreman signed it and handed it to me. Although my hand was trembling with nervous energy, I managed to scribble out my signature as well. As I did so, the foreman's name caught my eye. His last name was Evers, Carl Evers. He knew what was on my mind when I shot him a bewildered glance.

"No relation. As you can see, I'm white, and it's pronounced 'Eevers' with a long *e*. I'm a professor at the medical school." Dr. Carl Evers, foreman of the grand jury that had reindicted Beckwith after twenty-six years and having the same last name (although pronounced differently) as the victim, taught medicine at the same hospital where Medgar Evers died. Before we could get Beckwith to trial, Dr. Evers was killed in an automobile accident.

Close to 8 P.M., on Friday, December 14, 1990, Dr. Evers handed over the sealed indictments of the session to Senior Circuit Judge William F. Coleman. As I put my copy in my files, I noticed something else about the indictment. As all indictments in Mississippi must, it stated that the crime charged—here, the murder of Medgar Evers—was "against the peace and dignity of the State of Mississippi." Truer words were never printed. This murder, though, was against peace and dignity, period—of mankind and the human spirit.

CHAPTER SIX

THE LAST FULL MEASURE

The ink of the foreman's signature on the indictment wasn't yet dry, and Beckwith kept talking, much to my delight. The world, thanks to the media, would soon see Beckwith for what he was. As *USA Today* reporter Lee Howard observed, "Byron De La Beckwith is a grandfatherly seventy-year-old, quick with a disarming smile and a twinkle in his eye. But the image falls apart as soon as he opens his mouth."

In an interview at his home in Signal Mountain, while awaiting word of the grand jury's action, Beckwith told Howard, "We need to reestablish a Confederate States of America as a white Christian republic. I'm not willing to lay my life down to rid evil from this country. I'm willing to kill the evil in this country." But, Beckwith noted, "I don't feel good. I don't hear good. I don't see good. I'm getting a cataract in my right eye and that's my shooting eye."

A reporter from the *Washington Post* was also in Signal Mountain interviewing various townsfolk concerning their perception of neighbor Beckwith. A man who ran a service station on the main drag recalled, "When my mother died, Beckwith came to the funeral, and he said to my nephew at the graveyard, 'This is the way a funeral ought to be: no niggers and no Jews.'"

Even after his arrest on Monday, December 17, at 8 A.M., Beckwith continued to show that the seventy-year-old grandfather still had a violent side. Being led into the Hamilton County jail in Chattanooga, he snarled at reporters and asked, "How many Jews are among you? I saw one nigra man." Pointing to one reporter, he asked, "Are you a Jew? You look like a Jew to me. You want me to shove that camera down your throat?"

Inside the courtroom, Beckwith told Hamilton County criminal court judge Joseph DiRisio that the murder charge was "nonsense, poppycock, and just something to incite the lower forms of life to force and violence against the country-club set."

Afterward, when asked about the prospect of a third trial, a feisty Beckwith responded, "Do I look like I'm trembling, smoking cigarettes, and biting my toenails? I look forward with the greatest anticipation of thrashing the people waging war against me. That'll be more publicity for my book."

"What in the hell is wrong with Mississippi?" Thelma Beckwith asked. "He's not going to Mississippi. I bet you, two to one, he won't."

In an extradition hearing the judge considers only the identity of the person named in the warrant, the validity of the charge, and whether the person charged was in the state when the crime occurred. Notwithstanding this narrow scope of an extradition hearing and Beckwith's bravado about returning to Mississippi to stand trial, he publicly vowed to fight extradition "tooth, nail, and claw." Judge DiRisio ruled against Beckwith in that fight in a court appearance the same day of his arrest. Hamilton County assistant district attorney Rodney Strong, with whom I had been conferring by telephone, said, "We pulled a tooth today. Now we're down to the nail and claw." Appeals followed.

Ed and I issued a statement hoping that the community would pull together "rather than become polarized along racial lines and that everyone will view this reprosecution with an eye toward the evidence rather than fixing upon the race of the victim and that of the defendant." We also expressed hope "that no one will automatically support nor condemn our endeavors. . . . If Beckwith is innocent, he should be acquitted. If he is guilty, he should be convicted. . . . It is that simple. Justice can only be served if there is a final conclusion, once and for all."

It didn't take long, though, for the white supremacy groups to make their feelings known. The *Clarion-Ledger* reported that Joe McNamee of Jackson, a spokesman for the Confederate Knights of the Ku Klux Klan in Mississippi, had announced plans for a rally and fund-raiser in support of Beckwith when he returned to Mississippi for trial. "We don't look at him as a murderer. We look at him as a hero," McNamee said.

The National Association for the Advancement of White People also announced its support of Beckwith. "The NAAWP views the indictment of . . . Beckwith [as] a travesty upon justice," said Scott Shepherd of Memphis, the group's national director. "It is our belief that this attempt to convict . . . Beckwith is nothing more than a plot to hide the true identity of the killer of Medgar Evers."

Ex-Klan leader and then–Louisiana gubernatorial candidate David Duke likewise jumped on the Beckwith bandwagon.

W. B. Johnson, owner of Johnson Oil Company in Durant, Mississippi, wrote to me: "It is my practice to write in support of elected officials when they fight for what is right and make stands whether popular or unpopular. In your case, however, I can find nothing that warrants any support from morally upright citizens. . . . The day will come when your pitiful existence will only be a memory."

Watkins Ellsworth "Wat" Overton III, of Memphis, was chagrined by our stand. He considered Medgar Evers "a negro radical revolutionary and racist."

This is an immoral, cynical, self-serving attempt by certain officials to commit a legal lynching. . . . It is an egregious example of an abuse of public trust and judicial power. It marks the man who commits these outrages as a renegade, a scalawag and a traitor to his own race. An affront to decent people, an outcast to be scorned and ridiculed by honorable men. In common language—white trash.

Virulent letters also came from the North. One from Sam Brown Jr. of Reading, Pennsylvania, was replete with such comments as "blacks are sub-humans" and "black supremacy vs. white supremacy = *WAR!*" Another letter, unsigned, but postmarked from Rochester, New York, was titled "Definition of a Nigger." It contained a virulent racist "description" and ended: "P.S. We would be duly honored if you would forward this 'paragon of truth' to Mrs. Medgar Evers. Thanks, you Jew-faggot!"

So much for any enlightenment from the North. Hate, ignorance, and racism are not pure Southern maladies. These afflictions of the soul abound everywhere.

Amid this environment, Crisco and I kept working.

"YOU MISSED THE BIG ONE!!" read the first line of the phone message that Jeanie had left in my box on January 16. Thelma Beckwith had called. "You and Ed ruined their family's holiday . . . and you . . . will be punished for this," it read. I didn't appreciate at the time just how right she was.

Like a hurricane, some disasters are predicted, permitting preparation before they wreak havoc. Others, like a tornado, often strike without warning. I should've seen the signs—they were all there—but I never saw the cyclone that rocked the very foundation of my family.

After seventeen years, my marriage completely disintegrated. Dixie said that she needed someone more supportive of her and in tune with her feelings. I was angry, hurt, and devastated, but I forced myself to think clearly, rationally, and methodically. The only thing of which I was certain was that I wasn't going to leave the children. Dixie immediately moved in with her mother, and on February 15, she agreed to an order awarding temporary custody of the children to me. I agreed to a no-fault divorce, and the final order would be entered on April 15.

Just as I was picking myself up in my personal life, I received a phone call that knocked me to my knees emotionally. The kids and I arrived home one night following one of Burt's Little League games. Burt was undressing to shower; Claire and Drew were climbing into bed. I sat down on my bed to untie my Nikes and noticed the message light flashing on the bedside answering machine. I reached over and hit the PLAY button, then finished taking off my shoes and socks.

"I'm nearby watching," began the voice on the machine. I jerked up and stared at it. What the hell? "I wouldn't miss this for anything. I hope you don't. You see, there's a bomb in your house. It's set to go off at ten o'clock. Ha! Ha! Ha!"

The clock was steadily ticking on a nearby shelf. Seven minutes before ten. My mind raced. A hoax or serious threat? Whatever the reality, my heart was screaming, "You can't take a chance, get the hell out!"

I jumped up, barefoot, and sprinted through the house. I burst through the bathroom door and told Burt to pull his pants up and run to the truck.

"Sir?" he asked.

"Just do it!" Claire and Drew were up by then wanting to know what was wrong. I picked up Drew with one arm and grabbed Claire with the other hand. "Nothing's wrong, sweetie, we're just seeing how fast we can make it to Granny's house. It's a drill," I said, fleeing to the truck, my gut wrenching at the thought of being watched as the message had said. Was there a bomb or was the call a ruse to flush us out of the house, like a covey of quail from their brush, only to gun us down?

We made it to the truck, no shots. Well down the street, I slowed and listened. It was straight-up ten o'clock, but no explosion.

Once at my parents' house, I sent the kids to bed. Daddy was already asleep, and in hushed whispers I related the message left for me to my mother.

"Have you called the police?"

"No. All I could think of was getting the kids out. I can't call or tell anybody, Mama."

"What the devil do you mean, Son?"

"It was a hoax, Mama."

"This time."

"I have to deal with things as they come. If I call the police or tell *any-body* about this, the media is going to get wind of it. Word on this will spread like wildfire, which will only give ideas to other crackpots. This one was a hoax. The next nutcase may opt for the real thing. And, what do you think Dixie would do with this? She'd have me back in court in no time seeking custody, claiming that my involvement in this case was putting the children in harm's way.

"I'm not willing to give up my children because of some cracker's idea of a sick joke. They've got my attention and I'll be extra careful, but you've got to trust me, Mama. You can't tell a soul. Okay?"

The kids spent the night there and I returned home. The house was intact, the neighborhood quiet. Armed with a flashlight, I searched the perimeter of the house, then every nook and cranny inside.

It was a hoax, but I nonetheless felt violated, angry, and afraid for my family. Was I making the right decision in not reporting it? If not, I'd never forgive myself. It is one I will always second-guess. I said more than one prayer that night, but from that night on, I kept my Smith & Wesson .38 close by.

While cooperating with the FBI on another case, Lester Paul Hockman, incarcerated in an undisclosed federal facility, informed Agent Daniel Lund that he also possessed critical information regarding Beckwith's assassination of Medgar Evers.

Although Hockman had lived most of his life in another part of the country, his work as a carpenter had carried him to New Orleans, Louisiana. The report stated that in 1978 he was convicted and incarcerated for a shooting. Assigned for several weeks to clean the receiving unit at Angola Penitentiary, Hockman claimed to have met Beckwith, who was serving time on his New Orleans charge.

Hockman told Agent Lund that "Beckwith liked him because both were of German descent and talked freely to him." Beckwith frequently spoke of a person he greatly admired named Smith.* Hockman recalled seeing the name on some of the Klan literature that Beckwith kept in his cell. Smith, according to Hockman's account, ordered the hit on Evers, "as well as several bombings that resulted in the deaths of innocent people." A proficient shot as a boy, Beckwith bragged to Hockman that he "did not even need to use the scope to shoot Evers, whom he shot once in

---

*The name Smith is a false name.

the back." Beckwith said that "he had watched Evers's house for some time before the shooting" and "that he alone had shot Medgar Evers."

Asked by Hockman about the church bombings, Beckwith reportedly said, "Niggers are like roaches. You've got to exterminate them." Hockman reminded Beckwith that women and children were in those churches, to which Beckwith responded, "Hitting churches gave the opportunity to catch bunches of females who needed to be eradicated because they bear children."

Hockman said that Beckwith spoke openly about the murder of Evers, saying, "He was not worried about being prosecuted because he had been tried twice and found not guilty." Beckwith was so radical, Hockman "became uncomfortable" around him and "cut down his contact with him."

"Looks like we might have something," Crisco said.

"Maybe," I replied. "But he obviously wants something, and a lot of stuff could've been learned from the news."

"He's definitely got baggage," Crisco responded, tossing a five-page rap sheet on my desk.

"Damn. This guy's convictions go back to 1945." I read the list: auto theft, robbery, breaking and entering, and assault. He had spent most of the time since the end of World War II in prison. He was currently doing time for assault with a deadly weapon, but his sentence at Angola was for attempted second-degree murder. One entry caught my eye. On a '68 three-count charge of burglary, armed robbery, and assault, Hockman was found "not guilty *by reason of insanity.*"

"Shit, Crisco, this bird is a real Froot Loop, man." I showed him the entry.

"And Beckwith's not? Sounds just like the sort of guy our boy would pal around with."

"You have a point, but the defense will kill us with this."

"Let me at least go talk to him."

I agreed, so on May 2, 1991, Crisco hooked up with FBI agent Mike Soohy and interviewed Hockman at the federal pen.

Hockman, now sixty-one, confirmed to Crisco his statements in the FBI report and then some. Beckwith told Hockman that he preferred to be called Baron.

"After several conversations with Mr. Beckwith I expressed a desire to join the Klan," Hockman told Crisco. "I had an uncle years ago who was in the Klan. Beckwith seemed to want to impress me as to the power of the Klan, what they could accomplish if I joined them. And, to that end, he gave me several brochures to read which were stacked, I'd say, two feet high all the way around his cell."

Crisco asked what Beckwith had said about Smith.

"He said that Smith gave him the orders to transport the explosives to those who actually exploded the device in the Selma, Alabama, church that Sunday morning the four little girls were killed."

"The report mentioned some statement about roaches," prompted Crisco.

"Frankly, I lost all interest in joining the Klan when he described to me about the four little girls being killed. I asked him, 'Why?' and he told me that niggers are like roaches and you've gotta step on them while they're young."

"And that's when you lost interest in joining the Klan?"

"I'm not exactly a pillar of society, but that goes too far."

"Did he say anything about whether the murder of Medgar Evers was a Klan-authorized killing?"

"He mentioned that he never did anything in those days without Mr. Smith's okay. Beckwith said it was his own idea to kill Evers and nobody helped him, but there was a Klan meeting when it was agreed on."

"Did he say anything else about Evers?"

"He told me that he had gotten the address where Mr. Evers lived from a cabdriver."

"Any other details?"

"He said he had spent all of his life hunting in the woods and he knew a killing shot as soon as he pulled the trigger. He said he knew the man was dead as he pulled the trigger. Before the shot even hit him, he said he knew he was dead."

"Anything else?"

"He said that the governor of the state at the time, whoever that was, assisted him greatly. He said he had a lot of local support, too; that two individuals, policemen I believe, provided him with a good alibi that he was in town some distance away, and he spoke of that as a joke."

If Hockman was telling the truth, it would be good testimony for us, but that insanity verdict scared me. The FBI put him on a polygraph at my request. The results were "inconclusive." Hockman was an enigma I'd have to deal with later.

While the extradition fight in Tennessee afforded me time to get my life back in order, as well as a chance to try some other cases, the delay took its toll on a crucial witness. In a letter dated May 2, 1991, Delmar Dennis told me neither he nor his family were "holding up well" and requested that I drop his name from my witness list. "I admire your courageous work," he wrote. "Perhaps your generation will be able to stop those sinister forces which seek to perpetuate hate and murder in the name of Christianity. God knows I did my part and I only regret that it was of little help."

I got Delmar on the phone and coaxed him into hanging in there with me. He asked, however, if I would get the word out that he was defecting. Déjà vu? I agreed only on the condition that this time he not go on national television and expose my statements to that effect a pack of lies, as had happened following my first visit with him the previous year.

Autopsy, to the average person, is understandably a word with negative connotations. Dr. Michael Baden, however, in his *Unnatural Death: Confessions of a Medical Examiner,* makes the introductory point that through an autopsy, forensic pathologists such as himself make the body speak and that "deciphering the message is an art as well as a science."

I've only attended one autopsy in my career, but it left me with a deep appreciation of Baden's work and his words. His autopsy of Medgar Evers in June 1991, almost twenty-eight years to the day after Evers was murdered, was the most surreal experience yet in the case.

I was familiar with the career of this world-renowned forensic pathologist and had heard his partner, Dr. Lowell Levine, speak at a forensic science seminar in San Francisco. Levine is an odontologist with quite a résumé of his own. Most notably, he assisted in the identification of the remains of Josef Mengele, the Nazi war criminal, in South America. He and Baden are codirectors of the New York State Police Forensic Science Unit. I met Dr. Baden in mid-May at the Mississippi Prosecutors' Association conference, where he and Levine were speaking.

Ed Peters is a longtime friend of Michael Baden's, and through that friendship we got the esteemed doctors to Mississippi. As officers of the association, Ed and I were honored to serve as the hosts for our guests.

Eventually the subject of the Evers case arose. Ed and I explained some of the problems caused by the passage of time. Dr. Forrest Bratley, the pathologist who had performed the autopsy of Evers in 1963, was alive and residing in Jackson, but because of his age we weren't sure if he would still be around by the time we got to trial.

"What will you do if Dr. Bratley expires?" Baden asked.

"We'll introduce a certified copy of the death certificate and have Dr. Bratley's testimony at the first trial read to the jury," I explained.

"That seems rather sterile in a case otherwise rife with drama, wouldn't you say?"

"I don't know what else to do."

"Any suggestions, Michael?" Ed asked. "You look like you've got something on your mind."

"Have you thought about an exhumation and second autopsy?" Before Ed or I could say anything, Dr. Baden continued, "You'd be surprised what can be learned."

"Even after twenty-eight years?" I asked.

"It's possible. I've yet to come up empty-handed with one." Baden cited the recent work he and Levine had done regarding Czar Nicholas II and his family.

"But what would you reasonably expect to accomplish in this case?" Ed asked.

"First, there's the likelihood of obtaining physical evidence. You don't have the bullet, but a wound caused by a high-caliber rifle like a .30-06 frequently leaves a starburst pattern of fragments from the bullet. Second, and most important for your purposes, is insurance. If Dr. Bratley can't testify because of illness or death, you can still call the pathologist who conducted the second autopsy. You say you don't have photos from the first one showing the entrance wound, exit wound, and trajectory?"

"That's right," I confessed.

"See, if you do it again, you will also have pictures."

"Yeah, but what would something like this cost?" Ed inquired.

Dr. Baden told us that he would do it at no cost, provided it was done at his home base, Albany Medical Center in New York.

Ed thought it was a good idea and I agreed. We would need a court order authorizing the expense of the exhumation and reburial, so Ed secured one from Judge Hilburn. My initial job was to get the consent of Myrlie Evers.

After the initial shock subsided, Mrs. Evers realized the importance of the endeavor. Dr. Baden had also asked me to give her his phone number. He wanted to ease her mind as much as possible and answer any questions she might have. Calling me back after speaking with him, Myrlie Evers gave her consent but added one condition. Her son Van, the youngest of the children, had no recollection of his father. His only memories were those passed along by his mother and older siblings, Darrell and Reena. The sole images etched in his mind of his father were from photographs. The condition attached to Mrs. Evers's consent jolted me. Van insisted on attending. It was, in his mind, his only chance to cast his eyes on his dad.

"But, Mrs. Evers," I pleaded, "it's been twenty-eight years. Casting his eyes on the body now probably isn't the image of his dad he needs to have burned into his memory."

"Bobby, oh how I know that. And I've said as much to him, but he's so like Medgar. He's not giving an inch, and this is his call to make." I had no control over the autopsy. Dr. Baden was the captain in charge of that ship. I decided not to press the issue with Mrs. Evers but to enlist Baden's help in talking with Van once we were there.

I sent Mrs. Evers a written consent form to sign and get back to me. In my cover letter, I assured her that "after talking with Dr. Baden, as well as the superintendent at the National Cemetery and all others concerned, this procedure will be carried out in a professional and respectful manner, with no fanfare."

Early on the morning of June 3, 1991, Crisco and I arrived at the office of Jack Metzler, superintendent of Arlington National Cemetery. Metzler had been kind enough to make arrangements for the exhumation and transportation of Evers's body to Albany by Arlington Funeral Home (not connected with the cemetery). We presented Metzler our paperwork, and while he perused the court order and consent forms, Crisco and I met Van, who was waiting in Metzler's office.

At 7:30 A.M., Metzler escorted us to the grave, located on a gentle slope, and within five minutes the exhumation began. While the backhoe did its work, we introduced ourselves to Ron Unger and Don Hendrickson, both of the Arlington Funeral Home. Ron and Don were to drive the hearse to Albany, followed by Crisco, Van, and me in a rental car.

Part of Judge Hilburn's order directed that the entire process be videotaped. Crisco handled that duty while I took still photos. I thought I was doing a credible job, but Van politely asked to take over. Learning that he was a professional photographer, I gladly relinquished the office Nikon.

I was amazed at the grave's depth. Metzler explained that at the time of Evers's burial graves there were twelve feet deep instead of the customary six feet. This permitted spouses to be subsequently buried atop the veterans. Lack of space prohibited burial alongside one another.

By 9 A.M., the casket was removed. After loading it into the hearse, Ron and Don seated themselves in front. Crisco got behind the wheel of our rental, and I made myself comfortable in the passenger seat. We had stored our briefcases in the trunk with our baggage so Van, who was quite tall, could stretch out on the backseat, but he insisted on riding in the hearse. Ron had shown him that there were no backseats, so Van climbed in the back and stretched out by the coffin.

We arrived at Albany Medical Center at 5:40 P.M. The drive had taken us between eight and nine hours. I have trouble with my knees when I ride over a couple of hours, and they were killing me. I could only imagine Van's discomfort.

We met Capt. Tim McAuliffe, Baden and Levine's boss with the NYSP, who had made arrangements with hospital personnel to maintain security of Evers's body. I wrote the date and my initials on the cardboard box containing the casket, which was then locked in the morgue. A guard was posted at the morgue door throughout the night. Upon each change in shift, the guard being relieved signed a sheet relinquishing custody to his replacement. A strict chain of custody was thus maintained. I signed the first entry surrendering custody to Steve Robinson, who had the first watch, and then Tim escorted us to the Holiday Inn.

Dr. Baden telephoned with some relieving news. He had spoken with Van and agreed to a compromise. Van would not be on hand when the casket was first opened. Once the condition of the body was known, Dr. Baden would telephone Van at his hotel room and give him a description. Van would then make his final decision on whether to take a look.

The whole group, sans Van, met at the morgue at 9 A.M., June 4. Fifteen minutes later, Dr. Baden was preparing to remove the cardboard box. Crisco had the VCR camera and I double-checked the Nikon to make sure it had a fresh roll of film. My stomach was doing flips. Was I going to embarrass myself and throw up? Worse, although I had never fainted, would this be the occasion? Such were my thoughts as I listened to Dr. Baden dictating his every move for Crisco's camera.

The dramatic moment arrived. It was time to open the lid and see what we had. Since the body had been in the ground for twenty-eight years, Baden had arranged for a forensic anthropologist to be present. If the coffin contained skeletal remains, the findings of such an expert would be crucial. Dr. William Maples, although based in Florida, had worked with Baden and Levine many times. He had also been in charge of examining and identifying the remains of our nation's MIAs as they were brought to Honolulu from Southeast Asia.

"Ready?" Baden asked. Everyone circled the casket. I stood out of the way on a stepladder positioned at the front of the coffin. I focused the camera, ready to shoot whatever appeared in the viewfinder.

"Okay, here we go," Baden announced. As he opened the lid, a collective gasp sounded throughout the room. The body was in pristine condition! Medgar Evers looked as if he had just been placed in the coffin, lid up, for a wake. I couldn't believe it, but then again I had never been to an

autopsy before. The import of what I was witnessing, however, was verified by the astonishment of the world-renowned experts.

"Boys, it's going to be a good day," proclaimed Dr. Baden as he slapped
me on the back. Still reeling from the coffin's revelation, I was almost
knocked off the ladder.

As cameras flashed, a grinning Michael Baden turned to Captain
McAuliffe. "Tim, send someone to get Van. There's no reason to even
call. Just go get him. This is incredible."

"Well, you guys sure don't need me," the anthropologist announced.
"I'm out of here." Dr. Maples was right. We were looking at Medgar
Evers just as he was when Myrlie had said good-bye to him for the last
time over a quarter century earlier. He wore a dark suit, white shirt, and
NAACP tie.

While we waited for Van, we took many photos, including one with a
copy of that day's *Albany Times Union* newspaper, which featured a front-
page article and headline: "Evers Suspect May Face Third Trial."

Dr. Baden credited the perfect condition of the body to several factors,
starting with an excellent embalming job at Collins Funeral Home in
Jackson. Since moisture is the greatest enemy in the body's resistance to
decay, the twelve-foot-deep grave on one of Arlington's slopes had aided
tremendously. "I'm a man of science, and that's the scientific explanation," Baden continued. "Beyond that, all I can say is . . ." He paused a
moment. "Are you a religious man, Bobby?" I nodded. "Then you can
appreciate the unscientific explanation." Indeed, I did.

Excited chatter quelled as Van entered the room. Those of us standing
around the casket eased away and stood along the wall. It was unspoken,
but clearly understood, that it was time for forensics, science, and law to
take a backseat to humanity. The youngest son of Medgar Evers edged up
to the coffin and beheld the visage that death had withheld from him for
twenty-eight years, the countenance snatched from the grasp of his
memory by that sniper's bullet that had come to have such an impact on
my life. The bullet that had taken Medgar Evers away was a weapon of
separation; but it also bound me with that young man reaching out
and, just for a moment, gently stroking his father's hair. He needed
this moment, and already I felt the mission was worth the time and
effort.

I was standing behind Van, and after fifteen minutes of total silence, I
noticed his shoulders slightly tremble. But for the stainless-steel furnish-
ings, the atmosphere was more that of a wake. I stepped forward to Van's
left, and looking at his dad with him, I placed my hand on the son's

shoulder. Instinctively he turned and embraced me. "Thank you," he whispered. "Thank you for me and for my family. It's something I'll always treasure."

Glancing over Van's shoulder, I noticed other silent tears, a spontaneous and honest display of human values and emotions during a historic and trying time.

"I know," I whispered to Van. "Now, in the words of your mother, let's keep doing what we can to get the SOB who did this." Van nodded and walked over to thank Dr. Baden and the others.

After Van's departure, the lower part of the coffin lid was opened, revealing a Masonic apron, an Elk's fez or cap, and, amazingly, cedar leaves that were still green and fragrant. These were photographed, removed, and rephotographed.

The body was then taken from the casket and the clothing removed. After James Booth, of the NYSP, took fingerprints of the body, the autopsy began at noon and lasted over five hours. By its conclusion, we had X rays showing a starburst pattern of lead fragments left by the exploding bullet as it tore through Evers's torso. We also had a vial of these fragments, which Baden had meticulously removed, one at a time.

Jurors love physical evidence. Because of all the things they see on TV, they expect it. There is no substitute for their being able to hold an item of evidence and look at it, rather than merely hearing about it. While we did not have the bullet itself, our jury would be able to see the fragments from Medgar Evers's body and hold them in their hands.

Just as important, if not most important, to me, were the photographs of Medgar. I was previously concerned that because of the age of the case, the courtroom presentation would be more of a political or historical debate than a murder trial. Homicide cases cannot be tried in a vacuum. The victim must be humanized for the jury, since by the nature of the case, the victim is the only person involved whom the jury will not see. Since Evers was understandably rushed to the hospital, we lacked crime-scene photos to humanize him for our jury. The photos taken that day in June 1991 filled the void. They would see the face of the man, the face that a cowardly, back-shooting Beckwith had refused to see.

Dr. Baden and I had promised to call Myrlie Evers and report the day's discoveries, so Crisco and I joined Michael in his office on the NYSP campus. It was late in the day and everyone would've welcomed a night's rest before returning, but arrangements were already made for a seven-thirty reburial the next morning. We had not counted on the procedure taking so long and had grossly miscalculated the driving time between Albany and D.C.

Even though I still needed to call Mrs. Evers, there was no reason to further delay the others. At 5:45 P.M., Ron and Don pulled the hearse out of the medical center and picked up Van at the hotel.

Dr. Baden gave Myrlie Evers the details of the day's events while I telephoned Ed at his house and did likewise. When Baden was finished, I spoke to Mrs. Evers.

"It was truly a remarkable day," I told her.

"Bobby, you know the misgivings I had, especially concerning Van, but I spoke with him this afternoon—he called me from his room after he left the medical center—and this has been so good for him. Thank you."

"No, thank you for consenting to this. It was an emotional risk for you, I know, but it paid off big." I then explained the importance of the lead fragments and the photographs of the pristine body for the jurors.

"You know, Bobby, it's like Medgar was saying, 'This is the final thing that I can give you: myself. Now take it and go do justice for me, my family, and the Mississippi I dreamed of.'"

I wondered whether any prosecutor had ever been asked so much. Myrlie Evers's book, *For Us, the Living,* derived its title from Lincoln's Gettysburg Address. I thought of another phrase in the speech: "the last full measure of devotion." Medgar Evers gave just that for his cause. I could do no less in the cause of justice and for the sake of the human spirit.

Dan Prince, a forty-six-year-old ex-tenant of the Beckwiths', came to our attention in mid-August. According to an article in the *Chattanooga Times* newspaper, Prince was yet another person to whom Beckwith had made some incriminating statements. I dispatched Crisco and Benny to Chattanooga for an interview. They met Prince at the DA's office there on August 21. I had a string of trials coming up, so I stayed in Jackson.

The Beckwiths had rented an apartment attached to their Signal Mountain home to Prince, a former city sanitation worker, beginning in November 1986 until an argument between them the following August. Prince confirmed to Crisco and Benny, "While talking with Mr. Beckwith on several occasions, he talked to me about the case in Mississippi. He never referred to him as Medgar Evers. It was 'that nigger.' He said he was tried twice and both times acquitted."

"What specific statements did he make about that?" Crisco asked.

"One particular time, when talking to him in his front yard about the case, he said he had a job to do and he done it, and he didn't suffer any more for it than my wife would if she was gonna have a baby." It sounded a lot like the statement of Beckwith's that Delmar Dennis had related.

"Anything else?"

"When they kicked me out of the apartment, he said that he was tried for killing that nigger, and his job was killing people and it was national and he wasn't gonna let some local like me mess him up."

"What was he referring to?"

"I was arrested for vandalism. Me and my wife were divorced. The house was vandalized and she put the finger on me. The police arrested me at the place I was renting from Mr. Beckwith. They kicked me out because they didn't want the police there. He didn't want any heat on him."

"Why are you now coming forward?"

"It bothered me a lot and I kept up on the story and was about sick and tired of hearing the man's stories that he's not guilty."

"Did he ever mention the Klan?"

"He said he was a member and gave me some literature—a couple of pamphlets on the Klan."

"Who did you first tell this to?"

"Dick Cauthern, *Chattanooga Times.*"

"Has anyone else contacted you about the statements you made to him that were in the paper?"

"Just your office."

"Are you willing to testify?"

"Yes, I am."

We now had four "bragging" witnesses, people to whom Beckwith had boasted of killing Medgar Evers.

I received messages during a house-burglary trial in the fall that Tennessee's assistant attorney general Kathy Principe and governor's extradition officer Rose Hill had called. Something was up. I returned their calls during the midmorning break. The Tennessee Supreme Court had okayed Beckwith's extradition. It was time to send Hinds County deputies to pick him up, so I notified Sgt. Tim Matheny of the HCSO warrants division.

By the afternoon recess, however, another message from Principe was passed to me at the counsel table. At the first opportunity I reached her at her Nashville office. Beckwith's Tennessee lawyer had already filed a petition seeking relief in the U.S. district court. Having taken over nine months to exhaust his state court remedies, Beckwith was just starting in the federal courts. I wasn't sure if our witnesses, especially Delmar Dennis, would stay on board for another nine months. We had to do something.

Kathy indicated that we might have a narrow window of opportunity. The matter was assigned to Judge R. Allen Edgar, who was expected to rule rather expeditiously, possibly within the next few days. If he ruled in our favor, and if our deputies were in Chattanooga when the order was entered, and if they could whisk Beckwith away and across the state line before his lawyer filed papers appealing to the Sixth Circuit Court of Appeals, we would legally have our man. All Tennessee courts, state and federal, would lose jurisdiction in the matter the second Beckwith left that state's borders. We would have to move quickly, though, because Beckwith's attorney probably already had the appeal documents prepared and ready to file as soon as Judge Edgar's decision was rendered.

There was a big chance that our deputies would make a dry run, wasting two days on the road. In addition to the likelihood that an appeal would be filed before they could transport Beckwith out of Tennessee, Judge Edgar might not rule for weeks or even months.

I felt we had to try it, but, of course, Ed and Sheriff J. D. McAdory made the final decision. Sgt. Matheny and Capt. Sammy Magee (who had originally worked on the case as a cop in 1963) would be dispatched for two days. If the judge had not ruled by then, they were to come home. Tim and Sammy made the trip in street clothes. Linda Hamilton, of the sheriff's office in Chattanooga, would be their contact person. She, in turn, would be in contact with Kathy Principe and Rose Hill.

The deputies left Jackson on Wednesday, October 2, and checked in with Linda the next morning. By 11:30 A.M., the phone call came. Judge Edgar had ruled in our favor. Sammy and Tim raced to the federal courthouse, and while Tim ran inside to get a copy of the order, Sammy kept his unmarked car running in front. With the order in hand, they sped to the Hamilton County jail, and with Linda's assistance, they removed Beckwith from his cell by 12:15 CDT.

Beckwith was irate and throwing a fit as he was rushed to the car, yelling that he was being kidnapped. The maneuver went as planned and happened so quickly that neither Beckwith's wife nor lawyer was seen. As inevitably happens, word leaked enough that a reporter was hanging around the area. Ushered into the back of the patrol car, an angry Beckwith was approached by the female journalist. Asked if he killed Evers, Beckwith snapped back, "Are you pregnant!" With that, his head was pushed inside the car, the door shut, and Tim shot out of town, speeding toward the state line. As they zoomed past Signal Mountain, Beckwith announced, "Well, I guess you can see there's no dogs up here. It's because of all the Vietnamese that swooped in here. Ate every last one of them."

All the way to the border, Beckwith was telling the deputies that "they" (whoever "they" were) weren't going to stand for his being abducted and would be waiting at the state line. Then he started laughing and said, "Don't you see the humor in it? They're gonna take us all back. I'm going to appeal and go free and you boys . . ." He paused to catch his breath. "Well, you boys will have my old cell serving time for kidnapping. Yes, sir. Ha! Ha! Ha!"

Tim had the cruiser speeding down I-59 at full throttle. He paid no attention to Beckwith's ranting, but he couldn't discount the possibility of the appeal being filed and state troopers waiting at the state line. Within minutes, though, the burgundy Crown Victoria zipped past a sign: "Welcome to Georgia, the Peach State." Sammy and Tim could now put the car on cruise control and relax. They were home free. To an astonished Beckwith, it meant defeat in another round of our bout. For the first few miles in Georgia, the usually loudmouthed Beckwith was stunned into a brief silence.

The hush was short-lived, as Beckwith began to complain about the speed at which they were traveling. Indeed, Tim was burning up the road, stopping only once to let their prisoner go to the bathroom.

Although not speaking of the case, as they cut across northern Alabama and angled southwest into Mississippi, Beckwith's conversation inevitably turned to race. The United States was being taken over by the "dusky races," who were actually cannibals eating their way to power. He informed Sammy, who is seldom without a cigar in his mouth, that the deputy was safe. "The niggers can't stand cigar smoke. But you," Beckwith said, leaning from the rear seat toward the cage and behind Tim's ear, "you better be careful; they'll eat you, my friend, in a minute!"

Word of his return to Jackson had spread far and wide by the time the car pulled into the Hinds County Detention Center at 6:35 P.M. Passing the horde of reporters outside the booking office, Sammy turned to Beckwith and told him, "As you can see, there are a lot of reporters out there. We're going to rush you in between the two of us, and you aren't going to say a damn word to anybody. You got it?" Beckwith nodded and they were out. Once amid the throng, though, his mouth went to work.

"Did you kill Medgar Evers?" asked one reporter who couldn't think of anything original.

Beckwith wheeled around to face the reporter. "Is he dead?"

"Did you kill him?"

"I didn't kill him. Did you kill him? Are you a Jew? You know I don't talk to no Jews. You look like a Jew to me."

"Did you kill him?"

"I don't know who killed the nigger and I don't care." Beckwith paused for a second. "I'm sorry. I told my wife I wasn't going to say *nigger* again. I'm going to call him a colored person because he really is not a full-blooded nigger." He was laughing and having a good time as he was led to the booking desk.

Crisco and I stood to the side and watched. During the booking, we talked with Sammy and Tim, getting the details of the trip. As soon as he was booked on the murder charge, Beckwith was taken before Judge Hilburn for an initial appearance. There, Beckwith was formally advised of the charge and his rights, particularly his right to counsel. Until he hired a lawyer, Judge Hilburn appointed two of the most competent lawyers in the state to assist him. Jim Kitchens was a forty-eight-year-old ex-DA from Copiah County, just south of Jackson, and Merrida "Buddy" Coxwell was a thirty-seven-year-old lawyer who had been quoted in the *Clarion-Ledger* the day after Christmas, 1990, following Beckwith's indictment amid speculation of who might represent the defendant, as saying that he would not personally take the case.

At the arraignment the next morning, Friday, October 4, 1991, both Kitchens and Coxwell announced to Judge Hilburn that Beckwith was indigent and that they were in for the duration.

As I finished reading the indictment aloud in the courtroom and Beckwith entered his not-guilty plea, I was very much aware that we had crossed our own Rubicon. There could be no turning back or change of heart.

The stage was set. Indeed, the *Meridian Star,* the newspaper of the east-central Mississippi town of the same name, where Imperial Wizard Sam Bowers, Preacher Killen, and other Klansmen had been tried on federal charges in the deaths of civil rights workers Schwerner, Goodman, and Chaney, had this to say:

> The return of Byron De La Beckwith . . . after a long extradition fight . . . sets the stage for one of the most dramatic trials in Mississippi, if not American history. . . . Some Mississippians may question the point of reopening the case after all those years. Mississippi is a different place now. Why not bury the pain of the past and move on? It's not that simple. Critical to putting the past behind us is con-

fronting it squarely. That includes, where possible, amending old wrongs. Otherwise, the dark corners of the past will never stay buried—they will keep resurfacing to haunt us. The Evers case is unfinished business. The effort to solve it once and for all is appropriate and necessary.

CHAPTER SEVEN

Slow-Grinding Wheels

The wheels of justice often grind slowly, frustrating prosecutors, victims' families, and witnesses. However, albeit ploddingly, justice moves surely. Our journey to trial was one of those snail-paced ventures, and three years of legal calisthenics ensued. The jail key had barely turned on Beckwith's cell door before his lawyers sought his release on bail.

While the idea of releasing a defendant on a murder charge, one who had resisted the court's jurisdiction as long as Beckwith had, seemed absurd to me, I couldn't take any chances. Not only would we present that argument to Judge Hilburn, but we would also make a court record of Beckwith's continued ties to, or sympathies with, various militant white supremacist groups. I wanted the court to see that he was not a harmless old man quietly living out his twilight years in the Tennessee mountains.

The bail hearing was more than a defensive proceeding where we fought to keep the indicted murderer in jail. Surreptitiously, I used it as a way to preserve the admissibility of some crucial evidence.

Ralph Hargrove was the only person who could authenticate the negative of Beckwith's car, from which the crime labs had developed the enhanced photos showing the Shriner's emblem hanging on the rearview mirror identified by Robert Don Pittman. Because of his age and health, I wasn't certain Hargrove would be around to testify by the time we got to trial.

If he testified at a court hearing in the case, authenticated the negative, and Beckwith's lawyers had the opportunity to cross-examine him, that pretrial testimony, in the event of Hargrove's disability or death, could later be read to the trial jury under the same evidentiary rule that enabled us to read the testimony of our deceased witnesses from the 1964 trial.

Hargrove was my first witness at the bail hearing. Not wanting yet to highlight the significance of the car negative, I camouflaged it among fifty-three other negatives, twenty-two photos, and seven slides of the crime scene, murder weapon, and fingerprint comparisons. Starting with the car slide, I meticulously had Hargrove identify each piece of evidence, including the murder weapon.

The criminal record of a defendant is always considered at a bail hearing. I next put on Bernard "Bernie" Windstein Jr., a retired New Orleans police lieutenant, who was one of the officers who had arrested Beckwith on Thursday, September 27, 1973, at 12:03 A.M., on the Lake Pontchartrain bridge because "he had a time bomb in his vehicle."

"Would you tell the judge what other firearms or weapons of any sort were found in there?"

"When he got out of the car, we took a fully loaded .45 automatic off his person. He had a thirty-caliber carbine with several loaded banana clips. He had a partially assembled .30-03 Enfield, a Japanese six-point-five-millimeter rifle, and a fifty-caliber machine gun barrel in the trunk."

"Describe the time bomb."

"It was in a black wooden box about two feet long by about eight by ten. It had five or six sticks of one-pound dynamite and a five-pound stick, seismographic type, along with a clock, battery, necessary wires, and blasting cap."

"What, if any, papers were found?"

"A map leading to the house of the victim, A. I. Botnick, who was local director of the B'nai B'rith Anti-Defamation League."

Certified documents from Louisiana were then presented to Judge Hilburn showing that Beckwith was convicted of the charge on August 1, 1975, and imprisoned at Angola from May 6, 1977, until January 13, 1980.

"Did you ever see this defendant after his trial and conviction?"

"Yes, sir. I had the occasion to go to Washington, D.C., on May 3, 1977, and return him to New Orleans as a fugitive." That information scored a point with the judge, who knew of the bomb conviction, but seemed surprised that Beckwith was considered a fugitive in that case, too.

Jim Kitchens brought out on Windstein's cross-examination that his client was allowed bail by the Louisiana court notwithstanding his residence in Mississippi. When I had the opportunity on redirect, I asked whether Beckwith had made any statement at the time about resisting the Louisiana courts "tooth, nail, and claw," as he had done in our case.

"Not to my knowledge."

Sgt. Tim Matheny followed, testifying that Beckwith was upset about having to leave Tennessee and come to Mississippi, certainly not acquiescing to the jurisdiction of the courts of this state. On top of that resistance, once here Beckwith refused to be fingerprinted as part of the routine booking procedure, stating that "he would fight anybody who tried to fingerprint him."

I had no trouble tying Beckwith to various white supremacist groups, thanks in large part to his résumé, letters, and newspaper articles that his wife had provided. I needed a knowledgeable person, though, to educate the court on how militant these groups were. Believing in white supremacy, however repugnant, is not illegal. However, if the cause is kept alive through violence, Judge Hilburn should know that before deciding to release an adherent to such violent beliefs.

The job fell on the shoulders of Don Wofford, an FBI agent of nineteen years, sixteen of which focused primarily on domestic terrorism cases, which he defined as those "in which individuals in the United States commit crimes for a religious or philosophical reason rather than normal reasons of greed, vengeance, and so forth."

Introducing Beckwith's résumé, I zeroed in on his participation in the "Identity Branch of Christian Service." I asked Wofford if he was familiar with the group.

"The Identity Movement," the agent explained, "was a group of people in the United States who believe that white Aryan people are God's true children, not the Jews. They make various statements in publications and in their church services that Jews are Satan's people and that any minority—blacks, Hispanics, or whatever—are also Satan's people; and that it's up to the white Americans to take over this country and control it."

"What, if any, place does violence have in their mission?"

"In early '83, the Identity Movement in Coeur d'Alene, Idaho, had several meetings in which it was decided that a group of them would go underground, sever their ties with the Aryan Nations Church, form a criminal enterprise, and go out and rob armored cars and commit crimes in the name of the war of the white people to take back the United States from what they called the Zionist Occupied Government, or ZOG. They did rob armored cars, committed a couple of murders, and subsequently were rounded up, arrested, and tried in Seattle. All were convicted."

Putting the résumé aside, I turned to a letter Beckwith had written to *Attack!* magazine, published by the National Alliance, a neo-Hitlerian, racist, and anti-Semitic group based in Arlington, Virginia, which seeks the unification of non-Jewish whites to build a "new order." This same group promotes *The Turner Diaries,* a book written by its leader, Dr. William

Pierce, about guerrilla warfare and violence against Jews and other minorities. In fact, the National Alliance refers to it as a "Handbook for White Victory." It fantasizes about the overthrow of the American government by "superpatriots" who kill these "enemies," the destruction of Israel, and the establishment of an "Aryan nation and world."

The book was important, Agent Wofford explained, "because The Order used it as a sort of blueprint or guideline for their criminal activities. It depicts a race war in the United States which white supremacists eventually win."

Indeed, the book would later raise its ugly head in the trial of Timothy McVeigh for the mass-murderous bombing of innocent men, women, and children in the Murrah Federal Building in Oklahoma City. Any assumption that Byron De La Beckwith is an almost extinct dinosaur, that he is the last of an ugly breed and crusade, is badly misplaced. The "Beckwiths" of the sixties are the "McVeighs" of the nineties. No danger can be subdued if we don't remind ourselves that it's a perpetual threat and not obsolete.

I handed the copy of *Attack!* to Agent Wofford and asked him to identify it. "It says it is the 'Revolutionary Voice of the National Alliance.'"

"One letter to the editor in this edition begins, 'Dear Compatriot Dr. Pierce.' Who would that be?"

"Dr. William Pierce, author of *The Turner Diaries*."

"How is the letter signed?"

"'Sincerely, BDLB, Angola, Louisiana.'"

"What reference is made in the letter to the killing of Medgar Evers or the killing of any black in 1963 Mississippi?"

"The writer says he was tried for his life in 1963 for killing 'Mississippi's mightiest nigger.' He then says, 'There is still work to be done by those of us who aren't too liberal to survive, and I can't do what needs doing while I'm in here.'"

I then got in, through Wofford, the copy of the Klan newspaper, the *White Patriot,* that Mrs. Beckwith had sent to me. It had a large photo of the Beckwith couple at the 1986 Klan Homecoming in Pulaski, Tennessee. Next, I handed Wofford a copy of the book *Vigilantes of Christendom: The Story of Phineas Priesthood,* by Richard Kelley Hoskins.

"What does the very front of that book say concerning the role of Phineas Priesthood?"

"It states, 'As the Kamikaze is to the Japanese, as the Shiite is to Islam, as the Zionist is to the Jew, so the Phineas Priest is to Christendom.'"

I then pulled out a letter written by Beckwith to the right-wing newsletter the *Hoskins Report.*

"According to Hoskins, who wrote that and to whom Beckwith wrote this letter in February 1991, by what means are these Phineas Priests to enforce their interpretation of God's law?" Agent Wofford explained that they believe they are called by God to right wrongs as they see them. "Would that include murder?"

"Yes." Wofford then explained that Hoskins quoted in his book a biblical event in Numbers, chapter 25, where Phineas, a priest of Israel, murdered a fellow Israelite and a Midianite woman for having sexual relations. Wofford said that that, according to Hoskins, is an example of the mission of Phineas Priesthood.

"How does this defendant end his letter to Hoskins?"

"It says, 'Phineas for President,' and then is signed."

Last, I presented the judge with an affidavit by Kathy Principe, setting out the chronology of Beckwith's defiance of extradition and a copy of a motion she had sent to me. The latter was filed on Beckwith's behalf in the federal court in Tennessee asking that the sheriffs of Hamilton County, Tennessee, and Hinds County, Mississippi, be held in contempt of court for allegedly kidnapping him. It also sought Beckwith's return to his state of sanctuary.

I pointed out to Judge Hilburn that the motion was filed *after* Beckwith's arraignment and his request for bail. Even as his lawyers were asking Judge Hilburn to release him, saying that he would not pose a flight risk, Byron De La Beckwith was continuing to fight Judge Hilburn's jurisdiction.

The defense called Byron De La Beckwith VII, the forty-five-year-old son of the defendant. He was eighteen when he witnessed his father's 1964 trials. He briefly described his father's military service, employment history, and heart problems. Beckwith had recently undergone surgery at the Vanderbilt University Medical Center in Nashville, according to his son, and all of his doctors were in Tennessee.

Asked by Kitchens how he would describe the relationship between his father and the grandchildren, the younger Beckwith replied, "Extremely well, sir. Unfortunately, the great-grandchild really does not know him because he's been incarcerated ten months in Tennessee and the child is only three years old. But he is quite aware of who his great-grandfather is."

"I bet he is," I whispered to Ed. "They've probably told them all since birth how proud they should be. 'Granddaddy is the one who killed Medgar Evers.'"

Would his father pose a special danger to anyone in the community if released on bail? "No, sir. He wouldn't do anything but spend ninety percent of his time preparing his case with his attorneys and with his great-grandchild and his children."

Beckwith VII's attempt to explain away his father's associations with the various violent organizations that Agent Wofford had earlier discussed were rather humorous.

"Are you familiar with any of the organizations that were mentioned? I mean, do you belong to them?"

"No, sir. I just assumed the Identity Church that he belonged to was like the First Christian Baptist Church we belong to, sir." A few spectators smirked.

"Do you," Kitchens asked, "interpret anything your dad was quoted as saying as being an expression of violence or intent to harm anybody?"

"No, sir. No, sir. He's not a violent person. He's well liked by both races." Open laughter filled the courtroom. "All these other things that have occurred, it's probably with age and health and the abuse that he's had, because prior to, I guess '71 or '72, the things that they accuse my father of being against—the Jews, niggers, blacks, however you want to express it—that didn't erupt until '71, '72, '75."

"Do you know of any place he could go in this country where his face would not be familiar to people?"

"No, sir. If they didn't recognize his face, he'd talk to somebody and that would give him away."

Ed's cross-examination provided a glimpse of what could be expected later at trial. It was thorough, pointed, and a brief blueprint for students of the art. A newspaper article mentioned that Beckwith expressed his intent to vote in Mississippi the next election, as he claimed "residency" in Carroll County. It provided the point from which Ed launched his cross-examination to show the defendant as a fraud and liar who couldn't be trusted if released.

"You say your father lived in Carroll County, is that right?"

"Yes, sir."

"How long since he's lived there?"

"A little over eight years, sir."

"You're aware that he's filed an affidavit stating that he's a resident of that county in order that he can vote there?"

"I knew there was something in the papers about it. But, you know, I really didn't get into that. I think it was a political movement or stunt."

"To make a sworn affidavit?"

"Are you saying my father made the affidavit?"

"That's what I'm asking you. Are you aware of that?"

"No, sir."

"And yet you say you know him very well?"

"Yes, sir."

"Then you know he doesn't own any property at all in the state of Mississippi, don't you?"

"At the time being, he doesn't, sir."

The point was made, so Ed immediately moved to something else. There was no hesitation, no flipping through notes. "You said you could tell he was deprived of his medicine while incarcerated. What medicine does he take and what are the jailers depriving him of?" The question was asked to cast doubt on the witness's credibility, to get him to back off from something. The answer led to something even better than anticipated.

"I don't know the exact names for the medicines, but I know that if he didn't get it at the proper time and in the proper doses that it made him short-tempered."

"Short-tempered. And you say he's not violent?"

"Anybody can have a temper and not be violent," Beckwith VII snapped.

"I see, like he did with your real mother in Greenwood. He had a very violent temper there, didn't he?"

"No, sir."

"Do you deny she lodged charges against him because of violence?"

"No, sir, I don't deny that."

In response to one of Kitchens's questions, Beckwith VII mentioned that he had attended both 1964 trials, which had ended in hung juries, an obvious attempt by the defense to cast doubt on our chances of getting a conviction. "The two hung juries that you testified about," Ed began, "what was their race?"

"Objection!" Kitchens was on his feet. "That's irrelevant."

Ed didn't wait for a ruling. "Then why did he bring it up, Your Honor?" The objection was sustained.

"Who came to the trials during those hung juries?" Ed didn't wait for an answer. "People like Governors Barnett and Johnson, were they there?"

"Your Honor, objection! That can't have anything to do with this bail hearing," Kitchens said.

"If it's not relevant, then I don't know why he brought it out about the hung juries, Your Honor."

"I'll sustain the objection, but you can make your record, of course, Mr. Peters." There was no jury present to be tainted by the answers.

"Thank you, Your Honor. I just think the record ought to be clear why the juries were hung."

Turning back to the witness, Ed established that defendant Beckwith would be closer to several hospitals known for care of heart patients and closer to his lawyers if he remained in Jackson instead of returning home to Signal Mountain or temporarily moving in with the son in West Point, Mississippi.

Ed shifted to Beckwith's affiliations and sympathies with the militant right-wing groups earlier discussed by Wofford. "You said that you are not a member of these organizations that your father has been talking about, but have you ever become acquainted with any of them?"

"No, sir."

"The Ku Klux Klan?"

"I've read a lot about it and I've seen a lot of it."

"Have you heard your father talk about it?"

"Certainly, and a lot of other men, too, sir."

"He's in favor of that type of organization, correct?"

"Different sectors of it, sir."

"You are familiar with the fact that he says we need to go back to that type of life, aren't you?"

"I'm sure I've heard comments similar to that for the last twenty years, sir."

"Thank you. Now you can explain why he says things like that."

"He tries to express his feelings and his way of thinking towards segregation and integration. He doesn't express himself like you or I would."

"Hopefully," Ed quipped.

"Our feelings might be the same or close, but he is more open."

"So, you feel the same way he does; he just says it, is that right?"

"Not entirely, sir. I disagree with a lot of things my father says and does and the way he does them, and I express that to him. But I still love him and he is still my father."

I *almost* felt sorry for him.

One of the things I learned early on from Ed about cross-examination is to hit on a topic, move to another, and then return to previous ones. Never let the witness feel comfortable predicting where you're going next. Adhering to this strategy, Ed abruptly returned to Beckwith's violent nature. "And you say the defendant is not a violent person?"

"Yes, sir."

"Are you familiar with the charges that he was convicted for in Louisiana?"

"I'm very familiar with the charges. He was convicted, but he had no intentions of going down there and destroying anybody, sir, as they say."

"Tell us then, since you're able to conclude that, why he was down there with five sticks of dynamite, a time bomb, and about five other weapons."

"My father didn't know that dynamite was in his vehicle."

"He was being bombed himself? Is that what your position is?"

"Yes, sir." Laughter erupted.

"Let me ask you something else your father said. Do you know what he would mean when he vowed to cause an ill wind to fall upon those who would prosecute him?"

"Yes, sir. I interpret that as hoping that we can get free, politically fight the liberal forces."

"So, it's your position that this is a political prosecution?"

"Oh, yes, sir. Most definitely, yes, sir."

"And what ill wind is it that is to fall upon me for reprosecuting him?"

"Didn't anybody name you, specifically, sir, but hope your political career will not venture from this and put you into the governor's mansion."

"The ill wind would be that I am unfortunate enough to not be governor; is that what you're saying?" Ed asked sarcastically.

"Are you aware of your father's habits within the last couple of years with regard to storing food away for the revolution?" Ed was trying to show the judge that, although fiction, *The Turner Diaries* was taken seriously by Beckwith, who was preparing for the race war it depicted.

"I laugh. Yes, sir."

"That *is* his state of mind, then? He's preparing for this white-versus-black revolution, right?"

"I believe Daddy feels stronger than I do that something is going to happen, and maybe he thinks it's going to happen in his lifetime, and I figure it's going to be another three or four generations. So I'm not too upset and worried about it."

It was time to wrap up, and Ed did so by sending a message. "You say that his great-grandchild is quite aware of who he is. What did you do to make him aware of who he is? Did you say, 'Your grandfather was the Imperial Wizard of the Ku Klux Klan?"

"Oh, no, sir. They are aware that he's been accused of things."

"You're not telling them what his philosophies are?"

"No, sir. We try to make him understand that his great-grandfather is being accused of things, and it's very hard." No joke, I thought, considering that they were drilling this propaganda bullshit into a three-year-old.

"I'm going to tell you something," Ed said, "and I'm an officer of the court, so I'm under oath to tell the truth here. I'm not running for governor, and I don't want it. And so, if you will, when you talk to those grandchildren, tell them that's *not* why he's being prosecuted. Okay?"

Of course, there was no response, and nobody expected Ed's message to be conveyed to all of the little Beckwiths, but the press corps was there. Through it, just maybe other young people could be reached. Just maybe they would one day get the real message of this extraordinary case.

Gordon Lackey, mentioned in an FBI report as the person who swore Beckwith into the Invisible Empire of the Klan, also testified at the bail hearing. He had a real attitude problem—a cocky ass from the very start—even in response to Kitchens's asking how old he was. "I am fifty-five, I think, sir," Lackey snapped.

"Mr. Lackey, what has been the nature of your acquaintance with Mr. Beckwith?"

"Many different relationships: business, social, church, fraternal." Asked his opinion whether his "fraternal" brother would flee if released on bail, Lackey responded, "If Mr. Byron De La Beckwith tells you he will be here, he will be here."

The problem was that Brother Beckwith didn't tell the judge that. In fact, he didn't say anything. Kitchens and Coxwell didn't put him on the stand. The only comments attributed to Beckwith that were conveyed to Judge Hilburn at the hearing were those vowing to fight the judge's jurisdiction.

"Would he pose a special danger or threat to any person or group in the community?" Kitchens asked.

"I know he is a gentleman who would defend his honor if called upon at any time, but I have never *seen* a single act of violence from this gentleman. Not one." The splitting-the-hair answer was not what Kitchens had expected, so he repeated the question.

"Other than to himself," Lackey responded, "none, and there only from conversing freely with the press and being misquoted. That's the only danger he's got."

"I'm sorry, Mr. Lackey," Ed barked, leaping from his seat and pacing like a cat around the podium. "I don't know how you know he's been misquoted in the news media. Tell us what exactly it was that was misquoted."

"That would be like asking, 'Tell me, Mr. Lackey, exactly what's in the Bible.' It's a long and lengthy story. I could not. I decline. Sorry," Lackey snapped in staccato fashion. He then looked in Beckwith's direction and grinned, very satisfied with himself.

Naturally, he denied swearing Beckwith into the Klan. Lackey had obviously raised Ed's hackles. Normally, Ed wouldn't have made a big deal about a person's age, but because of Lackey's smug, contentious attitude, my boss wasn't about to let it slide. "And you say that you *think* you're fifty-five years of age, is that right?"

"Born September twelfth, 1936, sir. I didn't have a calculator. Sorry."

"Is your memory impaired in some way that you don't even know how old you are?"

"No, sir. I have a very good memory. I just didn't do the arithmetic on it. At my age, it's just not as significant to me as it is to some other people because I'm not running for office." I had never seen a witness show such disdain and smirk so much.

"You haven't had any disability?"

"For a very short period of time. I'm not a medical practitioner, but they call it myocardial infarction."

"How long ago was that?"

"Objection," Kitchens said. "I can't see where this gentleman's health is relevant."

"I'm trying to find out something," Ed explained. "For the first time, I've got a witness who doesn't know how old he is." Spectators chuckled.

Although it was already apparent, Ed nonetheless ended his questions by showing that Lackey was anything but an unbiased, objective witness whose testimony was worthy of any credibility. "Have you attempted to assist him in obtaining legal counsel?"

"I don't have the financial ability to help him do anything."

"Did you the first time he was tried?"

"He had good legal counsel in Mr. Hardy Lott and Mr. Stanny Sanders."

"Do you know how those attorneys were paid?"

"Totally by contributions from friends, and probably the same friends who put the great banner over the Yazoo River bridge in Greenwood when he came home after the second trial that said, 'Welcome Home DeLay.'"

"Were you one of those people?"

"Same people. I would be one of those people, yes, sir."

Judge Hilburn found insufficient evidence that Beckwith's release would pose a threat or danger to anyone or the community. The judge, however, was not persuaded that Beckwith, if freed on bail, would be in court as needed. Noting the lengthy time that had already passed and expressing an unwillingness to risk a similar lapse, Judge Hilburn denied bail, at least for a while, and the case was set to be tried on February 10, 1992.

While Crisco began the arduous task of notifying our witnesses of the February trial date, I proceeded to trial against another murderer. Another trial, another conviction. Life went on, even amidst gearing up for the biggest trial of my career.

The '91 holiday season came and went more rapidly than usual for me. There was no trip to Florida, no taking off the week between Christmas and New Year's. Crisco and I hit 1992 in stride for the final push to a February trial that wasn't to be. Judge Hilburn granted Beckwith's request for a continuance. His lawyers claimed they did not have sufficient time to prepare. A new trial date was set for June 1.

The postponement until June affected our prosecution much in the same way that a football defensive unit calls a time-out to "freeze" a placekicker. We were pumped up, the adrenaline flowing. Witnesses had made arrangements with their families and employers to be here. Crisco had coordinated travel arrangements and lodging. Now, everything was canceled and rescheduled for June.

Returning to Jackson from trying a death-penalty case on the Gulf coast, Ed and I found that Kitchens and Coxwell had filed a motion asking Judge Hilburn to reconsider his earlier decision denying Beckwith bail. Submitted with the pleading were affidavits of various people stating they had known Beckwith anywhere from ten years to his "entire life-time" and that they had no doubt that he would appear in court, as required, if released.

An all-star cast vouched for DeLay: Travis Buckley, the attorney who had represented Beckwith on the Louisiana explosives charge and who had defended Imperial Wizard Sam Bowers in the federal civil rights prosecution for the deaths of Goodman, Chaney, and Schwerner; Greenwood lawyer Hardy Lott, who was Beckwith's lead attorney in the 1964 trials; L. E. Matthews, who, according to FBI reports, had succeeded Bowers as Imperial Wizard upon Bowers's incarceration for the 1964 deaths of the three civil rights workers in Neshoba County, had made the bomb found in Beckwith's car in Louisiana, and had owned the property near the Byram swinging bridge where Beckwith gave his pep talk about the Evers killing; and Danny Joe Hawkins, who, according to the FBI, was a Klan muscle man with Tommy Tarrants and was later convicted in federal court for conspiring to overthrow a foreign government.

Since he didn't testify at the earlier bail hearing, Beckwith's lawyers attempted to plug that hole by also submitting an affidavit signed by him assuring Judge Hilburn that he would be in court as needed and waiving extradition. It was an obvious effort to get that promise before the court without being subjected to Ed's cross-examination. Even at the hearing on the motion for reconsideration, the defendant sat mute.

The judge took the matter under advisement, but was ultimately unwilling to chance the defense's request. The lawyers then sought relief from the Mississippi Supreme Court, but in an order signed by presiding justice Dan Lee, that court, too, refused to release Beckwith.

While Judge Hilburn was contemplating his ruling, the NAACP finally found its voice. Until then, we hadn't received one phone call or letter of support or encouragement from the organization. Finally, Stephanie Parker-Weaver and the Jackson Chapter issued a press release urging the judge to refuse to release Beckwith.

The press release did not, however, signal universal support among all blacks. Almost eighteen months earlier, an African-American elected official told me as much in the courthouse, proclaiming, "Myrlie Evers ain't in charge here no more. We're running things now." And in mid-March 1992, Ed received an anonymous letter from "a concerned black person in Jackson," stating, "It seems highly insignificant to bring up something that was done so many years ago with all the present or existing cleaning up to be done. It makes no sense to put the man on in his grave. . . . I repeat, it makes no sense, whatsoever, to bring up something that was done so many years ago. . . . Sincerely, Anonymous Human Citizen, PS Silently, without public knowledge."

Everyone in our office was well aware that crime, as life, death, and taxes, proceeded on. We were all busy trying cases. Ed and I had just finished a death-penalty trial, and at the time the letter arrived from our "Anonymous Human Citizen," I was in the middle of a kidnapping trial. As soon as I got a conviction in it, I had a bank-robbery report on my desk to review for the next grand jury.

In April 1992, we were still receiving reports from the FBI files on Beckwith. One report included a discussion between Beckwith, L. E. Matthews, and an informant about the Evers murder. The three men were on a 1973 scouting trip to New Orleans to plan the Botnick bombing.

Beckwith was asked how much time would be involved in planning the hit:

> Beckwith told Matthews it had taken him about 5 weeks to get lined up on Medgar Evers, to which Matthews responded that Beckwith botched the job—that after all the planning, he had to go off and

leave his gun at the scene. . . . Beckwith claimed that he hid the gun . . . and that he probably would have been all right if the previous owner of the gun had not gone to the prosecuting attorney's office and reported that he had sold it to Beckwith.

Since the informant was dead, the only way I could get any of these admissions by Beckwith in front of a jury would be through Matthews. I hardly expected him to come clean, but I understood that he was in bad health, and there was always the chance, however slim, that he would do so before facing his Creator. He didn't.

I was as anxious as anyone to get Byron De La Beckwith's trial over with and behind me. It wasn't to be anytime soon, though. The defense prevailed upon Judge Hilburn to postpone the trial once again. It was rescheduled for September 8. Arrangements were again canceled. Some witnesses were understanding; others were frustrated and angry. They, too, were ready to put this behind them.

Trials are normally conducted in the county where the crime occurs. The prosecution, at least in Mississippi, can never ask that a trial be held elsewhere, but the defendant may make such a request if he can show, "by reason of prejudgment of the case, or grudge or ill will to the defendant in the public mind, he cannot have a fair and impartial trial in the county where the offense is charged to have been committed." If the defendant proves this to the satisfaction of the trial judge, venue may be transferred "to a convenient county, upon such terms . . . as may be proper."

Beckwith's lawyers filed such a motion. The county from which the jury would be selected would be a crucial, if not *the most crucial,* issue to be decided by the judge. Granted, the case had received extensive publicity, but we wanted to bring other factors before the judge for him to consider prior to making a ruling. We also wanted some input on where the case would be tried, if not in Hinds County. We had a hearing on the matter in mid-July.

As expected, the defense concentrated on the sheer volume of the publicity, introducing copies of newspaper articles and videotapes of television newscasts concerning the case. They also called a couple of hired private investigators and a part-time deputy sheriff who testified that, in their opinion, Beckwith could not get a fair trial in Jackson. Although he was out of town and did not testify, Kitchens surprised us by presenting Judge Hilburn with a sworn affidavit from Charles Tisdale, the African-

American owner and editor of the *Jackson Advocate,* the city's oldest newspaper serving the black community.

The defense also noted that a bronze life-size statue of Medgar Evers was recently unveiled at the public library named in his honor and located on the major city thoroughfare that bears his name.

Through Bill Minor, a newspaper journalist who had covered Mississippi news for forty-five years and had attended the 1964 trials for the New Orleans–based *Times-Picayune,* I attempted to show Judge Hilburn that the publicity surrounding the earlier trials was as great, if not greater, than that now. Beckwith, I argued, couldn't complain that he hadn't received a fair trial then. If he could get one amid that massive publicity, my reasoning went, he could certainly get one in 1992.

I also attempted to show that, regardless of the publicity, it had not adversely affected Beckwith. A March 6, 1992, article in the *Clarion-Ledger,* which I introduced into evidence, reported that 70 percent of the people who responded to a survey conducted by the paper favored Beckwith's being released on bail. Jeanie Stewart, our office receptionist since November 1989 (the month after we first began our investigation), testified that the DA's office received "many, many calls" about the case over those years, all condemning *us,* not Beckwith.

"Jeanie, of the 'many, many' phone calls you received, do you recall even one commending the position the State of Mississippi was taking?"

"No, no. They were angry that we were prosecuting the case."

The feedback our office received indicated that any grudge or ill will in the public mind was not toward Beckwith, the indicted murderer, but rather toward us, his prosecutors.

I also put on several people who testified that Beckwith could get a fair trial in Jackson and that he himself had generated much of the publicity about which his lawyers were now complaining.

White fear of violent rioting by blacks, such as witnessed by the nation in Los Angeles at the close of the Rodney King trial, was also invoked by the defense. I put on several well-respected black professional people—a retired schoolteacher of thirty-one years, a Realtor, and a government lawyer—to alleviate this paranoia. African-American citizens in Jackson deserved more credit than that.

Groundless as it was, though, the white fear, especially among merchants, was there. A large security force would be necessary, "just in case," and the responsibility of forming such a task force fell on the shoulders of newly elected Hinds County sheriff Malcolm McMillin. Security would be manageable if the trial was held in Jackson, the sheriff advised Judge Hilburn, but would be a logistical nightmare if conducted in any other county. Crisco testified that such a move would cause a similar catastrophe regarding travel, lodging, and the protection of prosecution witnesses.

If we had to go to another county, we had to do everything we could to stay out of Klan Country, the small enclaves scattered around the state where, though inactive, some of the "old-timers" and their sympathizers still lived.

I suspected the real, unsaid reason for Beckwith's wanting a change of venue had less to do with publicity (after all, the news reached everywhere in the state) than it did with Hinds County's 52 percent black population. As a safety net to fall back on, I planted a seed with the judge. If Beckwith's request to move the case from Hinds County was strictly due to publicity, and not an effort to go from a county with a slight-majority black populace to a "whiter" one, then the case should be moved to a county with a racial ratio similar to Hinds County's.

My suspicions of the defense's motive were confirmed when they objected to Crisco's advising the court of the racial ratio of Hinds County, according to the most recent census. The objection was overruled, and Judge Hilburn ruled that venue would be changed, but the jury would be drawn from Panola County in north Mississippi, with a racial makeup similar to Hinds County's. The trial would take place in De Soto County, Mississippi, just south of Memphis, Tennessee. This was highly unusual, but done to get a jury not exposed to local news, and to select them from a county with a similar racial makeup. It would be inconvenient, but it could have been much worse.

I still hear comments that crimes of the past should be left to the past, that we have enough crime today to worry about. The statements carry with them the assumption that if a case from the past is prosecuted, there is no time to pursue those of today. Not so. I worked nights and weekends on the Beckwith case so I could keep up with my regular caseload. In the six weeks of the 1992 summer criminal session, I tried three more murder cases and an aggravated assault. Four more violent offenders were convicted and locked up. Yet, the letters of protest kept coming.

Beckwith's book, *Glory in Conflict,* was finally out, and several people around the courthouse (although not in the DA's office) even sent copies to him in the jail to get his autograph. I wouldn't buy one or even let it in my house, but I did read it to see if he had made any more remarks that I could use against him. It cleared up a lot for me, such as the identity of the real killer of Medgar Evers: Lee Harvey Oswald.

By this time John Kelley was the agent legal counsel at the Jackson FBI office. John was extremely helpful and accelerated the flow of information. We finally had a friend there who didn't make us ask for things before knowing they existed.

One such report revealed another informant, Dick Davis, who on the afternoon of October 21, 1969, had received a phone call at his home in Winter Haven, Florida, from Beckwith. A boat salesman at the time, Beckwith was in the area working. He explained to Davis that he was from Greenwood, Mississippi, and shared a mutual friend with Davis from Columbia, South Carolina. The friend, a member of the United Klans of America, had met Davis at a Klonvocation in Tuscaloosa and had given Davis's name and address to Beckwith and told him to look Davis up if ever in Winter Haven.

They met at a Lum's restaurant on NW Sixth Street. Davis drank coffee while Beckwith ate supper. Beckwith told Davis that he was a member of the White Knights of the Camellia in Mississippi. He related to Davis a conversation he had had with Imperial Wizard Sam Bowers a few days before. He said that Bowers, since the wounding and arrest of Tommy Tarrants in Meridian, was contemplating organizing a new underground unit within the Klan to engage in "guerrilla-type warfare" against Mississippi's Jews.

Davis's report indicated that Beckwith spoke a lot of "the good that a group of men can do individually when they are dedicated to the cause. He said that one man in any one area should spend his time dreaming up things that need to be done," such as "pouring plaster of paris down the commode of Jewish-owned establishments, restaurants, and such." Beckwith also advocated "burning Jewish homes and bombing Jewish synagogues."

Davis described Beckwith as speaking "brightly" about "killing certain Jews, Negroes, and extremely liberal whites." Children of these groups were not excluded from extermination. Beckwith told Davis that "the six-year-old Jewish child should be destroyed just as quickly as the adult Jew and more quickly than elderly Jews. . . . An eighty-year-old Jew," he said, "cannot father children, and therefore is not the threat to the white race that a six-year-old Jewish child is."

Speaking of his arrest and trials for Evers's murder, he neither admitted nor denied carrying out the killing. Davis noted, however, that Beckwith, "in advocating selected murder as a partial solution to the right wing's problem, stated that he would never ask a man to do anything that he himself has not already done."

Kelley assured me that the FBI would have Davis available to testify.

★ ★ ★

My personal life also took a positive turn, as I started dating someone.

I first met Peggy at one of the local hospitals where she worked as an RN in the emergency room. My daughter, Claire, had suffered a head injury at the school gym. Peggy got my immediate attention. She was gentle, caring, and humorous. I learned in our conversation that she was divorced and had three boys: Jared, fourteen, Joel, fifteen, and JJ, nineteen. I couldn't believe that she was the mother of a nineteen-year-old. She was, and still is, beautiful.

Our relationship grew and is still blossoming. We were good friends long before we were lovers. God sent me a companion, a pal, a real soul mate, when I needed one most. Peggy was a stabilizing force for me through the Beckwith years with her unwavering support.

Late in the summer, the defense filed the much anticipated motion to dismiss, claiming that Beckwith had been deprived of his right to a speedy trial. Tacked on to that was a claim that his rights against double jeopardy were also violated.

The defense team was caught off guard when Judge Hilburn indicated the prosecution could call its first witness and I announced that, according to our research (and I cited the cases), there was no speedy-trial issue since Beckwith had not been an "accused" until his 1990 indictment. The issue was due process. The burden was on the defense to prove that the initial prosecution was abandoned with the specific intent *at the time* to gain a tactical advantage, and that Beckwith was prejudiced by the delay to such an extent that he could no longer present the same defense.

Kitchens and Coxwell quickly huddled with their client and called Beckwith to the stand. Kitchens began by asking him if he recalled the outcome of the 1964 trials. "Yes, sir," he snapped. "We had two hung juries, both of them in my favor, one more so than the other. The second was extremely favorable." He was released on bail and the case dropped until his indictment in December 1990, whereupon "the powers in power threw me back in the Bastille and said, 'Sorry.'"

Beckwith was a bad witness, as his attorneys had probably feared. They had been looking to cross-examine our witnesses, rather than expecting the ball to be tossed immediately into their court. Beckwith was impossible to control and their worst nightmare. At one point during Kitchens's examination, Beckwith answered with the question, "May I interrupt you, sir?"

"No, sir, you may not," the annoyed defense attorney responded.

Asked how he would rate his memory of events surrounding the case, compared with it in 1963 and 1964, Beckwith said that on a scale from one to ten, he'd say about 50 percent. I guessed that meant a five. But Beckwith, evidently not realizing that his lawyers were trying to show that he couldn't mount a defense due to a lack of memory, added that the transcript of the first trial that we had provided him was a help in refreshing his memory.

"To what extent, sir?" Kitchens asked.

Beckwith replied that of the 50 percent that he couldn't otherwise remember, the transcript helped another "thirty, forty, fifty percent."

Kitchens asked if Beckwith remembered making the statements attributed to him by Dick Davis in Winter Haven, Florida. I'm sure Kitchens expected him to say no. Instead, Beckwith responded, "If he was a boat dealer I might have talked to him. That's the only business I had in Florida, was talking to boat dealers and trailer dealers, marine dealers."

Questioned about Delmar Dennis's reports, rather than just denying making the admissions, Beckwith went further and locked himself in a lie: "I have never been with Delmar Dennis at all." We had the dated autograph he gave to Delmar that night. The FBI had verified that it was Beckwith's genuine signature. Kitchens was aware of this and soon shut down his questions to his bigmouthed client.

Ed had a few questions of his own. Beckwith had already testified that he might have met with Dick Davis in Florida. Ed sought to obtain a similar admission regarding Beckwith's trip to Parchman with Peggy Morgan to see Klansman Cecil Sessums. "How do you know Cecil Sessums?"

"I can't recall, but I do know Cecil Sessums."

"Did you go to visit him in the penitentiary?"

"I went to the penitentiary to visit some people, and I would say that they were men accused of being to the far right, but I don't know who or what persons or what day it was or anything about it, and I don't know why I was asked to go to the penitentiary because I have never been there before and I couldn't even draw you a map as to how I got there."

"If in fact you went to visit him with Peggy Morgan, would you say you don't remember that?"

"I don't remember any Peggy Morgan. I remember a woman or a girl, a wife of a man, and that's all I remember."

That was enough, I thought. Ed had locked him in on at least admitting that he had taken the trip. Peggy Morgan wasn't making up the visit. Still, Beckwith would not hush.

"I just told you that I went to Parchman in the company of some other people because I didn't have a car and *somebody* said they wanted me to go there to see *somebody*. And I think it's on the record that I went there. That's all I know about it."

Asked by Ed if he had not worn the murder of Medgar Evers as a badge of honor, Beckwith said he was "still mad about it, indignant about it." Ed asked if he was enraged. "I will not look with kindness upon those that attack me."

"We are not asking you to look with kindness on it. We are asking you to answer the questions. Okay? Will you answer the question?"

"Little short questions. I will give you little short answers. Glad to do it, sir. Want to cooperate with you. I know you've got to make a living."

Kitchens had gone through Beckwith's health problems, including his hearing difficulty. Beckwith tried to emphasize it with Ed. "You don't seem to understand that I don't hear well." But again, he went too far when he added, "I never have heard well."

"So, then," Ed fired back, "you had the same impairment at your trials in '64 that you have now."

Beckwith, more interested in sparring with Ed than in thinking about his answers, waded further into deeper water. "I certainly did have impaired hearing as soon as I got out of the Marine Corps, and I told all my doctors about it and they said, 'Well, it's not that bad.'"

Later, Beckwith mentioned that he had been writing "five to twenty letters a day" since his arrest.

"Who are you writing to?"

"I have a file, and I will go get it and bring it to you if you want to look at it."

"Fine."

"I would say at least five hundred. . . ."

"Fine."

"Or maybe a thousand."

"Your Honor, we ask that he produce the file."

"No, sir!" Coxwell said, coming to his feet. "We object on attorney-client privilege."

"It's not up to his lawyers, Your Honor," Ed replied. "He says he wants to produce it."

"We're giving him advice to invoke the attorney-client privilege on any materials in his room," Coxwell said.

"And," Ed continued, "he hasn't said the lawyers were the ones receiving the letters. That's not attorney-client privilege, Judge."

"I'm going to sustain the objection," the judge ruled.

"We think it's relevant to his mental capacity and memory," Ed continued. "They are saying that he's a vegetable and we want to prove otherwise."

"Move along," the judge warned.

One of the prejudices that may be suffered by a defendant during a delay in a prosecution is embarrassment or scorn. "Are you telling us that up until these charges were dismissed [in 1969] that this was traumatic to you and your family, embarrassing to you and to them?"

"You've got it exactly right."

"Didn't you run for lieutenant governor?"

"In 1967."

Ed brought out that, even before the charges were dismissed two years after that, Beckwith was so embarrassed for himself and his family that he offered himself for public service, continuing to put himself in the limelight.

As to scorn, or the lack of it, Ed presented Beckwith with a copy of an article from the *New Orleans Times-Picayune*. Published upon Beckwith's release in 1964, the article quoted him as saying, "You don't know how good it is to be back here. When we arrived at Tchula, there was a sign saying 'Welcome Home DeLay,' and when I got to the outskirts of Greenwood, there was another one. It brought tears to my eyes." Ed asked him to read it and tell the court if the quotes were accurate.

"Could we see the article?" Kitchens asked. "I haven't seen it."

Beckwith kept on talking while his lawyers tried to read the article. "That's something from a foreign newspaper—"

"Be quiet, Mr. Beckwith!" Kitchens ordered.

After Ed repeated the question, Beckwith claimed, "That's a misprint." Instead of stopping there, he hurt himself by specifying the error: "It brought tears *of joy* to my eyes."

"Are you still contending that, when you got out of jail on these charges after the second trial, you were embarrassed, and that you were an outcast? And, as a matter of fact, you received a hero's welcome back to your area, didn't you?"

"How would you want me to answer that, sir?"

"Truthfully."

"People were overjoyed that they stopped spending money and we got good results. That's what happened. They were pleased."

"The trial that caused you such shame and embarrassment, is that the same trial that Gov. Ross Barnett came up to you during the trial and shook hands with you?" Kitchens's objection was sustained, so Ed tried it another way: "Did it cause you humiliation for the governor of Mississippi to come in and shake hands with you during the trial? Is that what you are saying was humiliating?" Again, a defense objection was sustained.

Whether a defendant asserts his right to a speedy trial while charges are still pending is another factor for the court to consider in this context. Thus, Ed asked Beckwith if he had his lawyers, from 1964 to 1969, file anything with the court to have a third trial. Beckwith advised that he only asked them to "throw the thing out."

"The juries that you had for those trials, were they all-white?" In response to Kitchens's objection, Ed explained, "The question is whether or not the state has unduly prejudiced this man by causing charges not to be brought then which are being brought now, Your Honor."

"I'll let him answer," the judge said.

Ed repeated the question. "I did," answered Beckwith.

I certainly don't sit in judgment on any of Ed's cross-examinations, but I prefer, once a defendant says what I want, leaving the matter alone and moving to something else. Once someone is hooked, asking the same question again only affords the opportunity for "waffling."

One mistake Kitchens and Coxwell obviously called to Beckwith's attention during the noon recess was his earlier statement about how beneficial the transcript had been in refreshing his memory. After lunch, Beckwith returned to the stand and Ed returned to the topic.

"You say that the prior transcript refreshed your memory thirty to fifty percent?"

Beckwith was ready this time. "We are going to cancel all of that. We going to strike that out of the record because I am not going to give such an arbitrary figure so carelessly to put in your purse. The longer I am put through these things my memory gets fainter and fainter."

The last sentence provided Ed room to fight back. "The more questions I ask you, the worse your memory gets, is that the way it goes? Does your memory get worse as I ask you questions? What's it gone down to now?"

"I'm going to cancel that off my record. That's you talking. Whatever is in my mind is bright and shining, and I am going to use it to my advantage. What I would like to dig up and protect myself with and can't, I am going to ask my lawyers."

"After you talk to your lawyers, are you going to just say whatever you think is best?"

"That's a very good statement."

Still testing Beckwith's memory, Ed asked if Beckwith remembered his lengthy interview with TV reporter Ed Bryson.

"I haven't seen or heard the tapes, but I recall Mr. Bryson coming and sitting three hours in our yard and asking me a lot of questions. So, let's listen to the tapes."

"Do you see him in the courtroom today?"

"I wouldn't know him if I were to see him. I don't know the man. But the thing is, I got his fingerprints, thank you. I don't need to see him. He's aged since then, surely. And *he* remembers what he said, agreed to do, and he has not done that." The man had to be crazy.

"You can recall the specifics of that agreement?"

"Is the man in court? If he is, let him stick his hand up so I will know. I want to talk to him."

"Answer the question."

"It was a verbal agreement."

"Do you remember the details of it?"

"I remember enough to know that I didn't get the tapes that he promised to give me, and he said—shall I say what he said that he would do?"

"Nothing is affecting your memory about that, then, is there?"

"I shall—no comment to that."

We won the hearing without calling a single witness. The only person to testify was Beckwith, whose performance on the stand adumbrated a trial showdown with Ed. That is, *if* there was a trial.

We won in the trial court, but Beckwith's lawyers succeeded in getting an emergency appeal granted by the Mississippi Supreme Court, which stayed all further proceedings. For the third time, the trial was postponed.

Frustration among our witnesses was at an all-time high. The repeated postponements were militating against our keeping everyone in our corner and willing to make the necessary sacrifices. It had been twenty months since Beckwith was indicted. Beckwith, the guy complaining about not getting a speedy trial, had caused every delay since then.

I prepared our brief for the state supreme court while the precedents we were relying on were fresh in my mind. Once that was done, I immersed myself in other files, preparing them for trials throughout the fall. We had a gang-related shooting, a capital murder, and an armed robbery against a guy whose alias was Doodoo.

Thursday, October 15, 1992, the Mississippi Supreme Court heard oral arguments on the speedy-trial and double-jeopardy issues. Each side was allotted thirty minutes. Kitchens and Coxwell split the defense's allotment. I argued on behalf of the state. I was nervous, but well supported. Ed and state attorney general Mike Moore joined me at the counsel table. Directly behind us were my family, joined by Myrlie Evers, who had flown in from Los Angeles the day before. It warmed my heart seeing my mother and Myrlie Evers talking and laughing together.

The courtroom was packed, and more people jammed the corridor outside. Peggy mouthed, "I love you," and I gave her a thumbs-up just as the bailiff called the proceedings to order and the seven justices who would make the ruling took their seats. Two justices, Fred Banks and Chuck McRae, had recused themselves. Although we were not privy to the reasons, I suspected it was because Banks, the sole African-American on the court, was a member of the NAACP's national board of directors with Mrs. Evers, and because McRae had sold his private practice to Jim Kitchens when he ascended the high court.

Once things got under way, I settled down and the time sped by. Each time a justice asked about the extraordinary time that had elapsed since the 1964 trials, I cited case after case that, in effect, said that it shouldn't matter. I realized the magnitude of the delay, I told them, but if the court really meant what it said in earlier cases, there should be a trial. "Those earlier cases and the legal standards set forth in them are not my words. The words are yours. I ask only that you follow them and be guided by James 1:22, 'Be doers of the word, and not merely hearers who deceive themselves.' " With that, I sat down.

Afterward, I walked outside in front of the building and talked with Peggy, Mama, my brother Mike, Burt, and Jared. I was facing the front door and noticed an older man in a dark suit walking briskly in our direction. He kept his eyes on me and reached inside his coat.

My first thought was that he was reaching for a gun. I had to get away from my family. I couldn't just stand there among them. If I was to be shot, it was going to be away from them. Nor was I going to run and leave them there. I dropped my briefcase, broke apart from them, and started walking fast straight toward him. Just as he was close enough for me to lunge at him, he pulled his hand from his coat and thrust it out for me to shake. I stopped cold in my tracks. I was confused. The gesture was cordial, but his eyes conveyed something sinister. I never looked away from them.

"I knew your father-in-law, Russel Moore, and I just wanted to meet you"—*It's okay,* I told myself, and shook his hand—"and to tell you that he's rolling over in his grave. It's good that he's not here to see that his son-in-law is doing everything that he can to wreck our society. He'd be so ashamed."

"That's where you're wrong!" my mother shouted. The gang was coming.

"You obviously didn't know the Russel Moore I knew," I said as the man turned and left. A security guard in the building must have been watching through the windows. He came outside and asked if everything was okay. I assured him that it was. With that, the case I had nurtured for three years was in the hands of seven justices.

Eight weeks later, on Tuesday, December 15, 1992, I received a call from "a friend of a friend" who claimed that the state supreme court would render its decision the next day. I was told that we had won the double-jeopardy issue but lost the speedy-trial one. There would be no trial. It was over, done.

My tip was wrong. The court rejected Beckwith's double-jeopardy claim outright and, by the slimmest of margins (4–3), decided not to decide the speedy-trial issue. The justices also ordered Judge Hilburn to reconsider releasing Beckwith on bail, even though the same court had earlier affirmed bail denial and even though all delays since then had been at Beckwith's request.

There would be a trial, but Beckwith was released on $100,000 bail (rather unusual for an "indigent" with court-appointed, taxpayer-paid lawyers), and the speedy-trial issue remained alive and well to come back to haunt us later, even if we got a conviction.

Kitchens and Coxwell had immediately petitioned the court for a rehearing, but it wasn't denied until April 22, 1993. Next, they petitioned the U.S. Supreme Court to review the double-jeopardy claim. That effort was rejected during the Court's 1993 July term.

In addition to getting my new family life off to a good start (Peggy and I married in February 1993), I spent the next several months, before the U.S. Supreme Court cleared the way for us to proceed in the Beckwith case, convicting other criminals: a rapist, an armed robber, and two murderers.

An unexpected event helped us in our case against Beckwith, and at his own hands. As soon as the U.S. Supreme Court declined in early July to review the state supreme court's ruling on the double-jeopardy claim, Judge Hilburn placed the case back on the active trial docket and moved the case to Panola County for jury selection and to De Soto County for a September trial. Neither county was happy about having to host any aspect of the controversial trial, and we weren't thrilled about having to move our entire operation 180 or so miles away to north Mississippi.

The ink on Judge Hilburn's order had barely dried when I started getting calls from officials in those northern counties and people in the Jackson area. Pamphlets advocating jury nullification in the trial (that jurors were not bound to base their decision on the law and the evidence) were distributed throughout the areas. Stamped on the cover of each one was "Compliments of Byron De La Beckwith" and his Tennessee address. Beckwith himself, who was out on bail, walked into a Jackson law office and handed one to a secretary.

We immediately filed a motion for Judge Hilburn to reconsider his ruling moving the trial. Following a hearing, the clearly and justifiably peeved judge ruled that the jury would still be selected in Panola County, but once selected would be transported to Jackson. We would try the case at home.

CHAPTER EIGHT

THE TRIAL, THE STORM, AND THE VERDICT

C old. Unusually frigid, bone-chilling freezing. That's what I remember most about the jury selection phase of the trial conducted in the north Mississippi town of Batesville.

We made the trip on Monday, January 17, 1994, the King holiday. Jury selection was scheduled to begin the next morning. Barbara Dunn made all the lodging arrangements. She, Judge Hilburn, bailiffs Steve Libenschek and Jeff Murray, Ed, and I stayed at one of those abbreviated versions of a motel, a Ramada Ltd. It was limited all right; all of the lightbulbs in my room were blown. I slung my bags on the bed and joined Ed in his room next door for a drink while the manager replaced the bulbs. At least the heat worked.

Having the assistance of jury consultants is not a luxury we've enjoyed before or since, but Pete Rowland and Andy Sheldon were so intrigued by the case that they had volunteered their services and soon joined Ed and me in his room. I still believe that jury selection boils down to common sense and gut feeling. Ed had picked enough winning panels over the twenty-two years he had been in office that I would have felt completely comfortable without any outside assistance. I was reassured, though, to hear them confirm our instincts, and they suggested some additional questions for Ed to add to his outline.

The courthouse in Batesville the next morning took on the appearance of a fortress under siege by an army of newspaper and television journalists. Trucks from all major networks were there. From the moment Ed and I got out of his vehicle, cameras snapped, microphones were shoved in our faces, and reporters bombarded us with questions about the historic trial. This was it, the time had come, and all that I could think about was getting inside out of the cruel wind.

Five hundred jury summonses had been issued. Probably half that number showed. The 250 people, combined with the media, packed the courtroom, leaving no room for other spectators. I was horrified to see Thelma Beckwith sitting in the first row with prospective jurors. Then again, I thought, as soon as she opened her mouth, she'd probably alienate them.

Myrlie Evers was recuperating from back problems, which prevented her from being there at the start, but she came a day or so later. By that time, the juror numbers had thinned some, and she quietly took a seat in the back.

Benny Bennett, who had been transferred by our new police chief, Jimmy Wilson, back to the police ranks from our office over our vehement objections, was there as Judge Hilburn's bodyguard. I noticed Benny slide in beside Mrs. Evers. She beamed when she noticed him. They had come a long way since the day she had unexpectedly encountered him in our office, zigzagging his new butterfly knife in the air. We had all come a long way.

Beckwith was beaming, too. If the trial was, as some thought, a three-ring circus, Beckwith viewed himself as the ringmaster at its center. Each day he wore one of several brightly colored sports jackets (I particularly recall a baby blue one and a red one), red-white-and-blue ties, and the ever-present Confederate-flag lapel pin. Since he was out on bail, he was free to roam as he pleased outside court. It wasn't uncommon to look up from our table during lunch at one of the town's cafés to see him and Thelma laughing and eating at a table beside us.

To the outsider, the jury selection is tedious, boring, and akin to watching paint dry. It is, however, *the* most important part of any trial and was particularly so in the Beckwith trial. Twelve strangers would make the critical decision. Regardless of the evidence and arguments of the lawyers, they would utter the words *guilty, not guilty,* or *hung. Everything* rested upon the dozen who would emerge from the human mass assembled in the Batesville courtroom.

Jury "selection" is a misnomer. It's more like jury "elimination." No lawyer has the luxury of deciding who will be on a jury. It's a winnowing, which started as Judge Hilburn went through the statutory list of disqualifications, exemptions, and excuses. Anyone, for example, over the age of sixty-five could claim an exemption and be dismissed. In this case, we weren't unhappy to see any of that generation leave. When the judge asked if serving on the jury posed any significant employment hardships, one man was excused because he had "to attend to some cows for a man."

Going through the medical excuses, one woman informed the judge, "I got an ill-deformed baby at home."

"You have a child with a deformity?"

"Yes, he plays with fires, so I have to watch him."

"Does the child have mental problems?"

"Well, out of one ear."

Some people said they couldn't sit in judgment of anyone's guilt or innocence and were excused. None knew Beckwith, but one white male said that his grandfather once bought a .30-06 rifle from the defendant.

"And," Judge Hilburn informed the jury pool, "for those of you who wish to seize upon this opportunity, anyone who wishes to admit being a habitual drunkard or gambler can be excused. Do I have any volunteers for that?" Laughter erupted in the courtroom. He didn't have any takers then, but I remembered an old man in a trial in Raymond who had raised his hand in response to the same question and was excused after insisting that he fit the bill.

Only one juror had not heard of the case. I wondered what planet she had been on. Ed asked the others if they had already made up their mind and knew how they were going to vote. Several hands shot up. We spoke with them further in the judge's chambers so the rest wouldn't be influenced by the responses.

"This trial is not about justice; it's about politics." "Thought the whole thing was senseless." "He's what, seventy years old?" "I think if Mr. De La Beckwith was black, we wouldn't be having this trial."

Such opinions weren't limited to native Mississippians. Consider, for example, the response of a retired naval officer originally from Montana, when Ed asked what his first thoughts were upon hearing of the retrial: "I was wondering just who's got anything to gain by the trial. Certainly, it is not the defendant, not anybody in the state of Mississippi. Somebody must have some reason for wanting a trial, but I didn't know who it was."

"And how does that make you feel?" Ed quizzed.

"Makes me feel uneasy. I believe I'd be looking around to see if it was you that had something to gain. If I was convinced that somebody had something personal to gain, I don't know if I would even consider what the evidence was."

I thought about all of the letters, comments, hateful phone calls, a bomb threat, and my divorce. What possible personal gain was to be had, other than knowing deep down you were doing the right thing?

Another white juror said, "I think somebody is trying to score some points."

"I assume you're talking about the prosecutor, who, of course, is me," Ed said. The juror responded yes, but added that she wouldn't feel that way if we had new evidence.

"Would you be as bold, if we have the proof, to look me in the eye and say, 'I was wrong; you've got the proof; it's not politics'?"

"I sure could."

By the same token, two or three blacks were excused, over our objection, because they told Jim Kitchens that they greatly admired Medgar Evers and appreciated the work he had done.

It would be a mistake, though, to assume that we wanted only African-Americans and no whites, as opposition to the trial wasn't limited to whites. One thirty-year-old black male, for example, who had never heard of Medgar Evers before we reopened the case asked Ed, "Why prosecute someone after all these years, regardless of what the evidence may show? This is the way I look at it: to me, I would say it's 'guilty' for taking someone's life, but it's 'innocent' for all the years that have gone by."

Another black male echoed the sentiment: "Why bring it back up, whether he's guilty or innocent? You know, wherever he's at, just let him stay, and I feel he's guilty."

When Ed asked, "Are any of you saying to yourself, He's already seventy-two years old, why are we fooling with him?" several black hands were raised along with white. Even though they believed Beckwith was guilty, they felt because of his age that he would be dying soon enough and facing God, the Supreme Judge. Let God worry about it.

Several African-Americans didn't know anything about the case. Although they had heard something about the trial on the news, they had never heard of Medgar Evers before, and didn't have a clue what kind of work he did. One such black referred to Evers as "Medgar Everett." Coxwell asked him if he had ever been a member of the NAACP. "No, I haven't."

"Did you know that Medgar Evers was?"

"No, I didn't."

"When did you learn that for the first time?"

"You just told me."

Another black male was asked by Kitchens, "As you were a young person growing up, did your parents ever tell you about Medgar Evers?"

"Not that I know of."

"Three or four years ago, if I'd walked up to you and said, 'Medgar Evers,' you wouldn't have known who in the world I was talking about?"

"I sure wouldn't have. I'd said, 'Who is he?'"

To somewhat prepare her for the worst, I apprised Mrs. Evers of these responses from the black jurors. "It was the same way in the sixties," she said. "So many who Medgar was trying to help shunned him." She realized the uphill battle we were waging, but urged me not to give up and to continue praying. Maybe, if nothing else came of this trial, people who had never heard of Medgar Evers or did not appreciate him would know who he was and have a greater respect for what many now took for granted.

Just as not every black was in our corner, not every white was in Beckwith's. One of the white females who indicated that her mind was made up was questioned further in chambers by Jim Kitchens: "What was your mind made up about?"

"The defendant's guilty," she declared.

"Thank you. I have no further questions."

Yet another white informed us, "I'm going to find him guilty because of the gun and his prints were on it."

A few were hard to read. For instance, one white said, "I don't know if the man's guilty or innocent. I just think he's an embarrassment to the State of Mississippi and would like for you to have left him where he was."

"I assume you've seen some interviews or something on television," Ed said.

"Just some of the ranting and raving."

While many prospective jurors were open and talkative about their feelings, they weren't the real threat. Once their opinions were known to us and if found to be so fixed that it would affect their decision, the judge excused them "for cause." There is no limit to such excusals.

Of the first thirty-six jurors left in the pool, after all excusals for cause, each side can excuse twelve of their choice for any race-neutral reason. The remaining dozen are the jury. The greater danger was that jurors might harbor ill feelings toward one side or the other or have strong opinions, but keep quiet. Pete and Andy had some good ideas for phrasing certain questions to flush out those jurors.

Beginning Wednesday morning, Ed asked each juror questions such as "What was your first impression or feeling when you first heard the case was reopened and going to trial after thirty years?" "How many of you feel that politics is behind this; the defendant can't get a fair trial after so long; you would be affected in deciding on a verdict by the defendant's health; it's a waste of taxpayer money; the trial is racially motivated?"

The questions prompted more responses from the otherwise reserved jurors. A white male, for example, told Ed, "It's a racial thing. It was racial then [in 1963] and it's racial now. It's a big waste of the state's money to even have the trial."

"What if the judge gave you an instruction and said, 'You're not to consider things like that.' How would you feel about that?" Ed asked.

"I'd feel like I was about as old as the judge is, and I might know as much as he does."

Coxwell, sensing that the judge was about to excuse this juror, attempted to rehabilitate him, but the juror held firm to his opinion. Asked by Coxwell if he could just *consider* a guilty verdict if hard evidence convinced him, the man replied, "I already have stated that I was opinionated about it, so I undoubtedly have already made my mind up as to which way I would go." The additional questions formulated the night before were apparently helping.

"Have any of you ever belonged to an organization that sponsors the superiority of the white race?" Ed next asked. No hands were raised, nor did we expect any. Most people wouldn't admit to it nor to being a racist, but the question itself was meant to cause the jurors to begin to distance themselves from Beckwith—a "we're not like him" strategy. Their silence to the question was not taken at face value, though.

Pete Rowland and two assistants had mingled around the town and learned of an issue that tended to split the county along racial lines. The southern part of the county was predominantly white and the north was mostly black. A bond issue to expand and improve North Panola High School had ignited opposition from voters in the southern sector and caused some racial friction. Ed asked jurors from the south how they felt about the bond issue.

He also asked each juror if they had children and what their ages were to see if any were of school age in 1970 when the public schools in the state were finally forced to comply with the U.S. Supreme Court's 1954 decision in *Brown v. Board of Education* and desegregate classrooms. Those people who had had school-age children were asked where the children attended school in 1970. Those who had pulled their kids out of the public schools and enrolled them in private academies to avoid integration were noted.

I suggested that Ed tell the jury that the evidence would show that Medgar Evers was the plaintiff in a school integration lawsuit, and thus indirectly responsible for Mississippi's schools being desegregated. Would that affect their decision? Would they feel that he was a troublemaker and got what he deserved? It paid off. One white male said, "That's a tough question." Two others said that, although he didn't deserve being killed, if Evers were even partially responsible for integration, it would probably affect their decision in the case.

Racial resentment arising in the workplace was also explored, as Ed probed to detect if any juror ever lost a job or promotion due to affirmative action. "Do you feel like you have to compete with blacks for a job?" Ed quizzed the whites.

Fear of what a juror's family, friends, boss, and coworkers might think was a concern. Most people, however, will not admit that others influence them, so our jury advisers suggested that Ed ask, "How many of you have talked to somebody about the case or heard other people talking about it?" Of those who offered a response, that of a white female is illustrative. Her mother had told her the trial was "ridiculous," and the juror had agreed with her. A friend told her the same thing, but urged her to still try and get on the jury because she would be "a part of history."

Ed also sought to ascertain which blacks worked under white supervisors, and from those, what comments were made once their supervisors had learned of their jury summons. Conversely, one white female worked with a black female (both were schoolteachers), a relationship that was weighing on her mind. Her African-American coworker had gone to college with Myrlie Evers, and the juror explained that she felt "kinda torn." In tears, she informed us, "I respect this lady and I have a feeling that if I go for you, she's gonna like that. If I go for the other, then I'm going to be hated."

I urged Ed to lay out the motive of the murder early on, attempting again to make it impossible for most of the potential jurors to identify in any way with Beckwith: "If the evidence shows that the victim in this case, when he was killed, was trying to get some changes made, trying to make it where black people could drink at water fountains, have equal access to department stores and rest rooms, be called 'Mr.' and 'Mrs.,' would anyone feel that would, in any way, justify someone killing him?"

Nobody raised a hand, so Ed finished by asking, "If that was his objective in life in the 1960s, would that influence you?" A white male raised his hand.

To illustrate that the ideal of justice is timeless and doesn't change, I got Ed to ask, "Is there anyone who feels that because things were different back in the sixties than they are today, this defendant should not be judged by today's standards; who feels that that's the way it was back then and he should be judged by the way things were then?"

A white male said that's exactly how he felt.

In a way, our procedure was the reverse from our normal approach to picking a jury. We usually want jurors to believe police officers. Here, however, we couldn't have them believing Holley and Creswell, Beckwith's alibi witnesses. Ed had to ask some questions that defense lawyers usually ask, such as whether anyone would automatically believe some-one because he's a police officer.

"No," a black female replied. "Any witness can lie, you know, just like the judge and lawyers and doctors, and, you know, preachers."

"Strike that," Ed joked to court reporter Kaye Kerr.

We couldn't give credence to the Klan, yet we had two witnesses who had been members. Ed had to ask if anyone would automatically disbelieve a Klansman. That Delmar Dennis and Dick Davis were informers helped, in some jurors' minds, to distance them from the Klan, but for others, being informers or "snitches" raised concerns about their testimony.

A few people said they couldn't consider a guilty verdict unless there was an eyewitness to the actual shooting.

In any other case, we would attempt to dismiss as many of the "maver-icks" as possible. These are jurors who look for an opportunity to strike back at a legal system they feel has wronged them or someone close to them. Since the defense usually seeks to eliminate the strong law-and-order people, the normal result is that moderates are left to serve on the jury.

Here, though, it soon became evident that, to a large degree, *we* would be striking the law-and-order people. The defense wouldn't have to. And, if they struck the moderates, the mavericks would be left on the panel. Our only hope was that Beckwith might not go for that. He was such a prima donna that he might look at them as "riffraff" and not con-sider them a jury of his peers.

We were implementing an entirely new strategy, and the chess match was well under way.

While we couldn't automatically depend on a juror simply because he or she was black, it was obvious at the outset that no blacks were wanted by the defense. Even those who felt too much time had gone by to con-sider a guilty verdict were released by the judge without objection by Beckwith's lawyers, who exerted no effort to rehabilitate them as was done with the whites. Ed couldn't resist commenting on the racial tactic.

An African-American truck driver who couldn't afford to miss *any* work, much less several weeks, sent word to Judge Hilburn while we were in conference in chambers that he really needed to be excused for that reason. Ed reluctantly agreed: "He's black and I understand that I'm cutting my own throat by saying this, but we've already cut him out of one week of work. We're gonna cut him out another week when all the other jurors are going about their jobs, but he can't because he's gotta be out on the road. As much as I hate to say it, I just don't believe we're being fair to him to do that."

When Kitchens concurred, Ed commented to the judge, "If he were white, I know they wouldn't agree." Kitchens objected. "I apologize," Ed continued, "and if they'll just spend half the time with any black juror as they have with a white, I'll take it back."

The defense was especially interested in what jurors had ever lived outside Mississippi, particularly outside the South. "We all live in Mississippi now," Kitchens told the jurors. "Have you heard that Mississippi is on trial in this case?" He was attempting to again rally the troops to resist outside attitudes and Yankee agitators, and I thought his approach somewhat effective as many heads bobbed up and down.

"I heard it on *Hard Copy* this week," one juror said.

The effect, however, lost some momentum with Kitchens's follow-up question: "Of course, we are all concerned with Mississippi's image all the time. But that wouldn't be part of what you would base your verdict on, would it?" Naturally, no juror would say he or she would, but I was grateful to Kitchens for planting the seed of concern for our state's image by asking the question. It was like saying, "Whatever you do, pay no attention to that polka-dotted elephant."

A juror's ability to afford the accused the presumption of innocence is always something defense attorneys spend a lot of time probing. When Kitchens posed the question to one lady, she asked him, "*Is* he innocent?" Another female responded, "I can't prove he's innocent."

"No, ma'am," the defense lawyer explained, "I'm not asking you to prove anything."

"I can't say he's innocent," she replied.

"You can't make that presumption at this point?"

"No."

When Kitchens posed the same question to a male juror, he replied that he could afford Beckwith that presumption "until you prove he's guilty."

"I don't intend to do that, sir," the defense attorney explained.

By Thursday, it was all too clear that nobody, so far, wanted to serve on this jury (except of course the lady who wanted to be a part of history), and everyone, judge and lawyers, began to get a little goofy. One juror, when Ed asked how he'd felt when he learned that he had to show up for jury duty in the case, responded, "Didn't affect me. I'm laid off, you know. I've got time to burn."

"Forty dollars a day?" Ed quipped, referring to the pay each juror would receive from the county.

"Yeah, beats nothing."

"I'd like to congratulate you on being the first juror that's said it was okay," Ed responded. "You don't know about eleven more people you can find like that, do you?" Everyone in chambers laughed.

Another juror was asked, "If you're required to go to Jackson and be housed in a motel there and trying the case for two weeks, is that gonna put you in a position where you're really financially strapped?"

"Would not," the juror responded. "I'm already broke." The courtroom fell out laughing.

Shortly after that exchange, we came to a female whom I'll refer to as Ms. White. We were speaking to the jurors one at a time in chambers, and Judge Hilburn asked Ed, "Who do you ask for next?"

"Ms. Vacillating White," Ed quipped.

When Ms. Vacillating White entered the room, she told Kitchens that she hoped she wasn't chosen "because I do not want to go" to Jackson.

"Yes, ma'am," Kitchens said. "Do you know anybody out there [referring to the jurors in the courtroom] who does?"

"Do you know anybody *in here* who does?" the judge asked.

Many times, to be certain, the levity gave way to frustration, and nothing is more frustrating than those jurors, such as Ms. White, who vacillate in their answers concerning their ability to be fair. They claim a fixed opinion one second, yet say they could still be fair. We call them wafflers, and Ed says if you ask what their favorite color is, the answer will be plaid.

After some responses along these lines by a white male, who then left the judge's chambers for Judge Hilburn to rule on any challenge for cause, the judge said, "Mr. Peters?"

"If you're asking me if I challenge him, of course. If I think you're going to sustain it, no, because the guy has no idea what's going on. The guy couldn't give a straight answer if you asked him what his age was." I remember thinking that the man must have been related to Gordon Lackey.

As plentiful as they were in the beginning, Ed had done a splendid job of getting most jurors who were biased against the prosecution excused for cause. Unless the defense could do the same with the blacks, our jury, unlike those in 1964, would include several African-Americans. The fact was not lost on Beckwith.

During a recess on Monday, January 24, Beckwith had an animated discussion in the back hallway with his lawyers. On my way to the bathroom, I could hear him telling his lawyers, "Looking up in that jury box is like looking up a stovepipe; all I see is black!" I walked on, hearing the defense attorneys urging their client to hold it down.

As I finished my business in the small rest room, the door opened. The quarters were so close, I had to back against the sink to let the door open. In stepped Beckwith, standing right in front of me, only inches away.

I stared into his eyes, pitch-black with no sparkle. I don't think I saw any iris; just black pupils like a shark's. Although I felt what a bird must while staring into the eyes of a snake, I was determined not to look away.

He broke the silent standoff. "Well, is this jury shaping up to suit you?"

"We'll just have to wait and see," I said, and stepped forward. Beckwith moved to the side, and as I walked toward the door, he replied, "That we will, my boy. Oh, yes, sir, that we will." He knew the onus was still on us. Even with several blacks, one person on the panel could hang it up, and he would walk free again, just as in 1964.

In a last-ditch effort to get black jurors to say they couldn't be fair, Kitchens added a few inflammatory questions as we talked to them individually in chambers. The judge, however, nipped it in the bud after Kitchens asked the first juror, "If it came to your attention that Mr. Beckwith [who was sitting by his lawyers] was a person who used the term *nigger,* and still uses it frequently, would that offend you and cause you to lean against him in the case?" Of course it would, and the judge excused the juror for other reasons.

Hilburn issued a warning, though. "I do want to caution you, Mr. Kitchens, that I'm not going to disqualify each juror that comes in here if you ask them that question for that reason alone." The clear message was that Kitchens could ask the question, but with the judge refusing to excuse jurors based on the answer, the defense would be stuck with their remaining in the jury pool after learning of such damaging information about Beckwith. The question wasn't asked again.

As soon as we arrived at the courthouse Tuesday morning, January 25, Ed and I were told that the judge wanted to see everybody in chambers. *Clarion-Ledger* reporter Beverly Pettigrew Craft informed everyone that a fax had been received in their newsroom purporting to be from an unnamed African-American member of the jury pool and stating that he had already made up his mind and would attempt to persuade other members of the jury to vote guilty. The fax had been sent from a pay machine at a local Kroger.

There was no Kroger grocery store in Panola County, but there was a

Kroger distribution center where one prospective juror worked. He was white. Although I didn't believe for a minute that Beckwith's lawyers had any involvement in it, I had no doubt that it was a deliberate stunt by some Beckwith sympathizer to get the judge to grant a mistrial. In fact, that's exactly what Beckwith's lawyers requested. The judge denied the motion and referred the matter to Panola County sheriff David Bryan for investigation. The investigation confirmed my suspicions. It was a hoax.

Court recessed Tuesday afternoon about three-fifteen. We had the forty-six jurors in the pool necessary to have the twelve who would serve on the panel, plus two alternates, after each side exercised their twelve peremptory strikes. Ed and I met with the consultants in his room, decided on the twelve we would excuse, and then predicted which dozen we felt the defense had to eliminate.

We toyed with one combination after another. No matter how we cut it, at least half the jury was going to be black. By no means did that alone assure victory for the prosecution. Any one juror could thwart everything we had done over the past four years, an entire term of office for Ed. With this jury, though, I felt we at least had a chance.

Each side was scheduled to exercise its challenges Wednesday morning. The jury would then be sworn in and transported by bus to their Jackson hotel rooms. With Ed's role in the jury selection closing, my job in presenting the state's case would soon start. Opening statements by the lawyers and testimony would begin Thursday morning at the Hinds County Courthouse. On Wednesday morning, while Ed finished the jury selection, I returned to Jackson to make sure that everything was ready to go on Thursday.

I had trouble going to sleep Tuesday night. Ed completely trusted me to prepare and present our case. Although I had done so many times in murder cases, none had had the scrutiny that attended this one. On my shoulders fell the responsibility of making or blowing our case. I knew its every nuance and intricacy, as well as its evidence, more so than any other human being. Why should I have been nervous?

Because twelve people who did *not* know all of the evidence and dynamics would render the verdict. It was my job to educate them gradually, to guide them methodically along the same trail I had followed for four years, to lead them inevitably to the assassin, and to ultimately convince them to take the bold step of a guilty verdict.

Could I do it? Would all twelve go along? Would it be victory or defeat? There was no middle ground. A hung jury in 1994 would be as much of a defeat for Mississippi as an outright acquittal.

I turned to my Bible that I brought from home and flipped through the pages. Page after page was turned, past one highlighted verse after another, until I came to the Thirty-seventh Psalms:

> Do not fret because of the wicked. . . . Commit your way to the Lord; trust in Him, and He will act. He will make your vindication shine like the light, and the justice of your cause like the noonday.

That was my assurance. I would continue doing my job, something that I could control. Beyond that, I couldn't afford fretting over Beckwith. I said a prayer and slept like a baby.

I caught a ride back to Jackson with a deputy. Arriving at our office around noon, I opened several letters that had come in during my stay in Batesville. The first few were positive and boosted my morale.

Instilling more pride in my pursuit was that Mississippi was being saluted in some letters from outside the state. They verbalized much of what I had felt all along, but hearing it from someone else meant much to me. It would have meant even more if fellow Mississippians had realized the tribute our state was receiving beyond its borders. These are excerpts from letters received from Jacksonians: "This trial is asinine"; "Something is rotten in Jackson in the justice system and you are part of it. This trial stinks"; "Nuts is nuts and this is nuts"; and "This trial is a disgrace."

Rep. Charlie Capps Jr., a longtime member of the Mississippi legislature and chairman of its powerful House Appropriations Committee, wrote in his individual capacity to Ed Peters:

> I cannot imagine your purpose, but for whatever reason, your indictment and proposed trial of Mr. Beckwith has done great and irreparable harm to our state. The State of Mississippi and thousands of private citizens have worked for several decades in an effort to change our image nationally, and I believe that this trial will destroy 30 years of work overnight.

Ed handed me the letter Thursday morning, just before I gave my opening statement to the jury. It infuriated me. Much as the state Sovereignty Commission worked against DA Bill Waller in his 1964 quest for justice, we had the House Appropriations Committee chairman (who, as such, was in charge of Ed's and my salary) trying, albeit unofficially, to demoralize us the day testimony started.

I considered writing to him and explaining our position and the positive aspects for Mississippi. But, although I didn't write, I wasn't going to let Capps get away with it. The only way he could possibly be proven right was if we lost. Capps pissed me off and I'm forever grateful that he did. I was pumped up and bursting at the seams by the time I stood before the eight blacks (three males, five females) and four whites (two males, two females) on the jury the morning of Thursday, January 27, 1994.

"Ladies and gentlemen, you're going to see from the evidence what this case *is* about, and likewise, what it is *not* about. You're going to see that it's not about trying to set an old wrong right; it's not about politics; it's not about whether this defendant can get a fair trial. This case is not even about a civil rights case that just incidentally involves a murder. It's not about the pluses and minuses of people's opinions in the civil rights movement of the 1960s.

"It's about a man whose life was snuffed out on June the twelfth of 1963, by a bullet that tore through his body. Medgar Evers was shot and killed. He lost his life by a bullet that was aimed out of prejudice, propelled by hatred, and fired by a coward from ambush at night.

"You're going to see, when it's all said and done, that the person who pulled that trigger from ambush and ended the life of Medgar Evers is this defendant, Byron De La Beckwith. And I'd like to take a few minutes this morning to explain how this came about and what happened.

"You see, in 1954, a landmark decision of the United States Supreme Court was handed down that in effect said that schools and public facilities could no longer be segregated; that people were to have equal access to them. Shortly after that, this defendant, who was an absolute self-proclaimed rabid racist—"

"Your Honor," Coxwell said, rising from his chair, "we object to the characterization of Mr. Beckwith and move for a mistrial."

"All right," the judge said. "Overruled."

I continued, "He embarked upon a one-man mission to purge society of anyone and everything that was for integration. This defendant embarked upon what he would later call a perpetual war against the enemies of this white Christian republic.

"And so around 1955, there appeared numerous letters written by this defendant to the editors of the various papers in the state, putting in print how he felt. You will see that there was absolutely nothing more important to him than pursuing segregation."

An objection by Kitchens was overruled.

"You will see letters written by this defendant where he proclaims that the enemies of the white race must be purged from society and the leaders of the NAACP exterminated.

"On the other hand, while all of this was going on, a man by the name of Medgar Evers was finishing school at Alcorn A and M. He had sought and been refused admission to the Ole Miss Law School because of his race."

"Objection," Kitchens said. "Counsel is arguing his case." Damn straight I was, and I could've hugged Kitchens for objecting to this part about the victim in front of the eight African-American jurors.

"Goes directly to motive," Ed explained.

"Let's move along," Judge Hilburn replied.

"In 1962, when James Meredith *was* successful in entering the Ole Miss Law School, Medgar Evers was instrumental in counseling and aiding him, all of which, as field secretary for the NAACP, brought Medgar Evers to the forefront. It made him the focal point of everything this defendant hated—everything this defendant said he would exterminate and purge from society, and on June the twelfth, 1963, he did just that."

Step by step, I informed the jury of the evidence connecting Beckwith with the murder.

"*His* car, *his* gun, *his* fingerprint, and certainly *his* motive.

"You'll see that because this defendant through the years thought he had beaten the system, when he thought it was all over with, he made incriminating statements to several different people he felt comfortable with.

"And when it's all before you, when it's all said and done, we're going to make one request to you based on the law and the evidence: simply hold this defendant accountable for what he did and find him guilty as charged."

Buddy Coxwell delivered the opening remarks for the defense:

"Mr. DeLaughter started off saying that this trial is not about this, and it's not about that, and it's not about the NAACP. But what he's basically going to be relying on is for you to convict Mr. Beckwith because of his opinions. But you're gonna find out that the state cannot prove to you beyond a reasonable doubt that Mr. Beckwith killed Medgar Evers.

"There's a lot of things the state will show during this trial that we don't have any dispute with. We don't have any dispute that Medgar Evers is dead and that whoever killed him was wrong to kill him. There will not be a lot of dispute from us about the crime scene.

"Mr. DeLaughter pointed out where he said Mr. Evers was killed. We may not dispute that.

"But by the time this case is over, you will have seen that it was physically impossible for Mr. Byron De La Beckwith to have killed Medgar Evers, because he was as far away from this location as you are from your homes right now at the time that it happened.

"You're going to find, through several police officers, who will testify that they saw Mr. Beckwith at a time it would have been physically impossible for him to have been here in Jackson shooting Mr. Evers.

"There may be testimony that Mr. Beckwith's fingerprint was found on the gun, but I want to remind you that the fact that his fingerprint was found on the gun does not mean that Mr. Byron De La Beckwith fired the shot.

"When you look at the evidence, I think you'll know in your own heart, regardless of what the state has tried to show you, that Mr. Beckwith is not guilty.

"Thirty-one years ago, he was in this courtroom and he entered a not-guilty plea. In 1991, he entered a not-guilty plea. I believe that's what the proof will show."

All successful prosecutions must tell the story of what happened, unfolding it before the jury in a logical sequence, one witness at a time. The better witnesses, as painful as it may be, actually relive the moment with such vivid detail and genuine emotion that all listening join along in the retrospective journey. For that moment, you are there with them, as an unseen observer of the events.

Myrlie Evers, I knew from her grand jury appearance, would be such a witness. I had promised the jurors in my opening statement that they would see what the case was, and was not, about. I wanted to come out swinging, jolting them to the reality of the horror and inhumanity of June 12, 1963. There was never any question who my first witness would be. Almost thirty years after she had last sat in the same witness chair, I called Mrs. Evers to the stand.

She had married Walter Edward Williams in July 1975, and before that she had been married to Medgar Wiley Evers. The names of both husbands were enunciated with emphasis and pride. Instead of turning away from the defendant, as many family members of the victim in homicide trials do, she gracefully turned and looked Beckwith dead in the eye as she uttered Medgar's name.

Myrlie and Medgar married on Christmas Eve, 1951. "We met on the campus of Alcorn A and M College the first hour, the first day, that I arrived as a freshman," she said. "Medgar received his degree in business administration in 1952. I completed two years of college there."

I began to lay the groundwork for Beckwith's motive behind the assassination. "Did he attempt to further his education after graduating from Alcorn?" I asked Mrs. Evers.

"Yes, he did. He attempted to enroll at the University of Mississippi Law School and he was rejected because of his race." Kitchens's prompt objection was overruled.

Medgar had continued selling insurance in Mound Bayou, Mississippi, Myrlie informed the jury, but because of the horrific treatment of blacks he witnessed as he traveled the dusty Delta roads, "he took on the position of the first field secretary for the NAACP in Mississippi."

"Would you explain to us what, if any, changes your husband was seeking to make, particularly just before his death?" Another defense objection was overruled.

"There were a number of things that Medgar was trying to do. One was the integration of schools. Another was opening up swimming pools or being able to go to restaurants; to use the public libraries; to be able to go to department stores and try on clothes, shoes, and hats; to be called by name instead of 'boy' or 'girl'; to have courtesy titles of 'Mr.' or 'Mrs.'; something as simple as having school-crossing guards for the children at the black schools."

Medgar befriended and counseled James Meredith in the latter's forced enrollment at the Ole Miss Law School in 1962, partially because of Medgar's position in the NAACP, but also because of his own rejection in the 1950s. Although many players were involved, Medgar was catapulted as the point man on the court for the NAACP. Ugly, threatening phone calls at home became so frequent after the Meredith "crisis," as it was referred to among white Mississippians, Myrlie and Medgar were forced to get an unlisted phone number.

We covered this ground not just for dramatic effect, but so the jury would understand, when they later heard the testimony of cabdrivers Speight and Swilley, why Beckwith had been unsuccessful in searching for Evers's listing in the phone book.

Against this backdrop, it was time to move to the murder. "When was the last time you saw your husband, Medgar Evers, alive?"

"June the eleventh, 1963, when he left home that morning to go to work. He left that morning after telling us good-bye with a very special embrace. Darrell was nine; Reena was eight; and James, or Van, was three. Medgar went out to his car and was out there for a second or so, and came back in and told us to be sure to take good care of ourselves and to be sure to watch President Kennedy's address that night, and hugged and kissed us all again and . . ." She was beginning to choke up. "And he left.

"He returned home," she continued, "on the twelfth of June. It was slightly after midnight. We heard the car, the motor of which we were very familiar, and the children said, 'There's Daddy.' We heard the car pull in the driveway, and this horrible blast." She paused, letting it sink in. The acoustics are terrible in the large historic courtroom, but you could've heard a pin drop.

"And the children fell to the floor as he had taught them to do. The baby was on the bed with me, and I bolted up and ran to the door, and there was Medgar at the steps with his keys in his hand.

"I screamed, I guess uncontrollably, and the children ran out shortly after I did, and they called, 'Daddy, Daddy, get up. Please get up, Daddy.'

"When I first got to him, there was another shot, and I remember dropping to my knees again, because I thought someone was trying to shoot me as well. Neighbors came and a couple of people put Medgar on a mattress and in a vehicle to take him to the hospital."

Proceeding with her through the photographs of the house, I introduced each one into evidence and circulated them among the jurors, who studied them with keen interest. I asked her about one showing T-shirts scattered along Medgar's blood trail.

"Those are T-shirts that Medgar had in his hand when he got out of the car. They were going to be given out to some of the demonstrators. They had the words on them 'Jim Crow Must Go.' "

Since some jurors weren't even alive in 1963 and others had indicated they knew nothing of Medgar Evers, I couldn't assume they were aware of what Jim Crow was or why it needed to go. "What did that have reference to?" I asked.

"To the laws that helped perpetuate segregation, the very laws Medgar was fighting to change."

It was time to lay some groundwork for the exhumation and second autopsy by Dr. Baden. I handed her two photos and asked her, "Do you know who this is?"

"Yes. This is Medgar in his casket." The photos taken when Dr. Baden had first opened the casket were introduced and passed to the jury. The testimony of Myrlie Evers, coupled with the pictures of her slain husband in pristine condition twenty-eight years after his funeral, personalized the case to the twelve jurors. The question of guilt or innocence was no longer a debate in the hypothetical abstract. On that note, I turned Mrs. Evers over for cross-examination.

Kitchens had to be careful. The jury had been visibly moved by Myrlie's testimony. As an ex-DA and seasoned trial lawyer, he knew any attempt to browbeat the victim's widow would prove disastrous.

Through a series of questions, he merely brought it to the jury's attention that one might reasonably infer from the many phone calls that a lot of people in 1963 Mississippi might wish to see Evers harmed. Beyond that, Kitchens actually filled in a gap for me.

Mrs. Evers had learned that the second shot that she had heard was fired by neighbor Houston Wells as an alert. I hadn't asked her about it because her knowledge of it was hearsay, but I certainly didn't object to Kitchens's inquiry.

Following her testimony, both sides released Mrs. Evers as a witness, which meant that she could remain in the courtroom for the duration of the trial. Unless released, witnesses may not hear the testimony of other witnesses.

Houston Wells was an invalid and unable to testify. I called neighbor Willie Quinn in Wells's place. Quinn lived in the same house he was in when Evers was shot. Located just behind Myrlie and Medgar's home, he, too, heard the shot and joined other neighbors in responding and accompanied Wells in transporting Evers to the hospital. En route, Medgar "kept saying, 'Turn me loose.' He stood up and I had to try to set him back down on the mattress."

B. D. Harrell Jr. was the captain in charge of the detective bureau shift at the police station when the call came in. Harrell was retired not only from the police department, but from the Jackson Public School System security corps as well.

The call came in around 12:30 or 12:45 A.M., he told the jury, "from a gentleman who identified himself as a member of the NAACP. He asked me had I received a call of a shooting on Guynes Street, and I said, 'Not directly.' He said, 'Well, let me assure you that there has been one.'" The caller provided Harrell with the address and explained that the victim was Medgar Evers.

Detectives John Chamblee and Fred Sanders were at police headquarters at the time and were immediately dispatched to the scene by Captain Harrell, who "also called radio and asked them to send a patrol unit."

One of those patrol officers was Eddie Rosamond. Rosamond and his partner, Joe Alford, were so close to Guynes Street they arrived at the Evers home in two to three minutes.

Rosamond testified, "Mrs. Evers was standing in the door and hollering, 'They shot Medgar, they shot Medgar!' He was lying kinda facedown in a fetal position in a puddle of blood. The first thing we did was to try to get him to the hospital. We got a mattress and used a neighbor's station wagon. We didn't want to waste any time calling an ambulance and waiting for them."

I called Charlie Crisco next to briefly testify to the chain of custody regarding the lead fragments that Dr. Baden recovered from the body, then called Baden himself to the stand.

Although the defense offered to stipulate to Baden's expertise in the field of forensic pathology, I wanted the jury to hear the details of his impressive credentials for two reasons. First, of course, I wanted the jury to realize that the man knew what he was talking about, and second, I wanted them to see that, in enlisting an expert of such notoriety and qualifications, the State of Mississippi had spared no effort in preparing a first-class case.

Dr. Forrest Bratley, the retired local pathologist who had performed the initial autopsy in 1963, still lived in Jackson and would, indeed, testify. I wanted, however, to send the jurors the message that this case involved an assassination. Baden was the chairman of the forensic pathology division of the U.S. Congressional Select Commission on Assassinations, appointed to reinvestigate aspects of the deaths of President Kennedy and Dr. King.

The body of our victim had been buried since 1963. I wanted the jury to know that Baden was the world-renowned expert who, in 1992, at the request of the Russian government, had examined what were believed to be the remains of Czar Nicholas and Alexandria of the Romanoff family murdered in 1918.

Baden testified: "Mr. Evers died of a single high-powered-rifle wound to the back that went through the right side about three inches off dead center, through the right lung, fractured two ribs in the back, and then exited through one rib in the front, just above and to the inside of the right nipple. The trajectory was about straight horizontal. That is, the bullet went through the body pretty much in a straight line, causing extensive internal injury."

After introducing the X rays, I had Dr. Baden mount them on a light box and point out, for the jury, the location of the lead fragments he had recovered and placed in Crisco's custody.

"On the right side of his chest, there's a starburst effect of little metal fragments, and this was very important for us to document, because that's evidence that a high-powered bullet, or at least a lead component, soft lead tip, had gone through his body and given this characteristic starburst pattern. So, even though the bullet is no longer present, little fragments of the nose of the bullet were there and I was able to remove them." Going further, Dr. Baden informed the jury the fragments were consistent with having been fired from a .30-06 rifle.

So the jury wouldn't give credence to any defense argument that an expert will say whatever the side paying him desires, I concluded my direct examination by asking, "Dr. Baden, what, if any, fee did you receive for your services to the State of Mississippi?"

"I guess a big bowl of gumbo this afternoon. My involvement in the investigation is part of a professional courtesy that the New York State Police is extending to the district attorney's office and no fees are involved."

Following the noon recess and a bowl of gumbo for Dr. Baden, Kitchens quickly went on the attack, questioning some of the doctor's findings. Bad mistake. The slash-and-burn tactic backfired several times.

"Now, you testified that they were pieces of lead, but you don't really know that for sure, do you?"

"I know this," Baden calmly replied, "by experience of seeing lead fragments on X rays. They have a very unique opaque quality, and by the appearance at the time that I removed them from the body."

Kitchens moved quickly to Baden's conclusion that the fragments came from a high-powered rifle and were specifically consistent with a .30-06. "Have you had any experience in testing firearms?"

"No," Baden said.

"Do you shoot, hunt, regularly?"

"No."

"Doctor, you said that you felt this wound was caused by a shot from a rifle."

"Yes, sir."

"You ruled out a handgun altogether?"

"Yes."

"What's your opinion about the velocity at which the bullet was traveling when it struck Mr. Evers?"

"Over fifteen hundred feet per second."

"Doctor, don't .357 magnum bullets travel at about the same speed?"

"Usually appreciably less. Handguns are up around about one thousand or eight hundred feet per second; a magnum maybe eleven hundred, twelve hundred feet per second."

"You don't really know a great deal about that to the point of being able to testify as an expert, do you, sir?"

"I would not testify as an expert about guns and ballistics, but I would testify as an expert about *the effects* of guns and bullets on the body. And in examining persons who have been shot, it's unusual to have a handgun cause this flying spread of lead that a higher-powered rifle causes, without knowing anything else about the weapon."

Baden's thrust-and-parry continued as Kitchens asked, "Now, Doctor, if you had never read anything about this case, you would have no way, whatsoever, of knowing what kind of bullet it may be, would you, sir, other than the fact that you found some lead fragments in Mr. Evers's body?"

"If I had known *nothing* about this matter, if this were a death of an unknown person with no history, I would have to say, as a medical examiner to the police, that you're looking for a rifle bullet, not a handgun bullet, that caused this injury, because of the fact that the bullet velocity caused this starburst effect, and that it had enough velocity to enter and exit the body. In my experience with two thousand murders a year in New York City, handguns don't cause this pattern, and rifles do cause this pattern."

Since some prospective jurors had indicated they would like to have some new evidence, something unavailable to prosecutors in 1964, I next called Dr. Forrest Bratley to explain to the panel that he had not taken X rays in the 1963 autopsy and, thus, did not have those of the starburst pattern of lead fragments, as did Dr. Baden.

The only photo I found of Medgar Evers from the 1963 investigation was one taken after he had died at the hospital. I introduced it through Dr. Bratley to show the exit wound in the chest.

In 1963, Kenneth Adcock lived with his girlfriend, Betty Jean Coley, and her mother, just off Delta Drive where Joe's Drive-In was located. Bored with nothing else to do late the night of June 11, Kenneth and Betty had walked to nearby Hawkins Field to watch the planes land. About 12:30 A.M., while walking back home along Missouri Street, they had just passed the triangular intersection with Guynes Street when they heard what Kenneth described as a "loud boom from my right. It sounded like a shotgun going off the side of my head." The blast was immediately followed by the sound of "somebody running fast." Kenneth could hear the sound of "leaves, bushes, and stuff cracking."

Scared, the young couple hurried down the street and heard a lady scream. Another shot, coming from their left and not nearly as loud as the first, followed. "Betty wanted to go see what the problem was," but Kenneth told her they were going home. The next morning they learned that Evers had been shot.

I asked Kenneth to mark on an enlarged aerial photograph of the neighborhood where they were when they heard the shot. It was just south of the small cluster of sweet gum from which the police had independently determined the shot had been fired. When asked to indicate the route of the shooter's flight, judging from the sounds Kenneth had heard, he drew an arrow from the sweet gum and pointing across the large vacant lot toward the far corner of the parking lot at Joe's Drive-In.

Betty Jean Coley had recently died. Her testimony in the first 1964 trial was the first delivered from the grave to our jury. Rather than have Ed or I read from the transcript, I opted for people to actually take the stand. I asked the questions prosecutors Waller and Fox had asked in 1964, and a surrogate witness responded by reading the answers. I selected these "witnesses" from our office ranks. Secretary Mary Lynne Underwood read for the deceased Betty Jean Coley, whose testimony mirrored that of Kenneth Adcock.

John Chamblee had retired from two careers since he'd last testified in the case—from the Jackson Police Department and the State of Mississippi Insurance Department's Arson Investigation Division. I was stunned by the toll the past three years had taken on the former detective.

Testifying before the grand jury in 1990, Chamblee was quick and certain in his answers. In fact, the copy of the partial police investigative file that we had given to him did little to refresh his memory simply because it didn't need refreshing. I had no doubt, listening to him discuss the details of the original investigation, that he knew and would never forget the fine points of the case.

Chamblee, however, had had some health problems since his grand jury appearance. Coupled with the passage of three more years, the effects were painfully apparent when he took the stand on Thursday, January 27, 1994. Nevertheless he managed to come through.

The evidence that he and Fred Sanders found at the scene, he told the jury, "showed that the victim was standing just about where the hinges on his front left door were, which put him about even with his windshield, because we found some blood and some fragments of body parts spread across the windshield and a little bit on the hood of the car."

Slowly, we went through more photos of the house, following the bullet's path as it burst through the front window, tore through the venetian blinds, crossed the living room, went through an interior wall into the kitchen, struck the refrigerator, ricocheted at a forty-five-degree angle to the right, and came to rest on a countertop. Each photo was numbered and the corresponding number was placed on an enlarged diagram of the house so the jurors could get a clear idea of the bullet's path.

Chamblee then explained how they had worked backward from that point to determine the spot from which the bullet had been fired. They learned from hospital personnel Medgar's height and the location of the entrance and exit wounds, including their distance from the bottoms of his feet. A detective of that approximate height was positioned in the spot where Evers had been standing when shot. Another detective held a flashlight in front of the bullet hole in the front window of the house and focused the beam on the chest of the detective standing in Evers's position at the approximate location of the exit wound. That detective then moved aside, and they followed the beam across the street to the same cluster of sweet gum pointed out earlier by Kenneth Adcock.

Chamblee described the area as they found it after sunrise. Someone "had been standing behind the three small trees and bushes that had grown up there recently because there was dew on the grass all around," but there was none in the cluster of trees where the grass was pressed down and trampled. A recently broken small limb created a head-high hole in the foliage. The break was still green. Whoever gazed out the hole had a clear view of the Evers house and yet remained concealed among the trees, tall grass, and brush. Police reports had mentioned a fresh horizontal scrape mark about shoulder high and speculated that the mark was made as the killer braced the barrel of the rifle against the tree for a steady shot. I asked Chamblee about it, as I had done at the grand jury, but at trial he said that he knew nothing about it.

He did recall seeing a Shriner's emblem in Beckwith's car after it was impounded, but he couldn't remember if he saw it "on the floor or on the window."

I shut down my questions at that point. John had covered the main things I needed from him, but it was such an arduous endeavor, I was afraid that points of interest were lost to the jury among the many "I don't know"'s and "I don't remember"'s. With the grand jury, John Chamblee had been like a learned professor lecturing a class. At trial, he seemed unsure and, at times, confused.

Each time he told me that he didn't remember something, I moved quickly to another topic. Kitchens, of course, did just the opposite on cross-examination, emphasizing how much Chamblee had forgotten. Kitchens was obviously trying to send his own message to the jurors: how can the defendant get a fair trial when one of the detectives in charge of the case has forgotten more than he remembers?

The harm wasn't devastating. John had said most of what I needed, and Fred Sanders could smooth things over later, if necessary. But things had been going so well throughout that first day of testimony I hated to end it on a note of such uncertainty.

I was surprised that few spectators, apart from the media and families of the victim and the defendant, were present. Charles Evers wasn't there. Myrlie's presence helped, but Charles, as a local resident, would have proven beneficial with the jury. I visited him that night at the local

FM radio station he owned and managed (which played excellent blues), hoping to coax him into coming for at least part of the trial.

Charles was wrapping up a weekly talk show when I arrived. Instead of being kept waiting in the lobby, I was shown to his office. I passed the time looking at the photographs covering the walls. Charles had worked his way from Chicago bootlegger to a political power in Mississippi. He was elected mayor of Fayette, a town just north of Natchez, then chancery clerk of that county. He had run statewide races for governor and U.S. senator. There were photos of Charles with the Kennedy brothers. One with JFK included Myrlie and her three children taken in the Oval Office following Medgar's burial at Arlington. Five months later the president was buried there, too. Reflecting Charles's subsequent shift to the GOP were photos with Presidents Reagan and Bush.

More prominently displayed than those of the presidents was one of Medgar, whom Charles had adored. After joining me in his office, Charles (who I guessed was about seventy, but still carried a large, muscular frame) told me how on cold winter nights he was the first to climb in the bed he shared with his brother to warm the sheets for him. There wasn't anything he wouldn't do for his baby brother, he said, but he did not go to the 1964 trials and he wasn't coming to ours either. Seeing my quizzical expression, he explained, "If I'm ever in the same room with Byron De La Beckwith, I know that I'd wrap my hands around that scrawny little neck of his and snap it just like a chicken's. And nobody, I mean nobody, would be able to stop me."

I wouldn't blame him if he did and told him so. We shook hands and I started to leave. "Bobby DeLaughter," he said. I turned to face him. "You and Ed Peters can get something I can't get. If I see Beckwith, all I can get is revenge. Y'all get justice for my baby brother, you hear?"

It was the first of several visits I had with Charles at his station over the years. He invited me back anytime for his talk show, and I took him up on it. Learning that I like blues, he invited me to a party on a large houseboat. He wanted me to meet a special guest and good friend, who was providing the music—the legendary B. B. King.

We received a jolt Friday morning when the *Clarion-Ledger* reported that the husband of the first alternate for the jury had ties with the Klan. Once in the courtroom, Ed vehemently asked the judge to excuse her from service and proceed with the second alternate if the need arose. Judge Hilburn took the matter under advisement, saying it was a moot point unless a member of the jury could not continue for some reason.

John Chamblee was not the only detective who was affected by time and age. Although O. M. Luke had always appeared in good health the several times I'd met with him, by 1994, he was bedridden. After tendering a letter from his physician to the judge, I put Doc Thaggard on the stand to read Luke's 1964 testimony.

Covering what Chamblee couldn't recall, Luke stated that on the side of one sweet gum "was an abrased part where something had struck it slightly, peeling off some of the bark." From that area, a search was gradually widened in an effort to find some physical evidence.

"I started to search, along with my partner, in the vicinity. There's a trail that leads off of Joe's parking lot. It was around eleven o'clock in the morning; the sun was right over my head. Searching as closely as I was, I saw something in this hedge that didn't look right. I took a second look, and I could tell it was the butt of a gun. So, I called my partner over and Captain Bennett.

"Then we called Captain Hargrove, our identification officer. It was stuck up in the vines, approximately twelve to eighteen inches. The vines were pulled back over the hole where you would have to be looking pretty close to see it. The gun was not dropped. It was well hidden and wasn't even touching the ground. It was suspended in honeysuckle vine, which was very thick. The gun itself was approximately twenty-five feet from the edge of the parking lot.

"Captain Hargrove took pictures of the gun, then a picture of me as I took it out of the hole. I took a stick and took the gun out in that fashion. I put my handkerchief through the trigger guard, carried it, and laid it on the backseat of the police car. No one touched the gun from the time I found it until Captain Hargrove examined it for fingerprints in his office."

To eliminate any defense claim that the gun could've been in the vines for a long time, Luke described the condition of its surface. "The gun was clean. Had a very small amount of dust on it, which any object would have at that particular time laying out in the weeds. The gun had not been wet. If there was a heavy dew or anything like that falls on it and you don't wipe it off pretty soon, this metal would rust pretty easily. The gun was perfectly cleaned, had been well cared for."

Fifty-six-year-old Thorn McIntyre was the twenty-five-year-old farmer who had telephoned the Jackson Police Department within days of Medgar Evers's murder to tell them that he had traded a 1917 Enfield .30-06 to Byron De La Beckwith.

I introduced the gun in evidence through McIntyre. The serial number on the gun matched the one on his invoice. McIntyre was positive that it was the gun he had traded to Beckwith because he only owned one

.30-06 rifle in his life, the one marked "Exhibit 36." Gingerly, the jurors passed it among themselves.

The scope wasn't part of the trade; it was added later. Thus, my next witness would've been John Goza, the man who had traded the scope to Beckwith, but he was dead. ADA John Davidson read the earlier testimony.

Goza operated Duck's Tackle Shop in Grenada, Mississippi, selling fishing tackle, guns, and other outdoor sporting goods, including a few telescopic rifle sights. Beckwith, whom Goza had known for ten to fourteen years, telephoned him the evening of May 12, 1963 (exactly one month before the assassination) and asked Goza how long he would be open. "He said he was coming over to do some trading."

Goza traded him a scope for a .45 automatic. The scope was a six-power Golden Hawk from United Binocular Company out of Chicago, the same kind found on the recovered rifle and bearing Beckwith's fingerprint.

In 1986, Captain Ralph Hargrove had retired after forty-five years with the Jackson Police Department. As at the bail hearing three years earlier, Captain Hargrove identified the entire array of photographs, slides, and negatives he had taken in 1963. When we got to the photos of Joe's Drive-In, the parking lot, and the area where Luke had found the gun, I had him mark the corresponding location depicted on the large aerial photo so the jurors had a coordinated bird's-eye view and close-up of each critical location.

Preparing to display Hargrove's slides for the jury, including one of the semicircular scar over Beckwith's right eye, I asked Judge Hilburn to dim the lights. When the bailiff turned them off, the judge's voice was heard in the darkened courtroom: "This is my first opportunity to put the media in the dark."

Overall, Captain Hargrove did fine, but his hearing had worsened over the past three years. When I asked him whose fingerprints he had compared with the one he had found on the scope, he said, "That I did what?" After repeating the question, he replied, "Oh, Mr. Beckwith's."

"Do you see him in the courtroom?"

"Yes, sir."

"Would you point him out to the jury, please."

"Did I what?"

"Will you point him out for the jury?"

"Yes, sir," Hargrove said, but he didn't.

"Will you point him out, please."

Finally he did. "He's sitting over at the end of the table."

If the trial had been delayed much longer, I'm not sure he would've been able to testify in person.

Hargrove explained to the jurors, "With fourteen points of identification, there's more than enough to identify the latent fingerprint as the fingerprint of Mr. Byron De La Beckwith."

On cross-examination, Kitchens asked Hargrove, "A fingerprint can be applied to a smooth surface without the person who made that fingerprint ever touching that surface, can't it?"

Captain Hargrove looked at the defense lawyer as if looking at a Martian. "Not to my knowledge."

"You have read about and studied so-called forged fingerprints, haven't you?"

"I don't know of any forged prints."

"And if Mr. Beckwith's fingerprint was on that scope, that doesn't prove that he fired that gun, does it, sir?"

"It doesn't prove that he fired it, no, but the fingerprint belongs to him."

Kitchens picked up the rifle. "And my fingerprints are on it now, aren't they, sir?"

"Well, they could be, and then again, they might not be." Hargrove explained that, unlike on television, finding a readable print anywhere on a gun is rare in real life. Despite his age, Hargrove held his own.

Midway through the cross-examination, Judge Hilburn adjourned court for the noon recess. As I stepped out of the elevator into our office lobby, receptionist Jeanie Stewart waved me over to her desk. "I'm not worrying you with all the calls coming in, but there's one that I think you need to call back." She handed me a pink message slip with the name of Mark Reiley and an out-of-state phone number written on it. I handed it to Crisco to check out while Ed and I ate a sandwich in his office and assessed the case.

"What do you think, boss?"

"You know you can't ever tell about a jury, but it's going better than I expected. I think we may actually have a shot at it. I've been reading all the stuff you gave me on Beckwith, and I've never had so much ammunition ready to use on cross-examination. Good job, boy. He's screwed whatever he does. The only way to avoid me asking him about all of this"—Ed motioned toward a crate full of Beckwith's 1964 testimony, his testimony at the speedy-trial hearing, letters, and videotaped interviews with the media—"is for him not to testify. And if he doesn't, the jury will never hear that bullshit story about his gun being stolen."

"You think he will?"

"He's got to. You've put his gun, with his scope, with his print, on the scene. The theft story is the only explanation he can offer, and *he* has to be the one to offer it."

"I think he has to, too, but for a different reason: he's Byron De La Beckwith and this is the show he's been waiting for. He has to perform."

"I don't see how he can't," Ed said, looking at the material again.

"Well, guys," Crisco said, walking in. "You're not going to believe this." Ed and I waited for him to continue. "It appears that Mark Reiley is with air traffic control at O'Hare in Chicago. It's shut down today because of snow. Since he couldn't go to work, Reiley was at home watching CNN this morning when a story came on about the case, Beckwith, Medgar Evers, the whole nine yards, and he recognized our boy Beckwith."

"From where?"

"Angola Penitentiary."

"What?"

"You heard me, but this guy's better, much better, than Hockman. Mark Reiley was no inmate. He was a guard, barely twenty at the time, and Beckwith tried to recruit him into all this white supremacy shit. To impress him and assure him nothing would happen to him if he joined the merry band, Beckwith told him he killed Evers and got away with it and he could assure the same kind of protection for young Reiley."

"Crisco, I trust your instinct," Ed said. "How did he *sound*? A nutcase, legit, or what?"

"He sounded very down-to-earth to me. I think it's at least worth checking out."

"Okay, then," Ed continued, "get him on the next flight down here for us to talk in detail with him and size him up." Ed instructed Crisco to speak with FBI legal liaison John Kelley, who was attending the trial, and enlist the Bureau's help in contacting the personnel office at Angola. We needed to know if and when Reiley was a guard there. Did his employment overlap any with Beckwith's term of incarceration? Did his job put him in an area where Beckwith was housed? The last thing we needed was to put on a witness and have it blow up in our face.

Back in court that Friday afternoon, Deputy Sheriff Shelby Barlow, the booking officer who had taken Beckwith's fingerprints upon his extradition from Tennessee, took the stand. I needed to enter those prints in evidence because I had a fingerprint expert from the FBI coming Monday.

Tommy Mayfield read the 1964 testimony of Hinds County sheriff J. R. Gilfoy. Former director of the Mississippi Highway Patrol and pres-

ident of the Jackson Gun Club, as well as sheriff, Gilfoy had been familiar with guns for some thirty years. During the 1963 investigation, the
sheriff's department had assisted police chief of detectives M. B. Pierce.
Sheriff Gilfoy was in Chief Pierce's office when Detective Luke brought
the rifle to Hargrove's office two doors down.

The sheriff was standing near Luke when the detective pulled the bolt
back, causing an empty shell to eject out of the barrel. Sheriff Gilfoy testified that he then "bent down and smelled the gun to see if it had been
recently fired." It had.

Tommy did fine reading the former sheriff's testimony, but his true
performance (and it can be called nothing less) came with his part as
deceased cabdriver Hubert Speight. Before our eyes, Mayfield *became* the
crusty-natured taximan from rural Mississippi.

"Would you state your name, please?"

"Hubert Richard Speight."

"How do you pronounce that?"

With a country-boy twang, Tommy said, "Spate."

Asked about his encounter at the bus station, Speight testified that he
was there, parked out front, about 4 P.M., on Saturday, June 8, 1963, the
Saturday before the murder. "I was parked in front of the bus station
when Mr. Beckwith approached me there, just walked up to the side of
the cab, and asked me if I knew Negro Medgar Evers, NAACP leader. I
told him that I did not. He went back into the bus station, and I saw him
looking in a phone book. He came back out with a map and told me he
had an address on Lexington Street and asked if I knew where it was. I
told him I did, but that couldn't be where the colored fellow lived
because it's an all-white section.

"He turned around and went back to the bus station." Beckwith came
out twice more asking Speight if it could be on Buena Vista, then Poplar.
Each time Speight informed him that those streets were also in white sections of town.

"Are you sure of the identification of the man?"

"I'm positive."

"Are you positive?"

"Yes, sir."

"Did you report this to the police?"

"No, sir, I didn't, but later on Mr. Swilley reported it. Swilley and I was
sitting in the car together when he approached it."

"How much later?"

"Shortly after they made the arrest. I come up here to see if I could
identify the man I talked to at the bus station. They carried me to the

police station. I stepped up there, and they had about six or eight all lined up together. I picked the man I was talking to out of the bunch—Mr. Beckwith."

When Coxwell read the cross-examination of original defense attorney Stanny Sanders, Tommy got even more into character.

"Mr. Speight, up until the night you testified about, had you ever seen Mr. Beckwith before?"

"No, sir, I did not. That is, if I did, I didn't know it."

"Do you remember when you first saw me before?"

"Yes, sir, I do."

"Who was with me?"

"I don't remember the man's name, but y'all came down to the boardinghouse to talk to me."

"And you were asleep, were you not?"

"That's right."

"And we stayed there and had about a thirty- or forty-five-minute conversation with you, didn't we, Mr. Speight?"

"Right."

"And we told you that we had seen where you had been subpoenaed, and we wanted to know what you knew about this matter, did we not?"

"Sure did."

"And, Mr. Speight, did you not tell us that you didn't know anything about it?"

"I did tell you that."

"You told us no, didn't you, Mr. Speight?"

"Yes, sir. I . . . I don't talk to two parties at the same time." The courtroom burst out laughing. "I also told you that I'd appreciate it if y'all would go ahead and let me go to sleep. As I say, when I talk to one attorney, I don't talk to another."

More laughter erupted.

"But you tell the truth whenever you are talking, don't you, Mr. Speight?"

"Yeah, but I can't tell both lawyers."

On redirect I asked the same questions former DA Waller had asked thirty years earlier. "By the time Mr. Sanders came to see you, had you already been up to my office and talked to me?"

"Yes, sir, I had."

"What did I tell you about Mr. Sanders or anyone else coming to see you? Go ahead, Mr. Speight."

"You told me if anybody come to talk to me not to tell them what we discussed and what we didn't."

"Were you following my advice when Mr. Sanders came out there?"

"I was."

I glanced at the clock on the wall behind the jury. It was only 2:40 P.M., and I was out of witnesses. Everyone else was scheduled to fly in over the weekend. There was no choice but to explain the situation to the judge.

Hilburn kept control of his court, but with years of expertise, he recognized the logistics Crisco faced in coordinating flights and lodging for so many witnesses, some of whom were also afforded security. Court adjourned for the weekend, but not before Ed advised the judge and defense lawyers of the noon news from Mark Reiley.

Discovery rules required us to make Reiley available to the defense lawyers for them to interview and we readily agreed to do so.

Since I needed to spend the weekend making sure everything was ready for all of our other witnesses and reviewing their testimony, Ed agreed to meet with Mark Reiley.

Reiley's call could not have come at a better time. Our other Angola witness, Lester Paul Hockman, was growing belligerent. Crisco and I walked over to the jail to see what his problem was.

Hockman was housed away from the other prisoners, in the hospital unit where Beckwith was held prior to his release on bail. Crisco and I sat in an examination room waiting for a jailer to retrieve our prisoner witness. Hockman had been cooperative when Crisco took his statement in the federal prison earlier, but he was everything but agreeable now. Since I had never met him, I stood and introduced myself as he walked in and asked how he was doing.

"I know who you are," he snapped, "and I'm not doing worth a damn."

"What's the problem?"

"I thought my lawyer and I made it clear that I was not to be held here. I was to come in, testify, and go back to a federal facility somewhere. I've been here two days and I'm not staying any longer."

I attempted to explain that predicting the precise date that a witness would testify in a trial involving so many witnesses was sometimes difficult; that although some may be called out of order, he was too important for me to do that. His testimony had to be with the other "confession" witnesses, and he would probably go on the stand Tuesday. He hit the roof, protesting that I was going back on my word.

"No, the only agreement I had with your lawyer was that I would convey to the U.S. attorney the extent of your cooperation for him or a judge to consider in any postconviction motions you may file in your case. I said I would keep you here only for a reasonable time for you to testify. I don't think you can say, under the circumstances, that I've been unreasonable."

"Well, the circumstances are about to change."

"Oh?"

"I want a specific recommendation to reduce my sentence—none of this 'he cooperated' bullshit. You owe me, man."

"I don't owe you shit." He was beginning to piss me off. "I'm giving you the chance to help yourself, take it or leave it."

He laughed. "You don't mean that. You're bluffing. You need me, man. I *am* your case. Without me, you ain't got shit."

"Where did you come up with that?"

"I read things, man."

"Well, you better subscribe to something else. Now, I've had a long week and I'm only going to ask you once: Are you testifying or not?"

"Not unless you request a reduction in my sentence and get me on the stand first thing Monday so I can get out of here and back to a federal facility."

I stood and turned to Crisco. "Tell the Marshal's Service we'll need Mr. Hockman for another week, maybe two, and first thing Monday morning remind me to call the U.S. attorney handling his case so I can tell him how this piece of shit backed out, was totally uncooperative, and tried to shake us down."

"Have a nice stay," I said to Hockman, and left. I could still hear his yells as I walked down the freshly mopped hallway: "You need me, man!"

Crisco caught up with me in the parking lot. "Well, you handled that with finesse," he said with just a touch of sarcasm.

"We don't need him. In fact, we're better off without him. There's no telling what he'd say on the stand. Besides, we're already depending on someone who sees a shrink, paid informants, and a drunk. How would tossing a career jailbird in the mix look? We'll go with Mark Reiley instead."

"What if he doesn't work out?"

"Then I'll just blame you."

"Jeez, you're killing me," Crisco mumbled as he took a swallow of Pepto-Bismol and drove off in his Blazer.

"Damn," I said aloud to myself, "what have I done?"

We kicked off the morning of Monday, January 31, with Russell Davey, a fingerprint specialist with the FBI for thirty-five years. After entering Beckwith's original 1942 Marine Corps fingerprint card, Davey advised the jurors that he had personally examined those prints with the ones that Deputy Barlow had taken when Beckwith was booked in 1991, and they matched.

Davey then informed the jury that he had compared the latent print found on the rifle scope with each of those fingerprint cards and determined the print on the scope and the one of the right index finger on the two fingerprint cards "were made by one and the same finger."

I asked Davey what other observations he had made concerning the print on the scope.

"Now, the surface that this print is on is a hard surface. It's not porous like a piece of paper. So, the minute amount of perspiration, face oil, or whatever was left by the print could easily be smudged or damaged, but this is a relatively good print. Also, there's not a lot of dirt, debris, or foreign substance on it, like an outdoor window or car would have on it. We quite often see that."

Kitchens had asked Captain Hargrove about forged fingerprints, and although Hargrove had said he didn't know anything about them, I was concerned that the question had planted a suspicious seed in the minds of the jurors. Davey, on the other hand, had experience with such forgeries, so I asked him, "What, if any, evidence do you see from the latent fingerprint that would lead you to believe it had been forged or was planted?"

"I saw nothing that would indicate that situation." There was no cross-examination by Kitchens.

Richard Poppleton served as a special agent with the FBI's firearms-identification unit, which, as he explained to the jury, dealt with "the microscopic examination and comparison of markings on ammunition to determine whether they were fired by a particular gun."

Before beginning his twenty-six years in the FBI Crime Lab, Poppleton had obtained a bachelor of science degree in mechanical engineering from Purdue and a master's in forensic science from George Washington University. He had previously testified as an expert firearms examiner some five hundred times.

Before getting into Poppleton's findings, I thought a brief mini-course was in order to make sure all of the jurors understood the bases of those conclusions. The determination of whether a bullet was fired by a particular gun, Poppleton explained, "is made possible because the tools used in the manufacture of gun barrels are constantly wearing down, inch by inch and gun by gun. In addition, a gun, after it is manufactured, can pick up different scratches and marks inside the barrel, even from a cleaning rod."

Even a gun that is never cleaned, explained the former agent, picks up markings through use. A comparison of all of these microscopic markings with the markings left in the soft lead of a bullet enables an examiner to determine whether a bullet was fired in a particular gun.

We didn't have the bullet that had ripped through Medgar Evers, but the FBI had retained all of Poppleton's copious notes, which he had with him while testifying.

"I found rifling impressions on this bullet of five lands and grooves, left twist, or in a counterclockwise direction. The land impression was the same as the groove impression—ninety-five thousandths of an inch. The land and groove impressions being equal is, in itself, quite unusual.

"What this means," he explained, holding the rifle for the jury to see, "is that five grooves in the barrel were produced by a rifling tool when it was manufactured that had five cutters on its surface, and each cutter was ninety-five thousandths inches in width, and it was pulled through the barrel, removing metal down to ninety-five thousandths inches deep. This, of course, is to make the bullet, as it comes out of the barrel, spiral like a football, so as to proceed in a straight trajectory or line. These rifling impressions are distinct to an Enfield rifle."

Poppleton further noted, "The rifling impressions on the bullet were exactly the same as those produced by the barrel of this gun. By that, I concluded this bullet was fired by an Enfield .30-06 rifle, Model 1917, and could have been fired by this gun. However, because the bullet was so badly mutilated and deformed, there were not enough sufficient microscopic marks for me to determine that the bullet definitely was fired in this gun to the exclusion of all other 1917 Enfield rifles. The microscopic markings I found on the bullet were all consistent with being fired by this gun, but just not enough for me to say that it definitely was.

"I would like to point out, though, that the bullet is also consistent with 180-grain soft-point bullets made by Winchester. This is the same type of ammunition as the six live cartridges submitted to me for examination [the live rounds found by Luke in the gun's magazine]."

Dr. Baden had held firm on cross-examination that the wound was caused by a high-velocity rifle. Since Kitchens had attempted to cast doubt on Baden's opinion by making it clear the doctor was not a ballistics expert, I took advantage of having such an expert on the stand to put the matter to rest.

"Mr. Poppleton, could that bullet have been fired by any other type of weapon, such as a .45-caliber handgun?"

"No, sir, it could not."

"What about a .357 magnum?"

"No, it could not."

Firearm examiners may also determine whether a particular weapon fired a particular empty cartridge. As explained by Poppleton, "The marks on a cartridge case consist not only of extractor or ejector markings, but it also has other types of markings left when it is fired. One type of marking left during the firing process is referred to as breech-face markings.

"They are made by the breech block of the gun that supports the base of the cartridge case into which the primer is inserted. That area of the base of the cartridge lays against the bolt when fired. When the primer is pierced by the firing pin, the explosion of the main powder charge in the cartridge expands and forces the soft metal at the base of the cartridge tightly against any defects in the face of the bolt. Those breech-face marks are characteristic of that particular gun and no other gun."

Poppleton testified that thirty-one of the fifty-three empty cartridges recovered from Thorn McIntyre were fired in that particular rifle, to the exclusion of all others.

Kitchens hit hard on our no longer having the bullet. Poppleton, however, was a veteran witness and maintained that the absence of the bullet had not diminished his original opinions reached in 1963 in any respect.

I had connected Beckwith with the rifle; now it was time to do the same with the car.

In 1963, Barbara Holder was a twenty-two-year-old carhop who worked at Joe's Drive-In. Although off Tuesday evening, June 11, 1963, she had gone to Joe's to hang out with friends. She got there about eight-thirty or nine and, after getting something to drink, went out to the carhop booth on the south side of the building to chat with Martha Jean O'Brien, who was on duty. Soon thereafter, Barbara noticed a car.

"This car came up behind the building and backed up to the corner of the lot. It was white and had a long antenna, a Plymouth Valiant, but it had a lot of mud on it. It pulled up to the back of the building close to the bathrooms and the gentleman got out and went to the men's room. Then it backed out to where it was originally parked in the corner.

"He was a white man," she went on, "about five-seven, five-eight, had on dark clothes and dark hair. That's all I saw. I had to leave and take a friend home. I don't know exactly what time it was, but I came back a few minutes before the drive-in closed, which was at midnight, and the car was still there in the corner." The driver was not in it, however.

I went through photos of the parking lot and of Beckwith's car with her. The car in the photos looked like the one she had seen.

Since Kitchens had earlier questioned police witnesses about the large distinctive trailer hitch on the rear of Beckwith's Valiant, I knew he was going to bring out, through the people who had seen the car parked at Joe's, that they hadn't noticed a trailer hitch. To defuse this, I asked Barbara Holder, "When it pulled into the corner, how was it parked?"

"It was backed in."

"At any time, did you ever get a real clear view of the back of the vehicle?"

"No, sir."

"Why," Coxwell asked on cross-examination, "did you tell Officers Benton and Black, in 1963, that you never saw the man get out of the car?"

"I don't remember why I told them that. That's been thirty years ago."

"Thirty years ago, your memory would have been better than it is today, wouldn't it?"

"That all depends, I don't know."

"So, as you've gotten older, your memory has gotten better?"

"I think so, yes, sir."

"You can remember things that happened back in 1963 better now than you could in 1963?"

"Probably, because I can't remember two weeks ago, but I can remember thirty years ago," Barbara replied, sparking some laughs. "I remember what happened *that* evening."

Following up on this on redirect, I asked, "Instead of taking it out of context, look at your earlier statement to Officers Benton and Black, starting where it says, 'I told Martha Jean O'Brien,' and read it to the jury."

"'I told Martha Jean O'Brien he would not blow his horn or blink his lights. I stood there for about five minutes, but he never got out of the car. He did not blow his horn, so I went on inside the café.'"

"So, the time you were saying in here that he never got out of the car was when you first saw him there?"

"That's my statement, yes, sir."

"Did you testify at the other two trials?"

"Yes, sir, I did."

"Did you tell the juries in those cases of the description that you've given to this jury?"

"Yes, sir, I did."

Ronald Jones, in 1963, was a sixteen-year-old friend of Robert Don Pittman's, son of the owners of Pittman's Grocery Store. After the store closed around nine the evening of Tuesday, June 11, the teenagers were flying a balsa-wood model airplane that landed on the store's flat roof.

After climbing up to retrieve it, Jones noticed a car driving slowly on Delta Drive. "It got my attention," he explained, "because it had a whip antenna on the back and I thought it was a police car. It was a white Plymouth Valiant.

"When I first saw it, it was going south on Delta Drive. It turned around right down below the store, and we were up on top, so I could see it turn around and go back north."

Jones said the car that he saw looked like the photos of Beckwith's car, but admitted on cross-examination, "I can't say one hundred percent it is or is not."

Before calling three other eyewitnesses about the car, I called David Adams of the Jackson Police Department and Joe Avignone of the FBI Crime Lab. They were the two forensic photographers who, at my request, had enlarged the photos of the car, zooming in on the rearview mirror.

The photos both men produced, magnifying the rearview mirror in the original by twenty times, clearly showed a Shriner's emblem hanging from the mirror.

In 1963, Ronald Acy was also a sixteen-year-old friend of young Pittman's. In fact, Acy worked for Pittman's parents as a meat-cutter in the store. After getting off work about 9 P.M., the Saturday before the murder, the two boys walked north to Acy's house to get his parents' permission to spend the night with Pittman. Walking back to the store, they noticed a car parked in what Jones described as "a little alley between the store and a line of trees." Just north of the trees was the parking lot of Joe's Drive-In.

"I would say it was a '60 to a '62 Plymouth Valiant or Dodge Lancer, a light gray or off-white. It had a long antenna that was folded down, and it had some kind of emblem hanging from the rearview mirror that really brought our attention to it."

"Why was that?"

"Well, it had some kind of big star on it, and some kind of big sword-looking thing running through it some kind of way. Anyhow, I thought it had diamonds in it or something another, and I told Robert, 'Let's get up there a little closer and look at it.' He said, 'Naw, might be somebody in there sleeping.' So, we didn't go no closer."

"What kind of emblem did it appear to you to be?"

"Back in them days, my parents did a lot of dancing at the Shriners', and that's what it looked like to me, some kind of Shriner's emblem."

"Is that the way you described it to the police in 1963?"

"Yes."

I handed him the photos of Beckwith's Valiant and asked how the car shown in them compared with the one he had seen the Saturday before the murder.

"It looks just like it."

Handing Acy the enlarged photos of the rearview mirror of Beckwith's Valiant, I asked how the emblem shown in them compared with the one he had seen on the car Saturday, June 8. "It looks like one and the same."

Robert Don Pittman backed up everything Jones and Acy had said, and more. Wanting to personalize the victim at every opportunity, I asked if he knew Medgar Evers. "He taught me how to play baseball out in my backyard."

Pittman was certain the car, which he and Acy had seen the Saturday before Evers was killed, was a white '62 Valiant. Additionally, he testified that he had seen the same car a second time the night of the murder, after seeing it around 9 P.M., driving up and down Delta Drive. Somewhere around 11 P.M., that Tuesday night, he saw it on the corner of Joe's parking lot.

Pittman looked at the photos taken of Beckwith's '62 Valiant and said, "It looks like the car." Shown the enlarged photo of the Shriner's emblem, he testified, "This is the emblem that I seen on the rearview mirror. Yeah, there's that star and the sword."

Coxwell handed Pittman a copy of his 1964 testimony and asked him to point out where he earlier testified about seeing the car the second time the night of the murder. "I don't see it," Pittman replied, "but I don't really believe anybody asked me about it that time." Although nervous, he was doing well. When I had gone over his testimony with him, I explained that he had to answer whatever the defense lawyer asked him, but he had the right after that to fully explain his answers. He'd learned the lesson well.

Coxwell continued to pepper him with questions the prosecutor asked in 1964 and then asked him again, "Is there anywhere in there, when you were called as a witness in 1964, that you testified that you saw a white Valiant parked on June eleventh, 1963?"

"No, sir, it's not in here, but I don't see the question about did I see it parked."

Frustrated, Coxwell asked it yet a third time. Pittman didn't budge. "Nobody ever asked me except Mr. DeLaughter. I can't answer something if they didn't ask me."

"Did you see a trailer hitch on the back of it?"

"No, sir, but I wasn't looking for one. It could have. The long aerial and emblem is what got my attention."

Coxwell brought out that Pittman didn't mention the emblem in his statement to the police. He first mentioned it in the 1964 trial, but Pittman was ready with the explanation: "That was the first time I was asked about it."

On redirect, I asked Pittman, who was only fifteen in 1963, "Why was it that you just answered the specific questions that you were asked back then?"

"My father said, 'Don't give them nothing they don't ask for,' and I obeyed him."

Having connected Beckwith's rifle and car to the scene, I moved to establish motive.

Adding a personal touch in establishing Beckwith's motive was Reed Massengill, a thirty-two-year-old writer and nephew of the defendant's. "He was married to my mom's oldest sister, Mary Louise Williams, and we carried on a correspondence by mail for about seven years, from April 1986 through November 1992, when he was being held in the Hinds County jail for this offense."

What generated the correspondence? Beckwith was trying to get his writer-nephew to pen a book about him. Toward that end, Beckwith provided Massengill with racist propaganda, Christian Identity tapes, copies of letters he had written, and the manuscript of a book someone else had started about him.

In a letter from Beckwith to the *Jackson Daily News,* dated June 15, 1957, the defendant wrote:

I'm not a prophet of doom, but things look pretty bad for the shady outfit called the NAACP. . . . Believe it or not, the NAACP, under the direction of its leaders, is doing a first-class job of getting itself in a position to be exterminated. I thank God for the Association of Citizens' Councils of America. Soon the cancerous growth, the NAACP, shall be cut out of the heart of our nation, and we will live happily ever after.

Another letter, addressed simply "To a friend":

The foul contemptible . . . person who . . . tells the Negro . . . that he's as good as anybody . . . should be ashamed to lie like that. Believing such a lie has put many a darkie in the river late at night; some at the end of a rope, stirring others of their race to unrest.

The Negro in our country is as helpful as a boll weevil to cotton. . . . They must be destroyed, with their wretched remains burned, lest the pure white cotton bolls be destroyed.

November 22, 1963, the day President Kennedy was assassinated in Dallas, Beckwith was in jail awaiting his first trial for assassinating Medgar Evers. From his cell, an elated Beckwith wrote his son, who was attending Chamberlain-Hunt Military Academy in Port Gibson, Mississippi:

Whoever shot Kennedy 'sho did some fancy shooting. . . . I guess when a few more of our enemies are gone, this will be a real fine world to live in. Wonder who will be next?

I bet Ole Medgar Evers told Kennedy when he got down there, "I thought you'd be along pretty soon." Ha, Ha, Ha.

He concluded by counseling his son not to let anyone see the letter.

The last letter, which Massengill read aloud to the jury, was written while Beckwith was incarcerated in Angola, on November 16, 1976, to his first wife, Willie, who in turn handed it over to her nephew Reed. "So, when you think of me, you see a man deep in debt, facing 5 years in prison, living like a nigger and as far in global, not state or county, Klan work as a 56-year-old man can be, and happy at it." Beckwith's words, penned in his own hand, would support the upcoming testimony of Delmar Dennis and Dick Davis concerning his Klan connection.

Kitchens asked Massengill on cross-examination, "Mr. Massengill, he didn't tell you that he killed Medgar Evers, did he?"

"No, sir, he did not, but since Mr. Evers was the leader of the NAACP at that time, one letter does mention him, although not by name."

"You don't know whether Mr. Beckwith had Mr. Evers in his mind or not when he wrote that letter, do you?"

"When he says the leaders of the NAACP need to be exterminated, it's not a great stretch of imagination for me to know who he's talking about. To look at any of the media from 1957 through '63 that deals with the NAACP in Mississippi is to associate that with one man, sir."

Kitchens also brought out that Beckwith wrote a lot of letters about many subjects other than segregation. "Mr. Beckwith is a very religious person, too, is he not?" Kitchens asked, not realizing the door he was opening for me on redirect. "Studies the Bible a lot?"

"He has said that he has," Massengill replied.

Kitchens closed his questions by bringing out that Massengill had published a book based in part on the data Beckwith had provided him.

It was my turn again. Redirect is limited to matters brought out on cross-examination that were not covered on direct. To ward off the objection I was sure would be coming from Kitchens, I asked Massengill, "Did I ask you anything about this defendant's religious beliefs earlier?"

"No, sir."

"Do you remember some questions Mr. Kitchens asked you about that and reading the Bible and so forth?"

"Yes, sir, I do."

"Okay. What are this defendant's religious beliefs?"

Sure enough, there was an objection, but Judge Hilburn overruled it.

"He later became involved in the Christian Identity movement, which believes that Caucasians are divinely charged to rule over the other races."

I recalled Dr. Bratley to advise the jury of his examination of Beckwith, following his arrest. At the request of Bill Waller, Bratley had examined Beckwith in jail on Sunday, June 23, 1963. He noticed an injury around the right eye in the shape of a semicircle, still pink, and estimated it to have been a fairly recent injury—anywhere from ten to thirty days old.

Handing the doctor the rifle, I asked if the injury was consistent in size and shape with the edge of the shooter's end of the rifle's scope. It was.

It was now time to put on the witnesses to whom Beckwith had made incriminating remarks over the years since his release. The first was Mary Ann Adams, the lady who, in 1966, was introduced to Beckwith at a restaurant between Tchula and Greenwood in the Delta.

"He came to the table with another man, who introduced him as 'Byron De La Beckwith, the man who killed Medgar Evers.' He stuck out his hand to shake my hand, smiling and nodding. I refused to shake his hand—said that he was a murderer and I wouldn't shake his hand. He got extremely agitated and angry—said he had not killed a man, but a damn chicken-stealing dog, and you know what you have to do with a dog after it's tasted blood."

I asked Mrs. Adams, once hearing this, why she hadn't reported it to the authorities. "Because I thought that he could not be tried again," she explained.

Coxwell asked her how she knew that Beckwith even heard the way he was introduced. "Because he was standing right beside the man who introduced him."

"How do you know he heard him?"

"Is he deaf?" The courtroom burst out laughing.

Dan Prince, the Beckwiths' former tenant, followed. "On occasion, when I was standing in his front yard—I don't remember how the conversation was led into—he made the statement that he was tried twice in Mississippi for killing that nigger. He said, 'I had a job to do and I did it, and I didn't suffer any more for it than your wife if she were gonna have a baby.'"

Under Coxwell's cross-examination, Prince readily admitted having had a drinking problem in the past, but insisted that it had nothing to do with being evicted by the Beckwiths. And although he'd gone to the *Chattanooga Free Press* with the information about the statement prior to advising law enforcement authorities, Prince steadfastly denied that he had tried to sell the information first.

After we recessed Monday afternoon, Crisco and I drove to the Holiday Inn to meet with Peggy Morgan and Dick Davis. The scene looked like something out of the movies. Crisco had put all of our out-of-town witnesses on one wing of a floor, and state troopers stood guard at the hallway's two entrances.

Peggy Morgan was even more scared than she was when Crisco, Benny, and I had first met with her in her Mobile apartment. After her ex-husband, Lloyd, had testified at the grand jury, she had received warnings from him on two occasions. "He told me I better not come here and testify. He said I was gonna wind up dead."

We had not been able to reach her in months. I wasn't even sure she would show up for the trial. Speaking with her in her motel room that night, I learned of the warnings and discovered that she had since been living in one motel after another in south Mississippi and Alabama.

Jim Ingram, the state commissioner of public safety, is a former FBI agent who first came to Mississippi in the 1960s to help break the back of the Klan. Jim was supportive of our endeavor and was glad to provide the security for our witnesses. The show of force paid off.

Finally feeling a sense of protection, Mrs. Morgan informed me for the first time that Beckwith had mentioned Medgar Evers by name on the trip to Parchman. Needless to say, the defense screamed bloody murder the next morning about a discovery violation. Since we had followed the rules and notified them of the new information at the first opportunity Tuesday morning, the judge allowed her to testify about it.

She told the jury about Beckwith's ride to the penitentiary with Lloyd and her. "Mr. Beckwith said that he had killed Medgar Evers, a nigger, and if this trip ever got out, he wasn't scared to kill again."

Kitchens, as expected, brought out that Mrs. Morgan suffered from an anxiety disorder and was on Xanax. She was subjected to child abuse at the hands of her father, and she had endured a tumultuous marriage before divorcing Lloyd. Her father was murdered, her mother froze to death, and Lloyd was carrying on an incestuous relationship with one of his daughters. Kitchens spared nothing in his attempt to discredit her testimony.

I next established the Klan connection. Dick Davis's role as an informant for the FBI had begun soon after he had attended a Klan meeting with a friend in Plant City, Florida. Although his friend joined that night, Davis did not. Within a few weeks, an article he read in *Reader's Digest* about the FBI and the Klan troubled Davis. Because the FBI took note of people attending such meetings, often running the license plates on the vehicles, merely attending could place one's name in FBI files forever. This worried Davis, so he called the FBI office in Lakeland, Florida, and explained that he had only attended one meeting out of curiosity and had no intent to join. "I just wanted to do whatever I had to in order to make sure that I wasn't listed as a Klan member."

The agent to whom Davis spoke seized on the opportunity and asked him to join the Klan to keep the FBI informed of the group's activities.

On October 21, 1969, Beckwith contacted Davis. "As I recall, he was selling boats at that time, and he telephoned me from Winter Haven Marine and said a mutual acquaintance had suggested that he look me up when he was in town."

They met at a Lum's restaurant, where Beckwith ate and Davis drank coffee. "He discussed his arrest, imprisonment, trials, and what he thought was necessary and a partial solution to the right wing's problem. I remember very distinctly that he said that he would never ask anyone to do anything that he hadn't already done himself."

"Well," Coxwell asked, "did you ever ask Mr. Beckwith, 'Did you kill Medgar Evers?'"

"No, sir, you didn't do that in those circles."

I appreciated the defense lawyer providing Davis with the chance to say that. It would also explain Beckwith's comments at the Klan meeting witnessed by Delmar Dennis.

Delmar, like Dick Davis, attended an information meeting of the Klan, curious about the group. Unlike Davis, Delmar joined in March 1964, being assured, as he related to the jury, "that we would never be asked to do anything that's illegal, immoral, or against our conscience, and I could live with that." It was naive thinking, as Delmar soon learned.

"I dropped out several months later when I discovered the Klan was, in fact, a violent organization. In June of '64, I attended a Klan meeting in Neshoba County, and when it was over, I rode home with some men who participated in the beating of some black people at the Mount Zion Church—blood still on their hands."

Delmar then told the jurors about being recruited in September by FBI agents Tom Van Riper and John Martin "to go back into the Klan, and to remain undercover and furnish information to the Bureau, which I did until October of '67. I became a Titan, which is an administrative office over a ten-county area of east Mississippi."

Asked about Beckwith, Delmar testified, "To the best of my memory, I think the first time I met him was August eighth of 1965, at a Klan meeting in Byram, Mississippi. It was a statewide meeting of Klan officers, both state officers and officers of local klaverns from all over the state. It was not open to nonmembers—to the general public.

"He was the featured speaker of the evening. I don't remember all the speech, but I remember that he was admonishing Klan members to become more involved, to become violent, to kill the enemy from the top down, and he said, 'Killing that nigger didn't cause me any more physical harm than your wives have to have a baby for you.'"

Delmar said that he normally reported his observations to the FBI—probably Van Riper—within twenty-four hours and assumed he had done so following this meeting. At the conclusion of Beckwith's speech, Delmar obtained his autograph with the date on it. I presented it to him to identify. He explained to the jury, "I wanted to establish that I did see him at the meeting that night. I thought it might be important sometime to prove that I was there when he was there."

Anticipating that Beckwith's lawyers would attempt to imply that Delmar was cooperating with us to write another book, I asked, "Did you contact our office with this information or did we contact you?"

"You contacted me. I certainly didn't contact you."

Lastly, I asked if he saw in the courtroom the man who had delivered the Klan speech.

"Yes, sir, I do. That's Beckwith over there."

"You have never seen in writing anywhere that the FBI wrote down the quote from Byron De La Beckwith that you just gave this jury?" Kitchens asked.

"That's correct."

"Yet, there are pages and pages of dialogue that you reported to the FBI of things various people said at meetings you attended?"

"Yes, sir."

"And you never did go into any of those meetings wired for sound, so to speak?"

"I never did."

"And Byron De La Beckwith never told you he killed Medgar Evers, did he?"

"He never said, 'I killed Medgar Evers,' that's true."

On redirect I asked Delmar why he didn't wear a wire at Klan meetings. "Because people were searched and it would have been extremely dangerous to have been caught with such a device."

The next two witnesses were called to verify certain points of Delmar's testimony. Former FBI agent Tom Van Riper explained that he was the FBI contact with Delmar Dennis, who was the principal informant in the FBI case code-named MIBURN (short for Mississippi Burning).

Van Riper said the two men communicated "almost daily" and verified that Delmar did, in fact, report to him certain statements that Beckwith had made at a Klan meeting regarding the murder of Medgar Evers.

The FBI did not convey the information to state authorities, however, because "the FBI would never have blown an informant as good as Delmar Dennis was in the MIBURN case, which was the most important thing happening at that time."

The other witness called to bolster Delmar's testimony was John Paulisick, an examiner of questioned documents with the FBI Crime Lab. After comparing the autograph presented by Delmar with known signatures of Beckwith's, Paulisick told the jury, "Byron De La Beckwith was responsible for preparation of the signature."

Thirty-six-year-old Mark Reiley, an employee of a company that manufactures and maintains communication equipment for air-traffic-control towers and weather stations, took the stand next. He was the young man who had called our office the past Friday upon seeing a CNN story about the trial.

"Whose face did you see on that news program?" Ed asked.

"Mr. De La Beckwith's," Reiley replied, pointing at the defendant, "the man with the dark blue suit."

"Where was he the last time you had seen him?"

Reiley explained that it was at Long Hospital in Baton Rouge, Louisiana, in late 1979. Reiley was then a guard at Angola State Penitentiary, and his job was to guard inmates sent to the Angola sick ward. The most memorable was Byron De La Beckwith.

"Tell us what relationship the two of you had," Ed said.

"He seemed to give me a lot of attention. I was very young—only about twenty-one. The youngest of the other guards was around fifty. He seemed very glad to see me. I remember, as soon as I walked in the room, he said, 'Hey, Young Blood'; that's what he called me."

Over the next several weeks, Reiley related, a close relationship developed between the young guard and the older inmate. "He seemed very interested in my life and my background. He knew I was lacking a father-type figure, and he definitely seemed like he would be more than willing to fill that role."

Beckwith discussed his religious beliefs with Young Blood. Blacks, explained Beckwith, were no more than "beasts of the field" and "whites were the chosen people to rule over the earth and be in charge of the beasts of the field.

"He explained to me that just as you might have to kill a deer or catch a fish for food, because that was their place, the beasts of the field, the blacks, were there to sow the field and take care of the earth for the chosen people, so if they got out of line, just like any other animal would, you should kill them and not in any way feel guilty about it."

One time, Reiley recalled, Beckwith pushed a button by his bed to summon a nurse. When a black nurse's aide responded, Beckwith informed her "to get a white person because he would rather a nigger not wait on him or take care of him."

Naturally, the comment angered and upset the lady, and they were soon screaming at each other. "And," Reiley said, "I was paying more attention to what he said."

"Why was that?" Ed asked.

"He was screaming at her, 'If I could get rid of an uppity nigger like nigger Evers, I would have no problem with a no-account nigger like you.'"

Even following this incident, Beckwith and Reiley continued the "Bible study." Reiley said that Beckwith "was trying to convince me that, since he was getting older, he needed younger people in his organization or movement."

"What was the organization's purpose or effort?"

"To show the world that whites were superior and blacks, if necessary, needed to be eliminated."

Finally, Reiley became disillusioned and started to question Beckwith on those beliefs. In an effort to validate his twisted views, Beckwith told Reiley that if anything he said was a lie, "he would be serving time in jail in Mississippi for getting rid of that nigger Medgar Evers." Instead, Beckwith informed Reiley, he had walked free, run for lieutenant governor, and had only people of wealth and prominence visit him.

Young Blood, though, was not persuaded and informed Beckwith that he was not interested in joining the movement. An enraged Beckwith, according to Reiley, "told me that he knew all along that I was a communist, nigger-loving bastard."

"And that's the last thing he ever said to you?"

"Yes, sir."

"Did you know who Medgar Evers was?"

"I had no idea at all."

"When was the first time you found out there was somebody who was interested in that?"

"This past Friday."

"What did you do when you first found out about that?"

"First, I called my wife to tell her that the guy I had told her about all these years, I just saw him on TV."

"What are you getting for testifying here?"

"Not a lot. I was lucky if I got a sandwich." Everyone laughed. During a heated exchange between Ed and Kitchens, Judge Hilburn leaned over the bench and asked Reiley, "Does someone need to get you a sandwich?" The increased laughter brought the arguing to a halt.

After unsuccessfully attempting to get the judge to strike Reiley's entire testimony, Kitchens brought out on cross-examination only that Reiley filed no formal report about Beckwith's comments, did not know what medication, if any, Beckwith was taking, and did not know for what illness Beckwith was hospitalized.

"I wasn't medical staff; they didn't tell us that."

Upon Mark Reiley's stepping down from the witness stand, I stood at 3:15 P.M., Tuesday, February 1, 1994, and spoke the words that I had seriously wondered four years earlier if I would ever be able to utter: "Your Honor, at this time, the state rests." Judge Hilburn adjourned court until nine Wednesday morning.

The defense began by reading the testimony of a deceased witness. Myrlie Evers's transcript cut both ways, aiding the defense as well as the prosecution. Lawyer-friend Crymes Pittman read the testimony of Roy Jones, who, at the 1964 trials, was the thirty-three-year-old owner of a neon-sign business and a volunteer with the auxiliary police in Greenwood.

He was on duty at the police department the evening of Tuesday, June 11, 1963, until 11 P.M. Asked what he did after work, he responded, "Well, me being new on the force, the fellas were always kinda helping me out on the different techniques you got about arresting and what have you.

One of the policemen was showing me how to handle different guys with a stick, and how you could hold them by the finger and what have you, and lead them around."

The image of Barney Fife, in an *Andy Griffith* episode, demonstrating his judo techniques on Andy flashed through my mind.

"What did you do then?"

"I got to thinking I'd better eat me a sandwich." Jones went to the same place on Main Street that Officers Creswell and Holley said they went to eat. On his way home, he testified, he saw Beckwith in his white Plymouth Valiant "in an alley by the Billups service station. He was sitting right there with his lights on, just like he was waiting for a car to go on by so he could pull out." Jones said it was 11:45 P.M., an hour and twenty minutes before the time, according to the 1964 testimony of Holley and Creswell, that they had seen Beckwith at the same service station.

I read some of the more pertinent questions that Waller had asked. Although knowing that the FBI and Jackson Police Department were investigating the murder, Jones did not contact either agency upon Beckwith's arrest to let them know that they had arrested an innocent man.

"Give me any other date, Mr. Jones, that you have ever seen Mr. Beckwith before in your life."

"Well, I couldn't pinpoint it by date."

"So, the only date you remember specifically that you saw him on a specific date was June eleventh?"

"That's right."

"And the only specific time you ever remember you saw him was at eleven forty-five P.M., on a black night, and he was in his automobile with his lights on?"

"That's right."

Former Greenwood police lieutenant Hollis Creswell, according to the defense lawyers, was too ill to testify. Since he was in good enough health to have testified in the grand jury proceedings without any difficulty, Ed objected to the reading of his 1964 trial testimony. The objection was overruled, so lawyer Crymes Pittman remained on the stand to read Creswell's previous testimony.

Creswell recounted how he and his partner, James Holley, had seen Beckwith in Greenwood at 1:05 A.M., June 12, 1963. The cops had pulled into the Billups station for cigarettes and noticed Beckwith getting gas in his Valiant at the Shell next door.

As with Roy Jones, Waller brought out that even though Creswell knew Jackson detectives Fred Sanders and John Chamblee were investigating the murder, he "made no effort to get his information into court or to any authorities, other than to Mr. Lott and one or two other officers in Greenwood."

James Holley looked as he did when Crisco and I first talked to him behind a Charter convenience store in 1990. It was Groundhog Day when Holley took the stand, and he reminded me of a big, pot-bellied woodchuck with a crew cut. He was Punxsutawney Phil in the flesh.

The direct examination by Kitchens was relatively brief and to the point. Holley merely reiterated Creswell's earlier testimony. According to Holley, upon learning of Beckwith's arrest ten days after the murder, he immediately realized that Beckwith could not have committed the crime.

"When Mr. Beckwith was arrested and you heard about that, what, if anything, about that made you think back to the early morning of June twelfth, 1963?"

"I knowed we saw him that morning, and later that morning we heard that the man had been shot and killed, and just putting two and two together."

"When that clicked in your mind, what did you do?"

"Didn't really do anything. I talked to some of the other officers I was working with, you know, and told them what I had seen."

Holley's direct examination concluded at eleven, and Judge Hilburn adjourned early for the noon recess. It was almost one forty-five when Ed started his cross-examination. He had had almost three hours to hone his strategy and questions.

"Are y'all first-name buddies?"

"No, sir."

"Why do you call him DeLay? Why don't you call him Mr. Beckwith?"

"I call him Mr. Beckwith most of the time."

Ed pulled out the transcript of my interview with Holley and pointed to it as he read aloud, "'And we just noted *DeLay's* car, and *DeLay* and the attendant were at the station.' Isn't that exactly what you told Mr. DeLaughter and my investigator when they came up and asked you what you were doing that night?"

"Sure, I saw—"

"DeLay."

"Sure."

"Your buddy, right?"

"My friend. Just like I hope you and I are friends."

"Pardon?" Laughter in the courtroom.

"I said just like I would hope that you and I are friends."

"What have I ever done to be your friend?"

"You've never done anything *not* to be my friend." Laughter again in the courtroom.

"Oh? I haven't ever done anything to cause you not to be a friend?"

"No."

"You remember me asking you questions before the grand jury?"

"Sure."

"Are you saying your testimony here and at the grand jury are the same as you gave at the last trial?"

"Sure."

"For instance, did you testify at the first trial that you'd never seen a Jackson police officer in Greenwood, period? Never talked to them?"

"I don't believe so."

Ed referred him to page 871 of the 1964 transcript. "Question: 'Hadn't there been some Jackson police officers at the police station in Greenwood?' And wasn't your answer, 'I have never met any of them, no, sir. I knew some of them had been there, but I haven't met any of them, not personally'? Now, is that the truth or not?"

"That's the truth."

"You deny that you testified at the grand jury that you talked with Officer Sanders of the Jackson Police Department?"

"Beg your pardon?" Holley asked, shifting his bulk in the witness chair. Ed repeated the question. "I may have chatted with him briefly at a shift change when he was in the station, but nothing concerning the case. He never asked me anything concerning this case."

"As a matter of fact, you and Lieutenant Creswell met with Mr. Sanders and Mr. Chamblee, detectives from the Jackson Police Department, on January twenty-fourth or twenty-fifth of 1964, in Greenwood, didn't you?"

"No."

"You deny that?"

"I deny that." I made a note to put Fred Sanders on in rebuttal.

"You deny that you talked with them where Creswell said, 'I know he didn't do it,' but did not give a reason?"

"I deny that, yes, sir."

"Look at page thirty-five of your grand jury testimony. Is your answer, 'Well, I know it was common knowledge, but to my knowledge, the detective that worked the case, I remember talking to them briefly one time'?"

271

"That's right. That's the only time that I ever talked to him."

"And now look at page thirty-eight. Question: 'And you did talk to him, but you wouldn't talk to him about this?' Answer: 'If I talked to him, I talked to him about this.' "

"About what?"

"This case that we're talking about. Same thing the grand jury was investigating."

"If I had of talked to him, I would've talked to him about it, sure."

"Question, page thirty-nine: 'You don't remember what?' Answer: 'The conversation with Mr. Sanders.' Question: 'Did you ever tell him that you'd seen Byron De La Beckwith at the service station when you talked to him?' Answer: 'I'm sure I did.' Did you talk to Detective Fred Sanders or not?"

"No, sir, I did not."

"So this thing you just said about talking to him between shift change, that's not true, is that right?"

"I said I'd never talked to him concerning this case."

"Mr. Holley, the questions we just asked and the answers you just gave, were those under oath?"

"Surely."

"Before the grand jury?"

"Surely."

"Now, I'm gonna ask you again. Did you talk to him or not?"

"As I told you, I don't remember."

"If you did talk to him, you told him that you saw Byron De La Beckwith in Greenwood with this car on the night of the killing, right?"

"I did not," he declared.

"Why didn't you?"

"Why would I have? I had no reason to tell him unless he asked me."

"You wouldn't have had any reason, as a sworn police officer, to tell an investigator on an important murder case that you knew where the person was at the time of the murder? Is that what you're telling this jury?"

"I think I would've been butting into his investigation, unless he asked me."

"You would've been butting into his investigation?" Ed asked incredulously, his voice booming.

"Right."

"If you're investigating a case, you don't wanna know who the alibi witnesses are, sir?"

"Sure, sure."

"Is that butting into somebody's case?"

"Sure, but I'm gonna ask."

"I see. So, you decided, 'I'm gonna play games. I'm gonna see if he asks me this,' right?"

"I was playing no games."

"Then why didn't you tell him?"

"He never asked me."

"Why didn't you tell him if he didn't ask you?"

"I didn't think he wanted to know."

"You think the Jackson detectives on this case just came up there to lean against the walls and stand around? What did you think they were there for?"

"To investigate the case."

"Then why didn't you volunteer any vital information you had?"

"They never talked to me."

"As a matter of fact, what happened was the defense attorney told you not to talk, didn't he?"

"I didn't go to Mr. Lott. He called me. I went to his office."

"What did you tell him?"

"Just what I'm telling you."

"Did you ever go to the DA's office and tell them what was going on?"

"No."

"Did you go to the FBI?"

"No."

"You didn't even go to your own chief at the Greenwood Police Department and tell him, 'There's a murder case and I know where the person they're saying murdered him was at that night'?"

"I didn't go to the chief and tell him that."

"But you did go to the defense attorney?"

"When he called me."

"How long was your buddy DeLay in jail and you let him stay there without telling one single law enforcement officer where he was that night?"

"I don't exactly know."

"Eight months? Ten months?"

"Somewhere along there."

"And you let your buddy DeLay stay in jail all that time and never once told a single person investigating it, 'You've got the wrong guy in jail'? Never once?"

"I did not."

Ed moved on to something else. Concerning auxiliary cop Roy Jones, Ed asked Holley, "If he had been at the Greenwood Police Department at eleven o'clock, checking out, you would have seen him, right?"

"I probably would have."

"Did you see him?"

"I did not see him."

"Other than officers that you worked with, tell us one other person you saw that whole night?"

"I saw Mr. De La Beckwith at one oh five in the morning."

"Tell us somebody else."

"I saw the service station attendant at the same time."

"What's his name?"

"I have no idea."

"When you were questioned under oath at the grand jury, you said you didn't know who got the cigarettes, you or Creswell, didn't you?"

"I don't know whether I did or not."

"Do you deny that you said, 'I don't know who got the cigarettes'?"

"No, I'm not going to deny that, because I don't remember."

"And now you're saying you did."

"I don't remember."

"Didn't you just swear under oath, right before lunch, that you went in and got cigarettes, and now you're saying under oath you don't know?"

"Maybe I did."

"After leaving from getting cigarettes, you were in a hurry to go and get your—I think you called it 'lunch,' right?"

"Well, whatever."

"You've called it 'lunch' every time you've described it, haven't you?"

"You can call it 'lunch' or 'supper' or whatever, but we got a sandwich."

"And you were in a hurry to go get your sandwich, right?"

"Before the store closed, I wanted to get it, sure."

"If you were in a hurry, why did you then go uptown and patrol around?"

"That—that's what I got paid to do," Holley stammered.

"So, you're positive you went up and did some patrolling around?"

"Sure."

"Do you deny that you've said that you went straight to the grocery store?"

"I don't believe I said that."

Ed showed him page seven of my interview with him. "Do you remember giving Mr. DeLaughter and Mr. Crisco a statement on May twenty-third, 1990?"

"I remember."

"And you were asked, 'So the last you saw him that night, he was getting gas?' and your answer was, 'At the Shell station.'" Holley nodded in agreement. "Then you were asked, 'When y'all left, did y'all head south or come back toward town?' and wasn't your answer, 'We headed north. We came north on Main here to this building right here'? You were talking about the grocery store, weren't you?"

"Yeah, yeah."

"Then you were asked, 'What did you do there?' and you said, 'We got us a little lunch,' right?" Holley nodded. "Mr. DeLaughter then asked you, 'Did you go straight from the Billups station?' and you said, 'Yeah. Straight.' Is that right?"

"That's right. We came straight by the store, went uptown, and came straight back."

"Excuse me, sir. Is there anywhere in there you said you went *by* the store, or did you say you went straight *to* the store?"

"We went straight by the store, went straight to the store, and straight by it, and came straight back."

Laughter in courtroom.

"What was unusual about seeing Byron De La Beckwith at that service station that night? What did he do unusual? What called your attention to him?"

"He was just there."

"He was standing there just like all the other people you saw that entire shift that night, right?"

"That's right."

"But you can't recall a single one of those people, except him?"

"Outside of my workers, no."

"Other than this defendant, and that was ten to twelve days later, right?"

"Right."

"And he did absolutely nothing to call his attention to you, right?"

"That's right."

"Now, tell us how he was standing."

"He was standing up by the car, with his foot up on the raised part where the gas pumps are."

"Which way was his car headed?"

"North."

"The same way y'all were going?"

"Yes, sir."

"Was he on the inside or the outside of that island?"

"On the outside."

"His car was on the outside, correct?"

"Correct."

"So, the car was between you and him?"

"Yeah."

"And you saw him with his left foot up on the island?"

"Sure."

"Saw through the car?"

"No."

"Saw over the car?"

"No."

"Saw under the car?"

"No."

Exercising his favorite strategy, Ed suddenly changed topics, returning to Holley's failure to say anything to the authorities.

"If you have vital information to an investigation of another police department, aren't you, as a sworn officer, supposed to share it with that police agency?"

"I don't think it's my responsibility to run him down if he's the investigating officer."

"You didn't have telephones?"

"Sure, we had telephones."

"Didn't have mail?"

"Sure, we had mail."

"That's the question. Shouldn't you at least have called or written?"

"Well, maybe I should."

"Do you know what a preliminary hearing is?"

"Yes, sir. To determine whether you've got enough evidence to proceed with a case or not."

"To determine whether or not someone was there and probably committed a crime, right?"

"Right, right."

"Well, did you go to the preliminary hearing and tell them this man wasn't there?"

"No, sir, I didn't go to it."

"Hardy Lott had already talked to you, hadn't he? You'd already told him that this man wasn't there?"

"Sure."

"So, were you asked by Mr. Hardy Lott to come down and testify?"

"Was what?" The man was thoroughly turned inside out. Ed repeated the question. "No, sir, he did not."

"And it was how long afterward that this defendant went on trial?"

"I don't know. I don't even remember when the trial was."

"So, you don't know the day he was arrested?"

"No, sir."

"But you do know the day he was in Greenwood?"

"I do know that."

"Wasn't the case much more publicized when he was arrested?"

"Sure."

Holley had been cross-examined, at this point, for one and a quarter hours. Judge Hilburn took a thirty-minute recess at 3 P.M.

When we returned to the courtroom, Ed resumed his cross-examination.

"Look at page thirty-nine. I wanna make sure we understand about Mr. Sanders. Question: 'Did you ever tell him that you'd seen Byron De La Beckwith at the service station when you talked to him?' Answer: 'I'm sure I did.' Is that true or false?"

"I meant if I had talked to him, I would have told him, but I never talked to him."

"Question: 'You know you did?' Answer: 'I'm sure I did.' Is that correct? Is that what you swore to before the grand jury?"

"It must be."

Ed moved back to the attendant. "Did you ever seek to find out who the attendant was that was pumping the gas there with your friend DeLay?"

"No, no, sir. I did not."

"It would've been easy to find out, wouldn't it?"

"Sure, it would have."

"You were cooperating with the defense attorney, weren't you?"

"Sure."

"And you never once went out and said, 'Hey, here's this attendant. Here's his name. This is who you need'?"

"No, sir."

"There with your friend DeLay. Didn't do that?" After no response from Holley, "Is your answer no?"

"No, I did not."

"What other cases did you investigate that night?"

"I don't recall."

"What arrests did you make that night?"

"What, what?"

Ed repeated the question.

"I don't know if I made one."

"You don't remember one thing you did on duty that night, except going to eat a sandwich and seeing your friend DeLay?"

"I remember patrolling, but nothing happened that stuck in my mind."

"Just seeing your friend DeLay?"

"I saw him at the service station that night, sure."

"Did you stop and talk to him?"

"No, I did not."

"Did you wave at him?"

"No, sir, I did not."

"Did Creswell wave at him?"

"I don't know whether he did or not. I didn't keep my eye on Lieutenant Creswell every moment I was in the car with him."

"You weren't watching Creswell, you were watching your friend DeLay. Is that what you're saying?"

Coxwell could stand it no longer. "Your Honor, I object to his characterization. His name is Mr. Beckwith and I object to Mr. Peters constantly characterizing that way."

"That's what *he* called him, Your Honor. I called him the same thing."

"Let's move along," the judge suggested.

"Judge," an exasperated Coxwell said, "I—I—I would like my objection ruled on, if it please the court."

"All right," the judge said, then turned to Ed. "You can refer to him as Mr. Beckwith."

Ed was not going to refer to any defendant as "Mr." "Or 'the defendant,' Your Honor?"

"Or 'the defendant,'" the judge said.

"Thank you." Returning to Holley, Ed asked, "How can you tell us that the defendant was standing there with his foot up on the curb and you can't even tell us if Creswell, your partner, who was in the car sitting within three feet of you, waved or not?"

"I do not know. That's the best I can tell you."

Holley was worn down. When Ed turned toward me, his back to the jury and judge, he winked. I turned around and silently mouthed to Mrs. Evers, "Watch."

"Mr. Holley, I believe at the beginning of the testimony you said that we're friends, is that right?"

"Said what?"

"That we're friends, you and I are friends."

"I said I hope we would."

"You still consider us friends?"

"Sure."

Walking slowly away from Holley, along the front of the jury box, Ed delivered "the closer."

"If I ever get in jail, will you promise not to leave me there for eight months if you knew where I was at the time of the crime?"

The courtroom erupted. Holley was as stunned as if he'd been struck between the eyes, and Kitchens was on his feet objecting and moving for a mistrial. "Your Honor," he said, "that's an argumentative question and just borders on the ridiculous and absurd."

To everyone else in the courtroom the ridiculous and absurd thing was the tale woven by Kitchens's witness. It had come completely apart. It wasn't 1964 anymore. Holley wasted no time making an exit. I don't know whether the big groundhog was spooked by his own shadow or frightened by the sun finally setting on an era where such lies were not so easily seen or, if seen, ignored.

Kitchens next called John Book, the coworker who had seen the scar over Beckwith's eye the day before the murder. His testimony didn't hurt our case at all, since we weren't going to argue that the cut came from firing the rifle during the murder. Beckwith testified in 1964 that he cut it on Sunday, June 9, 1963, while target practicing with the gun at the Greenwood Police Department firing range. We were content with that. It showed he was sighting the weapon in preparation of the murder. Putting Book on the stand also allowed Ed to establish during cross-examination that all Beckwith talked about with Book the day they were together was segregation and guns.

Thursday morning, Margaret Ellis, Kitchens's law partner, read the prior testimony of carhop Martha Jean O'Brien, concerning the white Valiant she had seen at Joe's Drive-In "between eight-thirty and ten" the night of the murder. "It drove to the back. The man got out and went to the rest room. And then he backed down in the corner." She described the man as "very tall, dressed in dark clothes, and in his early twenties."

On cross-examination, I had Ms. Ellis read O'Brien's testimony identifying a photo of Beckwith's car as the one she had seen that night, a fact of which she was "absolutely positive."

Following a short recess, and before the jury returned to the courtroom, Kitchens announced, "The defendant now wishes to call Byron De La Beckwith, the defendant, by means of the purported transcript." Beckwith was the only person who could take the stand and claim that his rifle was stolen after target practicing with it on the Sunday before the murder. If he didn't say it, the jury would never hear it, but the last thing the defense attorneys desired was for Ed to do with their client what he had done with Holley. If they could get Beckwith's earlier testimony read to the jury, as had been done with "unavailable" witnesses, the jury would hear his stolen-rifle claim without his being cross-examined. The defendant, his lawyers argued, was "unavailable" due to his lack of memory.

After much consideration during another recess, Judge Hilburn overruled the request, but stated that he would "allow the defense the latitude of presenting evidence recorded at the previous trial through the transcript in the event the defendant's memory, in fact, fails him in that respect."

Abruptly the defense rested. Groans permeated the courtroom. Ed disgustedly flipped his pen in the air and let it fall on the counsel table.

"Does the state have any testimony in rebuttal?"

We put on Fred Sanders to tell the jury about the two times Chamblee and he met with Holley and Creswell.

"Was this case discussed with them?" I asked.

"Yes, sir."

"Before or after the arrest of this defendant?"

"It was after the arrest."

"At any time during those conversations, Mr. Sanders, what, if any, mention was made by either Hollis Creswell or James Holley that they knew for a fact that this defendant could not have committed the murder you were investigating because they had seen him in Greenwood on the night and approximately at the time that this murder occurred?"

"No, sir, that was never said by either one."

In an effort to show some possible justification in Holley's failure to notify the authorities of his claim, Kitchens asked Sanders, "For most of the twenty years you were on the Jackson Police Department, there was no such thing as giving the defense attorneys copies of police reports, was it?"

"That's true."

"Likewise, there was no such thing as defense attorneys giving information about their case to the other side, was it?"

"That's true."

My only follow-up question to Sanders: "Was it common practice for sworn police officers to conceal material information in a murder case that they knew was being investigated?"

Over Kitchens's objection, Sanders was allowed to answer. He said emphatically, "No, sir, it was not."

It was Thursday, February 3, 1994, and all evidence in the third Beckwith trial was before the jury. Judge Hilburn recessed at 2:40 P.M. The jury was sent back to the hotel, but after an hour break the judge went over jury instructions with the lawyers.

The only thing left for me to do in finishing this long journey to justice was to deliver a closing argument tying everything together, but more importantly guiding the jurors to see that a guilty verdict was just as crucial in 1994 as it was in 1964. The killing couldn't seem like ancient history. The trial couldn't be considered a day late and a dollar short. I had to convey the revulsion I felt for Beckwith's dastardly deed and make the jurors, all twelve of them, feel it, too.

As Robert Keith Leavitt put it, "People don't ask for facts in making up their minds. They would rather have one good soul-searching emotion than a dozen facts."

That Thursday night at home, I pulled the various notes I had kept for this very purpose and finalized an outline for my summation. At ten Friday morning, February 4, 1994, after three weeks of trial and four years of work, it was show time. Psyching myself up for the occasion wasn't difficult. In fact, I felt on fire.

"When we started the testimony a little over a week ago now, I stood before you and I told you that when all the evidence was in, you would see what this case was about and what this case was not about. Now you know that it *is* about an unarmed man arriving home the late hours of the night, having been working, coming home to his family—his wife, three small children who were staying up, waiting on him to get home—getting out of his automobile with his back turned, and being shot down by a bushwhacker from ambush. He crawled from that automobile where he was gunned down, alongside the carport, trying to make it to his door, in this puddle of blood, with his keys in his hand, and his wife and children coming out when they hear the shot, and his three children stating over and over, 'Daddy, Daddy, please get up.' That's what the case is about. This man being gunned down and shot in the back in the dark from ambush, not able to face his self-appointed accuser, his judge, and his executioner.

"And the court has given you several instructions, and this instruction tells you what the case is about legally. It's about whether or not this defendant killed and murdered Medgar Evers on June the twelfth, 1963. It doesn't say 'unless the defendant is of a certain age,' because no man, ladies and gentlemen, is above the law. And if we start making decisions that don't have anything to do with the law, eventually, where do we draw the line? Do we say in this case, 'We're gonna draw the line when the person is seventy-something,' and in another case if they're sixty-five? No man, regardless of his age, is above the law.

"And it doesn't say 'unless you find that this offense was committed over thirty years ago.' Because you see, ladies and gentlemen, what we're talking here, this type of offense, this type of murder, this assassination by a sniper from ambush, is something that's timeless. This is something that spans the races. It is something that every decent human being should absolutely be sickened by, whether you are black, white, Hispanic; it doesn't matter. Murder by ambush is the most vile, savage, reprehensible type of murder that one can imagine.

"This isn't about black versus white or white versus black. This is about something that is reprehensible to decent minds. This is about society, civilized society, versus the vile, society versus the reprehensible, society versus the shocking. This, ladies and gentlemen, is about the State of Mississippi versus this defendant, Byron De La Beckwith.

"Now, who could do such a thing? I'll tell you: the person who wrote, 'The Negro in our country is as helpful as a boll weevil to cotton. Some of these weevils are puny little runts and can't create the volume of damage that others can. Some are powerful, becoming mad monsters, snapping and snarling and biting the cotton. They must be destroyed with their wretched remains burned, lest the pure white cotton bolls be destroyed.'

"Well, in Medgar Evers, the field secretary for the NAACP, the focal point of integration in 1963, this defendant saw, in the scope of this gun you see, the main boll weevil that needed to be eliminated, lest the pure white cotton bolls be destroyed.

"So, who could do such a shocking thing? His opinion has not changed one iota from those words. How do we know that? Exhibit seventy-one, written in November 1976: 'as much involved in Klan activity as a person can be.' He was on a one-man mission to exterminate what he considered to be the most important, in his words, 'boll weevil' of that time.

"So, we know from the evidence that on the Saturday before Medgar Evers was gunned down, this defendant was in Jackson; couldn't find his prey's residence. Why? Because Medgar Evers, by that time, had to get an unlisted phone number. He couldn't just go to a phone book and look up his number and his address. And so he was at the Continental Trailways bus station trying to find out where he lived. We know he went up to some cabdrivers trying to find out. We know after that his car was seen parked on the north side of Pittman's Grocery on Saturday trying to find where Medgar Evers lived; drove to the location and walked into that vacant lot, getting things ready.

"We know he went back to Greenwood, got his rifle, got the scope that was on there that he had just bought from John Goza a month before this, went out and target practiced, getting those crosshairs, those sights, set for his target. He got that scar over his right eye when the recoil of that scope jammed his eyeball. He went to work on Monday—worked all day—and what was on his mind? What did John Book tell you? All he wanted to do was talk about integration and guns. He couldn't keep his mind on his business that day.

"The next day was *the* day, and his car was seen by those teenage boys again. This car, his car, was seen parked in that corner with the rear end backed into it, where all he's got to do is get out, walk down that path as shown in the pictures, get to this clump of trees, and wait.

"While he's waiting, he takes his hand and breaks off this branch here, and what does he have? He has a hole. And what do you see in that hole? A perfect view of the driveway of Medgar Evers. And he waits.

"After midnight, Medgar Evers, unsuspecting, gets out and gets his T-shirts out of the car. This defendant takes this rifle, braces it up against a tree, finds Medgar Evers, his prey, in this scope, and he pulls the trigger and ends his life in one fatal shot.

"After he does his dirty work, and he's on the way back to his car, perchance if he's seen or stopped, he can't afford to have this rifle with him, so he takes it and sticks it in the honeysuckle vines behind this hedgerow, gets in his car, and leaves.

"We're not just talking about some 1960s-model white Valiant. It also has a long aerial on it. And what else did Robert Don Pittman say, not only to you, but also in this same courtroom thirty years ago? 'The thing I remember most about it, when we got up close, was that emblem on the rearview mirror.'

"And so what did we have the FBI do in recent years? To go back and get the negative from this photograph, enlarge this area here, and let's see if it has any type of emblem hanging from it. And, lo and behold, there she is. Now, a person's words may be one thing, but a picture speaks a thousand words.

"*His* gun, *his* scope, *his* fingerprint, *his* car, and lastly, but certainly not least, *his* mouth. When he thought he had beaten the system thirty years ago, he couldn't keep his mouth shut with people that he thought were gonna be impressed by him. Six people have given you sworn testimony that at various times in different locations, none of whom knew each other or came across each other at any time, what he has said about this. He wants to take credit for what he has claimed should be done, but he just doesn't want to pay the price for it.

"And so, not only do we have his car, his gun, his scope, his fingerprint, his mouth, we've got his own venom, which has come back to poison him just as effectively as anything else.

"And why did any of this happen? For what reason was Medgar Evers assassinated? For what he believed. For wanting things like what? To be called by name, instead of 'boy.' To go in a restaurant, to go in a department store, to vote, and for his children to get a decent education in a decent school; for wanting some degree of equality for himself, his family, and his fellow man, and for them to be accepted as human beings with some dignity.

"When that kind of murder happens, ladies and gentlemen, no matter who the victim, no matter what his race, there is a gaping wound laid open on society as a whole. Even where justice is fulfilled, that kind of murder, that kind of wound, will always leave a scar that won't ever go away. Justice is sometimes referred to as that soothing balm to be applied to the wounds inflicted on society, and where justice is never fulfilled, and that wound can never be cleansed, all it does is just fester and fester and fester over the years.

"And so it is up to the law-abiding citizens and the law of the State of Mississippi that the perpetrator of such an assassination be brought to justice, so that the decent, law-abiding people of this state will maintain a new respect for the value of human life, and that our state will truly be one that is of the people, for the people, and by the people, no matter what your race, color, or creed is.

"One of the defense attorneys, early on in the jury selection process, asked whether or not any of you had heard something to the effect of the eyes of the world being on Mississippi or Mississippi being on trial. I'm not sure what eyes are on Mississippi, but this I do know: justice in this case is what you twelve ladies and gentlemen say it is. So, in this case, in effect, *you* are Mississippi. So, what is Mississippi justice in this case, ladies and gentlemen? What is Mississippi justice for this defendant's hate-inspired assassination—assassination of a man that just desired to be free and equal?

"If you analyze the evidence, use your common sense that God gave you, examine your heart, your consciences, and base your verdict on the evidence and the law, then you will have done the right thing. If you base it on the law and the evidence and in the spirit of human dignity, there's no question in my mind that whatever you come out with, it'll be the right thing, because I have faith that it will be to hold him accountable, and the only way to do that is to find him guilty.

"From the evidence in this case, the law that you've sworn to apply, it can't be but one way if justice is truly going to be done. And so, on behalf of the State of Mississippi, I ask that you hold this defendant accountable. Find him guilty, simply because it's right, it's just, and Lord knows, it's just time. He has danced to the music for thirty years. Isn't it time that he pay the piper?

"Is it ever too late to do the right thing? For the sake of justice and the hope of us as a civilized society, I sincerely hope and pray that it's not."

There was no way, as pumped up as I was, that I could sit through the defense closing arguments without standing up and saying, "That's bull-shit!" So, for the only time in my career, I left the courtroom before the defense lawyers delivered their summations. Drinking repeated cups of coffee, I paced the hallway behind the courtroom. At noon the rear door opened, and bailiffs Steve Libenschek and Jeff Murray escorted the jurors out. Steve said that Judge Hilburn wanted them fed first, so they would not start deliberating until 1:30 P.M.

Our juries, unlike those in some other parts of the country, rarely deliberate more than a few hours before reaching a verdict. As I thought that we annihilated the defense with our evidence, I didn't expect this jury to do otherwise. At six-thirty, though, after five hours, the jury had yet to reach a decision. The judge brought the jurors back into the court-room and informed them that he was recessing court and sending them to their hotel for the night. They would resume deliberations at nine the next morning. I left the courthouse dejected.

The storm that I had sensed approach, from the moment of my com-mitment to this case, hit with a mighty vengeance that Friday night. Never before had I witnessed one strike with such fury. Something cata-clysmic was at hand—the day of reckoning.

What in the world could be hanging up that jury? Whatever it was must have to do with something other than the evidence. I was not only alone physically. I *felt* alone. The emotional lift of the morning and the hope of the afternoon had long since evaporated. I was worn-out in every sense of the word.

Desperate to get my mind on something else, I pulled Faulkner's *The Unvanquished* from the shelf. One observation penetrated the mental veil separating his words from my preoccupation with the trial: "Victory without God is mockery and delusion, but . . . defeat with God is not defeat."

★   ★   ★

A few people were already in the DA's office when Peggy and I walked in a few minutes after nine. Among them were Burt, my brother Mike, and nephew Jim, who is a year younger than Burt. I was pleasantly surprised to see them but warned, as I had with Peggy, that we were in for a long day.

At 9:20 A.M., I walked back to Ed's office to see if he was in. He was, and I told him that I'd be in the library if he needed me.

Other people from the office began to trickle in. Idle chitchat pervaded the office. Every now and then the phone would ring and whoever answered it would say, "No, not yet. It's much too early, though. . . . Yeah, it could be a long day." I glanced at the clock—9:35. The phone rang again. This time I heard Nancy Lee, our victim assistance coordinator, calling my name. "Bobby!" Nancy entered the library. "They've got a verdict."

Everything, for a few seconds, stopped: my heart, my breath, and time itself. It had to be not guilty. If they were unable to unanimously convict by the end of the previous day, it would take longer than thirty-five minutes this morning for the majority to change the minds of any holdouts.

"Go tell Ed, will you, Nancy?"

Turning to Peggy and Mike, I said, "I need to go down the back stairway with Ed. Y'all go on down, and after the verdict, no matter what it is, come back up here immediately and wait for me. This is the safest place in the building, and there is no telling what's about to break loose."

I gave Peggy a kiss and hurried to the stairs, where I met Ed. He gave me a pat on the back. Nancy had told him that Myrlie Evers was not at the courthouse yet. Nobody, not even she, expected a verdict this early in the day. We got to the second floor and walked down the hallway behind the courtroom to Judge Hilburn's chambers.

Ed asked the judge if he would please wait until Mrs. Evers and the family arrived; we understood they were on the way from the hotel. The judge agreed, and Ed and I walked into the courtroom via the rear door.

No one was seated at the defense table, but other than that, the place was packed—even the balcony, which was where the press had been relegated. Deputies lined the walls, all with walkie-talkies in hand. I recalled how only a handful of people—mostly family and friends of the various participants in the trial—had come to watch during the first few days. The crowds had grown, however, as word spread that we were trying a real murder case with all of the evidence, vitality, and drama that normally attends such trials. This trial was one of substance, not merely a political show with smoke and mirrors. I was especially gratified to see the large number of students there.

Ed and I took our places at the prosecution table and waited for what seemed an eternity. My palms were sweating and my insides were convulsing. The rear door opened. Beckwith, flanked by Kitchens and Coxwell, entered, and they took their places at the defense table. They appeared as confident as I was nervous. Someone leaned over the rail behind us and whispered that Mrs. Evers had just arrived. Before either Ed or I could stand to tell Judge Hilburn, the rear door opened again. It was 10:15 A.M.

"All rise!" Bailiffs Libenschek and Murray entered, followed by court clerk Barbara Dunn.

"Ladies and gentlemen, when the verdict is read, there will be no demonstrations or any type of emotional outburst," the judge warned.

Nodding to Libenschek, Judge Hilburn said, "Bring the jury in." One by one, they filed in. The judge, as is his practice, had them stand in front of the bench, facing the judge. "Ladies and gentlemen of the jury, have you reached a verdict?"

"We have, Your Honor." The black minister spoke, which meant that he had been selected foreman by the other jurors.

Judge Hilburn continued, "The clerk will read the verdict."

The yellow piece of paper was handed to Barbara. I closed my eyes with my hands cupped around my face. Was the world holding its breath, as I was mine?

"We, the jury, find the defendant guilty, as charged."

Yes! Sweet Jesus, thank you. To God be the glory, great things He hath done. The judge's admonition was ignored. There was a brief outburst from the audience. A stern look from the judge restored silence. The muffled voices of the deputies, barely audible as each relayed the news into his walkie-talkie, reminded me of a wave at a ball game. "Guilty, guilty, guilty . . ."

As the news reached the deputies stationed in the hallway outside the courtroom, jubilant cheers and thunderous applause erupted, making it evident that the hallways, like the courtroom, were packed. Unlike those in the courtroom, however, people in the hallways repressed nothing.

The judge thanked the jury for their diligent and difficult service and finally discharged them. Everyone in the courtroom remained seated until the jurors had made their exit.

"He's not guilty!" Thelma Beckwith wailed. "And y'all know he's not. The Jews did it!" How many times had she screamed that to me over the phone every Saturday morning at six-thirty? I thought how so very far we had come since those early days.

"Will the defendant please rise and come forward for sentencing."

Judge Hilburn's words snapped me from my reverie. Kitchens and Coxwell flanked Beckwith on either side. Gone was Beckwith's smirk and cockiness. "Mr. Beckwith, by mandate of the laws of the State of Mississippi, it is required that I sentence you to a term of life imprisonment." Then, looking at me, Hilburn added, "If you'll prepare the order, please." My pleasure.

"By mandate of the laws of the State of Mississippi." Those words reverberated within me. Mississippi, the state that I love, after all was said and done, had pulled through. Mississippi had taken a stand for decency, race relations, and justice. How proud I was to have been a part of it.

Ed and I stood, shook hands, and exchanged congratulations. We left through the rear door and climbed the three flights of stairs to our offices.

I didn't see my family anywhere, and Ed and I were needed back downstairs in the press conference room, which was really an empty courtroom that had been assigned to the media.

We were greeted with cheers and applause, and after making a brief statement and answering a few questions, we returned to the office. I was relieved to see the smiling faces of my family.

Prosecutor Linda Anderson came in and said that Mrs. Evers was giving her press conference, but had asked her to tell me not to leave until she came up to see me. So, Peggy and I sat and talked, wept a little for joy, and laughed. We, in short, just let it out.

I didn't want to rush Mrs. Evers. She had waited so long for this moment, and I wanted her to bask in it for as long as she desired. But I was tired. I had ridden one hell of an emotional roller coaster, and I was ready to get off.

I knew Mrs. Evers would be in town until Tuesday or Wednesday of the following week, so I would definitely see her before she returned home. I asked Linda to just tell her that I was worn-out, but promised to see her before she left town. In fact, she could call me later that day.

Peggy and I went down the back stairway. As we reached the first floor, Mrs. Evers entered the stairwell. She wore the biggest smile I had ever seen. Tears streaked her cheeks, but the eyes were no longer sad and haunting.

She swept me up in her arms in a motherly way, and I could feel her shaking with exuberance. "Thank you, Bobby. Thank you so much for me, my family, and for Medgar. He can rest in peace now." My eyes welled up as I returned the embrace. Turning to Peggy, Mrs. Evers continued, "Mrs. DeLaughter, you're just going to have to excuse me, but I have come to love this man as one of my own sons. Thank you for being there for him and supporting him. Believe me, I know how tough it is to do that. What can I say? We just love him."

"I do, too, Miz Myrlie, I do, too," Peggy responded.

When we got home, I changed clothes, sat on the couch, and flicked on the TV. News of the verdict was on every local channel. I expected as much. What I didn't expect, though, was the jury foreman's explanation of how the panel had reached a verdict so quickly that morning. He said that the first thing the jurors had done after the doors had closed behind them that morning was to hold hands and pray for the guidance of the Almighty. Once again, as had happened several times since late 1989 on this case, I broke out in goose bumps. I felt the Lord was telling me, just as is stated in Exodus 19:4, "I bore you on eagles' wings."

I was given a lot of credit for obtaining the conviction, but a quote of Sir Isaac Newton's came to mind: "If I have seen further, it is by standing on the shoulders of giants."

A montage reeled through my head of all the giants upon whose shoulders I had stood to make all of this possible: John Chamblee, Fred Sanders, Capt. Ralph Hargrove, and the other detectives of the Jackson Police Department; district attorneys Bill Waller, Jack Travis, and Ed Peters; the white-male jurors in both 1964 trials who had the integrity and intestinal fortitude to stick by their guilty votes; Judge Russel Moore; from the media, Jerry Mitchell and Ed Bryson; Dr. Michael Baden and the personnel of the FBI Crime Lab; courageous witnesses Thorn McIntyre, Delmar Dennis, Dick Davis, Peggy Morgan, Mary Ann Adams, Dan Prince, and Mark Reiley; and last, but not least, Myrlie Evers.

Peggy and I had weathered the storm by leaning on each other, standing on the shoulders of giants, and soaring on the wings of eagles.

Epilogue

Wedging between last-minute shoppers and edging down the aisles of Northpark Mall, I realized the futility of my mission. Hard as I tried, I couldn't concentrate on the holidays. All the memories and emotions of the past eight years coursed through every vein. It was almost 4:30 P.M. The state supreme court's decision would have been made public hours earlier. Time to leave and face the consequences.

The last time I felt so low was when I ran for appeals court judge. The court was newly created in 1994, so I would not have to face an incumbent. I thought that, with my years of courtroom experience, my chances were promising. It was a disaster.

I recalled an interview with a journalist a few days after the verdict. He wanted to know what I saw as the legacy of our prosecution. I thought the conviction had the potential to do a lot of good for justice and race relations. The opportunity was in our hands, but it remained to be seen what we did with it.

Enough of the voting public hung it around my neck like a millstone. I didn't campaign on my involvement in the Beckwith case, but I quickly became familiar with hard stares, men who refused to shake my hand, and a few ladies who threw my literature back in my face as they realized, *You're the one who persecuted Beckwith!*

I should have seen it coming, but I didn't. I lost the election, clobbered, two to one.

I was devastated, not because I had lost (after all, it was my inaugural political outing), but because the underlying reason was this one case. Thelma Beckwith had predicted as much.

I was also pierced to the core by those who didn't bother to vote, especially the blacks. I felt abandoned. It did not escape my sense of irony that I had prosecuted the murderer of the man who had died securing voting rights for blacks, and they had stayed away from the voting booths in record numbers.

I wasn't the only one in my family who paid a price for my involvement in the Beckwith case. My father, for instance, lost several business clients across the state by taking up for me.

It really wasn't until after the release of the movie *Ghosts of Mississippi* that many people realized that our motives were not political and appreciated our efforts. Hardly a day goes by now without someone writing or telling me as much. I may even consider another run at a judgeship in 2002. The response has been that positive.

The initial release of the movie, as Willie Morris chronicled in *The Ghosts of Medgar Evers,* created a stir in some circles that caused me almost as much stress as the case ever did.

The main criticism was not that the story told by the movie was incorrect. Indeed, as Willie Morris observed, it was 85 percent accurate with the other 15 percent very much in keeping with the spirit of the events. The objection of most critics was that it was the story from *my* perspective, and I am white.

Notwithstanding some inevitable criticism, the movie did a lot of good. The power of film is awesome, and it conveyed to millions the many important messages that I always felt the case contained. True, the story began thirty years ago, but it addressed ideals of the present and future.

Certainly, the verdict was liberating for the Evers family, bringing closure, the relief that only justice can bring, and the freedom to move on with life. On a larger scale, it brought another type of closure for Mississippi and the New South. Beckwith's cell door slammed shut on a sad saga that was all too long in the making. It broke the shackles that had made us prisoners of our past. As David Sansing, one of my history professors at Ole Miss, said following the verdict, "Mississippi is now free at last!"

Without doubt, most Mississippians, as most Americans, are decent, well-meaning people, but being "good" is not enough. Upon the shoulders of such people falls the burden of courageously stepping in, righting wrongs, and unveiling demagoguery for what it is. All that's necessary for evil to prevail is for good men and women to do nothing.

Probably the most frequently asked question of me about this case is "Why did you do it? What kept you going with such commitment? It had to have been something much deeper than just doing your job or 'the law.'" I don't know that I can give a short answer, but I believe that my personal experience highlights a conviction that we must not allow ourselves to become shackled to the letter of the law alone. "The law," said Henry David Thoreau, "will never make men free; it is men who must make the law free."

One of the greatest jurists in American jurisprudence, Learned Hand, similarly noted, "I often wonder whether we do not rest our hopes too much upon constitutions, upon laws and upon courts. These are false hopes; believe me, these are false hopes. Liberty lies in the hearts of men and women; when it dies there, no constitution, no law, no court can save it." We must keep alive the *spirit* of the law and what George Washington described as "that little spark of celestial fire called conscience."

Leaving the Northpark Mall, it finally dawned on me. I obviously had no control over the Mississippi Supreme Court. The good that had been accomplished came because of the prosecution by the State of Mississippi and because of a verdict by a cross-section of its citizens. Let the court do what it would now. No court could ever take that away.

Turning the ignition and firing up the heater, I took a deep breath and soon was among the bumper-to-bumper traffic. It was a few minutes past five. I turned on the radio, caught the end of a weather advisory, and then heard, "And wrapping up our hourly news, for those of you who are just now getting off work and joining us, the Mississippi Supreme Court rules in the Byron De La Beckwith case. . . ."

"Damn," I grunted. "Just what I need to hear."

"By a four-to-two vote, the conviction of Beckwith, for the 1963 murder of civil rights leader Medgar Evers, has been upheld."

"Upheld?" I whispered, then shouted, "We won!" Like a maniac, I laughed uncontrollably, beating the steering wheel and screaming repeatedly, "Yes! Yes!" Tears of joy trickled from the corners of my eyes, and I said a prayer of thanks.

Where was a phone? I veered to the right into Popeye's and quickly dialed the office of Pat Flynn, the assistant attorney general who had argued the appeal. "Please be in, please." She answered on the fourth ring. "Is it true?" It was. She had a copy of the opinion waiting for me.

I hung up and dialed the DA's office. Crisco was on his way out, but agreed to retrieve the opinion from Pat. It would be on my desk. Almost an hour later I was reading it. The 115-page majority opinion, authored by my schoolmate and Fordice appointee Justice Mike Mills, closed with this beautifully crafted observation:

> Miscreants brought before the bar of justice in this State must, sooner or later, face the cold realization that justice, slow and plod-

ding though she may be, is certain in the State of Mississippi. Today's ruling represents the final act of this sovereign State's attempt to deal with a maelstrom born out of human conflict as old as time. The legal and law enforcement communities of this State must be applauded for their energetic, patient and long-suffering efforts, beginning only minutes after the shooting of Medgar Evers, to squeeze some justice out of the harm caused by a furtive explosion which erupted from dark bushes on a June night in Jackson, Mississippi. Final resolution of this conflict resulted from voices, both present and past, who showed the courage and will, from 1964 to 1994, to merely state the truth in open court. Their voices cannot be ignored. We affirm the finding of the jury that Byron De La Beckwith VI murdered Medgar Evers on the night of June 12, 1963.

The days of Jim Crow or legally sanctioned racism may be gone, but as John Perkins and Thomas Tarrants observed in *He's My Brother,* the fruit those days produced remains. Although the types of racial barriers that Medgar Evers fought have collapsed, a Color Curtain in this country still separates. It is found in every state of the Union. One need only scan the daily headlines across the country to learn of racial unrest or distrust, if not outright brutality. If we confront it, instead of pretending it doesn't exist, our contemporary Color Curtain can meet the same fate as the Berlin Wall, the Iron Curtain, and Jim Crow. But we must be steadfast in our resolve, as was Medgar Evers, in treating one another as human beings with dignity.

On a recent drive with Charles Evers and author Willie Morris through the Mississippi Delta, on the way to speak to a group of high school students, I took the opportunity to ask Charles what his brother would think of today's Mississippi.

Medgar, he said, would be both proud and saddened. "He'd be proud of the way white folks and black folks get along, for the most part. Thirty years ago, it would be dangerous for you and me to be seen together riding like this. But, you know, we haven't had a race riot, much less a racial killing, in twenty-five or thirty years. There are plenty of places in the rest of the country that can't say that. They can't look down their noses at Mississippi anymore, and Medgar would be proud of that."

"What would he be sad about?"

"The extent that blacks don't take advantage of the opportunities he died trying to open up for them, like voting, staying in school, and getting an education. He'd be sad at the way they're killing each other." Charles shook his head in disbelief. "Do you realize that more young black men have been killed by other young blacks than the Klan ever hoped to kill? If young blacks really want to honor my brother's memory, they will stay in school, stay off drugs, vote, and make something of themselves. When they go and kill each other and this other mess, they're not honoring Medgar. They're fulfilling every prediction and bigoted stereotype the Klan ever made."

Prosecuting Beckwith was not living in the past or reliving the 1960s, as some critics claimed. It was facing and conquering it, so we could continue moving on. Likewise, taking responsibility for past race relations is not about paying monetary reparations or indulging white guilt.

It's living a lifestyle *now* of compassion, justice, and reconciliation that matters. We can't erase our negative history, but we can control the present, and consequently the future, by building friendships across racial lines. We can live in a way that leaves behind a *new* legacy for our children and grandchildren.

The Beckwith verdict exemplified what can be accomplished when we unite in putting our shoulders to the wheel. Blacks and whites have got to have faith in our courts and in our democracy. Where one race is left out, taken for granted, or loses faith, there is no democracy; there's only *hypocrisy*.

Reprosecuting Beckwith was like yanking a curtain off a long-ago-covered mirror, forcing everyone exposed to the case to look deep within themselves. Some felt hope and encouragement. Others didn't like what they saw. Perhaps that accounts for some of the anger vented toward Mr. Peters and me. We all stand before the mirror. We are responsible for what is reflected and accountable for the decisions we make. There is no escape. Making no decision is making one, and our choices will have far-reaching consequences.

President Kennedy, on the very night Medgar Evers was slain by a racist, said, "We face a moral crisis as a country and as a people." Although it may no longer take the form of a sniper's bullet, racism still threatens the moral fabric of our country.

Healing racism can occur only through positive and voluntary association with others who are different. But racism has been here for hundreds of years; it will not change quickly. Although we have come a long way in thirty years, it requires patience, understanding, and prayer.

POSTSCRIPT

My dream of becoming a judge came true on December 2, 1999, when I received a call from Governor Kirk Fordice's chief of staff. The governor had appointed me to the Hinds County Court bench to fill the unexpired term of my friend and neighbor, Judge Chet Henley, who had died of a heart attack the previous month. It was Governor Fordice's last judicial appointment before leaving office.

On December 10, 1999, Judge L. Breland Hilburn, who had presided over the Beckwith trial, administered the oath of office during a ceremony held in the same courtroom in which all three trials had taken place. It was packed with family, friends, colleagues, and other well wishers.

Times do change, and life is good.

If I were dying, my last words would be: Have faith and pursue the unknown end.

—Oliver Wendell Holmes

Just because we cannot see clearly the end of the road, that is no reason for not setting out on the essential journey. On the contrary, great change dominates the world, and unless we move with change we will become its victims.

—Robert F. Kennedy

Index

Index

Index

BOBBY DELAUGHTER is a judge in the Hinds County Court, Jackson, Mississippi. He graduated from Ole Miss Law School in 1977 and is a former assistant district attorney and a past president of the Mississippi Prosecutor's Association. He is a graduate of the FBI's National Law Institute and has served as lawyer-in-residence at the Pepperdine University Law School. He lives in Terry, Mississippi.